Freire for the Classroom

A Sourcebook for Liberatory Teaching

Books by Ira Shor

Critical Teaching and Everyday Life
*Culture Wars: School and Society in the Conservative
    Restoration, 1969–1984*
A Pedagogy for Liberation (with Paulo Freire)

Freire for the Classroom

A Sourcebook for Liberatory Teaching

Edited by
IRA SHOR

Afterword by
PAULO FREIRE

BOYNTON/COOK PUBLISHERS
HEINEMANN
PORTSMOUTH, NH

BOYNTON/COOK PUBLISHERS, INC.
A Subsidiary of
HEINEMANN EDUCATIONAL BOOKS, INC.
361 Hanover Street   Portsmouth, NH   03801-3959
Offices and agents throughout the world

© 1987 by Ira Shor

First Edition

91 92 93 9 8 7 6 5 4 3

Library of Congress Cataloging-in-Publication Data

Freire for the classroom: a sourcebook for liberatory teaching / edited by Ira Shor;
    afterword by Paulo Freire.
    p.   cm.
    Bibliography: p.
    ISBN 0-86709-197-5
    1. Teaching. 2. Literacy. 3. Education—Political aspects.
    4. Education—Social aspects. 5. Democracy. 6. Freire, Paulo,
    1921-   . I. Shor, Ira, 1945-
    LB1025.2.F73 1987
    371.1'02—dc19   87-18622
                                                               CIP

Printed in the United States of America

16276163

Acknowledgments

Permission to reprint the following copyrighted material is gratefully acknowledged.

Elsa Roberts Auerbach and Denise Burgess. "The Hidden Curriculum of Survival ESL." *TESOL Quarterly*, Vol. 19, No. 3, pp. 475-495. Copyright © 1985 by Teachers of English to Speakers of Other Languages.

Nan Elsasser and Patricia Irvine. "English and Creole: The Dialectics of Choice in a College Writing Program." *Harvard Educational Review*, 1985, 55-4, 399-415. Copyright © 1985 by President and Fellows of Harvard College.

This is a great discovery, education is politics! When a teacher discovers that he or she is a politician, too, the teacher has to ask, What kind of politics am I doing in the classroom? That is, in favor of whom am I being a teacher? The teacher works in favor of something and against something. Because of that, he or she will have another great question, How to be consistent in my teaching practice with my political choice? I cannot proclaim my liberating dream and in the next day be authoritarian in my relationship with the students.

PAULO FREIRE
A Pedagogy for Liberation

Preface

In April, 1964, the Brazilian military overthrew civilian rule, ending a period of optimism and cultural democracy in that nation. Paulo Freire was then leading an ambitious and successful literacy program. He was training literacy teams to set up "culture circles" around the country, where the "dialogic" method of teaching propelled peasants and workers into reading, writing, and social awareness. During the coup, Freire was arrested, imprisoned for seventy days, moved from jail to jail, and then forced into exile with his wife Elza and their five children. Thus began Freire's long career outside his native Brazil. He went from Bolivia to Chile to Massachusetts to Switzerland, with many stopping points along the way. In 1980, with a new democratic opening in Brazil, Freire and his family were finally able to return. But he kept traveling through the 1980s, revisiting the friends and colleagues he made during his long exile, and speaking to new groups interested in critical pedagogy. His ideas for problem-posing education and critical consciousness have had an international impact. In September, 1986, in Paris, Freire received the UNESCO Prize for Education, one more testimonial to his global reputation.

This volume presents some of the most interesting work being done in Freirean teaching here in North America. Many teachers in the U.S. are dismayed with the traditional pedagogy dominating the curriculum. They and the students are uninspired by the standard syllabus, with its dull texts, required tests, rote memorizing, abstract subjects, and basic skills approaches. Many are looking for alternative methods which set creativity and empowerment as their goals. The Freirean approach offers hope as well as a history of application; it is a theory of learning and social change along with practical teaching techniques tested in diverse settings. This volume is thus a sourcebook for what has been done as well as an invitation for creative and hopeful teachers to reinvent the methods for their own classrooms.

As editor of this book, I want to thank the contributors for their ingenuity and determination. They kept alive the promise of education in this difficult period for teachers and students.

I. S.
New York City
July, 1987

Contents

Freire for the Classroom

A Sourcebook for Liberatory Teaching

Editor's Introduction: Using Freire's Ideas in the Classroom—How Do We Practice Liberatory Teaching?

IRA SHOR

Brazilian educator and philosopher Paulo Freire has a growing audience in North America. On his visits to the United States and Canada, Freire's seminars have been noted for their lively crowds. Can a social pedagogy emerging from the Third World truly work in the North? What are Freire's ideas? How do we adapt them for our classrooms? These are some of the questions this book will try to answer. In the coming pages, creative teachers influenced by Freire's methods will report on their classrooms. They and others are pioneering an area of education that is still a frontier.

This is a good moment to strike forward in new directions. An education crisis has been declared in the United States by the highest policy-makers and authorities, since the landmark report *A Nation at Risk* burst from the Reagan White House in 1983. The years following brought a flood of further reports, task forces, commissions, and legislation. But several waves of reform may make a bad situation worse. The mechanical, authoritarian remedies offered by the new reformers cannot solve the current dilemmas of education. They were developed without teacher-student involvement, in a routinely undemocratic fashion. Official circles and thinkers failed to come up with creative answers. Their efforts need to be replaced by critical approaches to learning and democratic models of social change. Freirean methods for empowering education are hopeful avenues worth exploring, as counters to the conservative reforms of the Reagan era. This current volume is one effort in that direction. It joins a body of knowledge and experience accumulating among liberatory teachers despite the regressive trends of the recent period.

Two overviews begin this anthology. The first, "Educating the Educators" (Chapter 1), is the uncut, original essay I wrote for the *Harvard Educational Review* (November, 1986). This complete paper follows the Freirean practice of placing educational issues in their historical and political setting. Freireans design curriculum by situating academic study in the immediate context of the students and in the larger context of society. In the opening essay, I discuss the roots of the new crisis in schooling and teacher education. Then, I propose *equality* and *desocialization* as foundational values to design critical pedagogy. Finally, I offer an agenda of practical themes that can underlie a Freirean learning program: democratic dialogue in the classroom, curriculum situated in the learner's reality, participatory teaching formats, and critical literacy.

The second overview, "Problem-Posing Education" (Chapter 2), by Nina Wallerstein, is from her book with Elsa Auerbach (Wallerstein & Auerbach, 1986). Even though this was written for ESL settings, Nina's lucid presentation of Freirean methods is a wonderful introduction for teachers in any discipline. She identifies the key steps in a Freirean process. Her insistence on the phrase *problem-posing* instead of *problem-solving* establishes the Freirean educator as a leader of probing critical inquiry rather than as a mechanical answer-giver with a preset syllabus. Nina's work is always full of helpful advice on how to apply teaching ideas in our real courses, and this chapter is hands-on.

The next essay, "An Interactionist Approach to Advancing Literacy" (Chapter 3), by Nan Elsasser and Vera John-Steiner, is an early contribution to Freirean studies in this recent period. It was not only path-breaking when it appeared in 1977, but it also intelligently synthesized two powerful approaches to pedagogy. The first is the sociolinguistic research of Soviet experimentalist Lev Vygotsky, who worked in the 1920s. The second is Freire's dialogic methodology. Using Vygotsky's theories of language acquisition and Freire's teaching strategies, they present a critical literacy course that was illuminating to me when I first read it. It also influenced the authors of the next piece in this anthology, who similarly integrate Vygotsky with Freire.

"Illiteracy and Alienation: Is Paulo Freire's Pedagogy Relevant?" (Chapter 4), by Linda Finlay and Valerie Faith, is another excellent example of theory used in practice. Linda and Valerie clearly discuss Vygotsky's ideas on the difficult transition from speech to writing and then offer a detailed report on a literacy course they taught to first-year college students. They also discuss the role of student alienation in the current literacy problem. Their teaching approach demonstrates the use of *generative themes and words*, that is, language and subjects drawn from student life are the materials for critical inquiry. Generative themes and key words from student speech offer the most open access to student concerns. By using these phrases and themes, Linda and Valerie offer a step-by-step example of how uncritical perceptions of experience can be transformed into critical understanding.

The generative-theme method is fundamental to Freirean literacy programs. It reappears in the next essay, " 'Strangers No More': A Liberatory Literacy Curriculum" (Chapter 5), by Kyle Fiore and Nan Elsasser. This is perhaps the most moving and poignant testimony in this book. Kyle and Nan tell about a writing class Nan taught for adult black women at the College of the Bahamas. This is a fine example of how to situate a course in the thematic concerns of the students while structuring academic exercises that develop critical literacy. The women were preoccupied with themes of domestic violence, rape, and sexual inequality in their society. The way Nan skillfully guided these generative themes into critical reading and writing is a real education for teachers.

The next essay continues demonstrating the generative-theme method for critical literacy. My report, "Monday Morning Fever: Critical Literacy and the Generative Theme of 'Work' " (Chapter 6), is taken from my book (Shor, 1987). In this selection, I use the generative theme of "work" to develop critical consciousness in class. Teachers in professional programs or in career courses might especially examine this report to see how the routine experience of "work" can be problematized in a critical literacy format. I present in detail how the course progresses through a variety of small and large intellectual exercises that offer students some critical detachment on a rather ordinary piece of life. For me, the helpful parts here are the ways in which literacy techniques are integrated into a consciousness-raising study of work.

The ideas of pedagogy situated in the real issues of student life and of critical curriculum inserted into the widespread problems of alienation and disempowerment reappear in Nancy Zimmet's essay "More Than the Basics: Teaching Critical Reading in High School" (Chapter 7). Nancy's report demonstrates an application of Freirean ideas in a public school. Her students at Newton North High are not the top 15 percent who so interested patrician reformer James Bryant Conant when he toured the nation's schools in an earlier period of reform in the 1950s. Nancy does not teach the cream of the crop who will be bullied and nurtured into becoming the future elite. She uses the immediate context of lesser status, inferior feelings, anger, and alienation as themes that help reverse some anti-intellectual results of mass education.

Following Nancy's report, Nan Elsasser returns with coauthor Patricia Irvine for an account of their teaching at the College of the Virgin Islands, "English and Creole: The Dialectics of Choice in a

College Writing Program" (Chapter 8). They make no direct reference to Freirean methods in this paper, but their teaching demonstrates their long-term study of Freirean approaches. Freire discusses (Shor & Freire, 1987) the need to critically study the everyday idiom of non-elite students at the same time the literacy class studies the standard usage or elite idiom of society. Nan and Pat offer an excellent example of how to do this. Ordinarily, non-elite students, both white and non-white, are at a disadvantage in school and society because their every-day language is different from the elite usage favored in the classroom and in the business world. However, a critical study of a native idiom, in this case Creole, simultaneous with a critical inquiry into Standard English, proves to be an empowering experience for the students. This report is a rich example of how to deal concretely with the language differences between teachers and students, while keeping in the fore-ground the social aspects of language use.

The problem of nonstandard speech in students versus standard usage in school and official life is only more exaggerated in the case of ESL classes. In the next essay, Elsa Auerbach and Denise Burgess offer a thoughtful and extensive survey of traditional texts in pro-grams for nonnative speakers, "The Hidden Curriculum of Survival ESL" (Chapter 9). The authors reject mechanical and manipulative varieties of *problem-solving* and *survival* ESL. They reveal the racial and class bias behind these apparently helpful materials. Instead, they urge a Freirean problem-solving approach authentically grounded in the situations faced by ESL students.

The Freirean notion of situating pedagogy in the real needs of the learners informs Nancy Schniedewind's "Feminist Values: Guide-lines for Teaching Methodology in Women's Studies" (Chapter 10). Nancy has written extensively on desocializing students from the sexism, racism, and class bias we all inherit from mass culture (Schniedewind, 1984). Her essay in this book is a helpful blend of theory and practice. She describes her courses in detail after discuss-ing the pedagogical principles she is trying to implement. Nancy has been influenced by Freirean approaches and makes direct reference to Freire in this paper. Besides being of concrete value to teachers, her report shows the intersection of women's themes, feminism, and Freirean learning styles. This book, also, demonstrates the major con-tribution made by women in developing Freirean applications of liberatory education. The common ground on which feminism and Freirean education meet may be the mutual interest in participatory politics, in the integration of social issues with subjective experience, in the use of interactive formats for consciousness-raising, in demo-cratic social relations for school and society, in the empowerment of non-elite groups, and in the critique of domination by elites.

The final selection in this anthology is Marilyn Frankenstein's "Critical Mathematics Education: An Application of Paulo Freire's Epistemology" (Chapter 11). Marilyn's essay has unusual depth. She demonstrates that Freirean problem-posing can be applied outside language, literacy, literature, and communications classes. These latter disciplines have made the most progress in the field of liberatory teaching. This makes sense given that language courses were the scenes of Freire's original literacy programs for peasants and workers in Brazil, in the 1950s and early 1960s. The extension of these methods to non-language courses is needed to balance the push forward into critical literacy classes. Marilyn is a leader in this project. Her essay offers a fine summary of Freirean theory underlying our practice. Then, she concretely shows how to design practical curriculum from these concepts, in a math course. Perhaps a second volume can follow this one—devoted to applications in the natural and social sciences, in professional programs and in career courses. There are teachers like Marilyn who are experimenting in nonlanguage courses, whose work I would like to learn from. I would be grateful to receive teaching reports at the Department of English, College of Staten Island, Staten Island, NY 10301.

Concluding this volume is an afterword by Paulo Freire, "Letter to North-American Teachers" (Chapter 12), written especially for this book. Paulo begins by asserting the political dimension of education. He goes on to consider differences between progressive and reactionary teachers. Further, he writes about our need to make the social relations of the classroom consistent with our democratic values. Following Paulo's letter is Cynthia Brown's essay, "Literacy in 30 Hours: Paulo Freire's Process in Northeast Brazil." I include this paper here because it is the best brief presentation of the classroom method originally used by Freire and his literacy teams. Cynthia's essay includes the drawings used by Freire to stimulate discussion in literacy circles for illiterates. This report first appeared in 1974 and has offered many teachers a lucid contact with the origins of Freirean methods.

We teachers have many needs and face many demands. Our classrooms are busy, complicated places requiring ingenious, agile minds. Hopefully, this book will be of some help to teachers who want to experiment with liberatory learning. This has been a difficult, degenerate period in school and society, so rich in budget cuts and official alarms and accusations of teacher-student *mediocrity*, and so poor in creative ideas and in resources directed to classrooms. This age may give way to forward-looking renewals and to progressive politics, or it may decline into even worse conditions and more austere conservatism in and out of education. No one can predict the future and no one book can solve all our day-to-day challenges in the classroom. We can only work for the future we want. The essays collected here show profound desires for liberatory learning in a democratic society. They are starting points and glimpses of what is possible even under trying conditions. But, these essays are not final words or prescriptions. They can be helpful guides to the creative invention needed in each course we teach. The words in this book will be a success when they are superseded by the work of many hands and voices in countless classrooms of illumination.

References

A Nation at Risk. (1983). Washington, DC: National Commission on Excellence in Education.

Auerbach, E., & Wallerstein, N. (1986). *ESL for action: Problem-posing at work.* Reading, MA: Addison-Wesley.

Schniedewind, N., & Davidson, E. (1984). *Open minds to equality.* Englewood Cliffs, NJ: Prentice-Hall.

Shor, I. (November, 1986). Equality is excellence: Transforming teacher education and the learning process. *Harvard Educational Review, 56*(4), pp. 406-426.

Shor, I. (1987). *Critical teaching and everyday life.* Chicago: The University of Chicago Press.

Shor, I., & Freire, P. (1987). *A pedagogy for liberation.* South Hadley, MA: Bergin & Garvey.

1.

Educating the Educators: A Freirean Approach to the Crisis in Teacher Education

IRA SHOR

Teacher education programs are disturbingly alike and almost uniformly inadequate .... This nation cannot continue to afford the brief, casual, conforming preparation now experienced by those who will staff its classrooms .... We will only begin to get evidence of the potential power of pedagogy when we dare to risk and support markedly deviant classroom procedures.

John Goodlad (1983)

Only a few teachers used the difficult decade of the 1970s to teach themselves and their students with some new methods .... It is easy to claim that a radical restructuring of society or the system of education is needed for the kind of cultural bridging reported in this book to be large scale and continuous.

Shirley Brice Heath (1983)

It is astonishing that so few critics challenge the system .... When one considers the energy, commitment and quality of so many of the people working in the schools, one must place the blame elsewhere. The people are better than the structure. Therefore the structure must be a fault.

Theodore Sizer (1984)

[F]ar too many teachers give out directions, busywork, and fact-fact-fact lectures in ways that keep students intellectually passive, if not actually deepening their disregard for learning and schooling.

The Holmes Group (1986)

Reform in the Name of Authority Since 1983:
The Roots of the Crisis in Teacher Education

Wisdom says where there is light there is heat, but experience shows that the opposite is not always true. The post-1983 waves of reform, "the great school debate" chronicled by Gross and others,[1] created the context for examining teacher education, but the reform movement so far has generated more heat than light. Perhaps it is understandable for discussion of root causes and forward-looking solutions to languish in conservative years. The Reagan Administration, which once declared *ketchup* a vegetable when it sought to cut school lunch budgets, released a report, *A Nation at Risk* in 1983, accusing students and teachers of an alarming *mediocrity*. Apparently, this mediocrity was helping Japan and Germany outpace our economy, even threatening national security. The antidote fit the regressive tenor of the times—more traditional courses, more mechanical testing, and a lust for *excellence* coupled with a token glance at equality.

After *A Nation at Risk* appeared, a second major salvo was fired by the influential Education Commission of the States in its report *Action for Excellence* (1983). It repeated the White House alarms on school decline and teacher quality, highlighting *the teacher gap*, that is, the shortage of qualified teachers to fill classrooms and the lower achievement of those entering the profession. Joining these key statements in that same year were many studies and documents; among the more widely-discussed were *Academic Preparation for College* (1983), *Making the Grade* (1983), *Educating Americans for the 21st Century* (1983), and *America's Competitive Challenge* (1983). This great stir from above provoked state-wide legislation and reviews of curriculum in its first assault on the crisis. Eventually, the reform campaign swept the sad condition of teacher education into its nets, in a "second wave" of the great school debate.

Fishy Nets: Why the Authorities Launched Their Reforms

Unhappy with the costs and the outcomes of schooling, the highest policy-makers turned their attention after 1983 to curricular reform, to restructuring their management of the teaching profession, and to teacher education. At this juncture, business and the military complained about the quality of graduates entering the workforce and the service, especially in regard to literacy and to work discipline.[2] From another angle, the new arms race and the high-tech boom in the economy created in the early 1980s an undersupply of computer workers and engineers (estimated at some 40,000 a year by the

Business-Higher Education Forum). This labor shortage could be solved by tipping curriculum towards technology and computer studies. Unfortunately, by 1986, sectors of the electronics industry were laying off workers in a period of economic *recovery*, sorry news for students who rushed to computer majors and for college planners who promote business needs through curriculum.

Still another labor factor brought curriculum and teacher education into the spotlight. By 1984, the teacher surplus of the 1970s had become a teacher shortage. Even though education programs had grown by 113 in number since 1973, by the 1980s they were producing *53 percent fewer* teachers.[3] Schools were experiencing disruptive spot shortages of teachers, especially in math, science, and foreign languages. Inner-city schools had unusually high turnover rates in their staffs each year. Substantial portions of the teacher corps were teaching out-of-license, with music majors instructing math courses, for example, as stopgap measures, in nominally temporary arrangements that became a permanent and irrational way of life. This teacher supply problem is expected to grow worse in the coming decade, so official *"man*power" planning required a look at what the professional pipeline can do to train new teachers and how the profession can be reorganized to get more from current staff.

With few exceptions,[4] the official reports explained away the real issues in the teacher shortage and in the decline of education, choosing instead "blaming-the-victim" formulas such as student-teacher "mediocrity," the need for "excellence" and higher "standards," the softness in a "cafeteria-style" high school curriculum, and the "breakdown of discipline" in school and the family. In reality, the current crisis was invited by budget cuts in public schools and colleges, which left class size too large, school buildings shabby, instructional materials in short supply, education programs unable to afford careful mentoring of student teachers, and new blood not coming into aging academic departments. Further, conservative educational policy imposed depressing programs of careerism and back-to-basics in the 1970s, making intellectual life in the classroom dull, vocational, and oversupervised.[5] These new curricula discouraged creativity and liberal education, inviting gifted teachers to leave the profession, while dissuading students from thinking of education as an exciting career. The vocational imbalance in college curriculum in the 1970s, when the job market for liberal arts majors and for teachers collapsed, when business and computer majors expanded wildly, steered a generation away from education as a forward-looking job. Those teachers already in-service faced austerity from Nixon through Reagan, leading to wage losses and to decay in their worsening schools. These depressing conditions in the public sector were characteristic of the recent conservative resurgence against the egalitarianism of the 1960s.

Two other real factors in the teaching crisis are higher wages in the private sector for some college graduates and the appearance of a new baby boom. Wages for technical-scientific graduates are better in the private sector than in education or in public sector jobs. This difference draws labor to industry, attracting teachers out of low-paying education jobs into better-paying corporate ones. In an economy unbalanced by military spending, there is a domestic "brain drain" of math, science, and engineering teachers from education into the booming military and electronics sectors of the economy.[6] Secondly, the rising birthrate made its predictable impact on the elementary grades by 1984, creating a demand for new teachers after a decade of economic and social policy that undermined public education. A sudden demand for labor is a crisis in education as in any other labor-short part of the economy. The $130-billion-a-year school system needs about *one million* new teachers, according to the NIE report, *The Condition of Education* (1984).

Evading issues of economic policy and the arms race, the "excellence" reformers promised a renewal from high-tech, traditional subjects, more required testing, career ladders in the teaching profession, and something called "education for economic growth." Such myths hid the causes of school decline, due not only to budget cuts, to the withdrawal of federal support for equality, and to the redirection of funds from social services to the military, but also to the dramatic failure of the corporate job market to inspire graduates with employment equal to their educations.[7] Only a few years before the White House initiative in 1983, the education scene was debating the terrible predicament of "the overeducated American." Besides Richard Freeman's 1976 book of that name, other studies by Ivar Berg, James O'Toole, Harry Braverman, Henry Levin, and Russell Rumberger pointed to a workforce gaining more education while the job market *deskilled* work through automation and *raised* the credentials needed for routine jobs.[8] Just how "overeducation" turned overnight into "mediocrity" was not addressed in the official reports. This would require less blaming of individuals and more critical looks at the corporate-education system. For example, the corporate policy of deindustrializing the United States in favor of cheap-labor sanctuaries in the Third World has profoundly affected education policy. Underlying the new reform wave is the corporate need for a new outcome from schooling—graduates ready for the narrow literacy needs of a computerized economy and workers adjusted to frequent job changes, lower wages, and routine labor, in a "high flex" business world. The major reports after 1983 took for granted that this brave new system would benefit teachers and students as well as business.

The System of Silence: Pushing Liberal Values to the Margins

By ignoring uncomfortable political questions, the recent reform wave had a remarkably unbalanced debate and legislative season. Official commissions and legislative groups, along with media coverage, followed a narrow line of traditional frameworks and authoritarian remedies.[9] These "get-tough" approaches caused visible dismay in out-of-favor liberal circles. Ernest Boyer (1983) complained in his Carnegie report that the new regimens forgot that "education is to enrich the living individual," while Theodore Sizer declared that the current reform wave lacked the compassion for students present in earlier periods of change.[10] Boyer, Sizer, and other skeptics like John Goodlad and Harold Howe II doubted the claims of the "excellence" camp with regard to illiteracy, the SAT decline, and the need for heavy doses of back-to-basics.[11] The liberal dissenters observed the strident emphasis on more testing of teachers and students, more required courses, fewer electives, a reduced federal role in guaranteeing equity, and the call for Standard English over bilingual teaching.

In a period dominated by conservatism, the liberal dissents were worthy of more attention than they received. Besides Boyer's report *High School* (1983), liberal departures can be found in studies by Sizer (1984) and Linda Darling-Hammond (1984a, 1984b). Two "premature" liberal statements from 1982 were Herb Kohl's (1984) helpful book on basic skills and Gene Maeroff's *Don't Blame the Kids* (1982), which offered critiques of the conservative politics behind the back-to-basics movement. These works appeared at the same time as Mortimer Adler's *The Paideia Proposal* (1982), but got far less attention than Adler's traditional proposals. Further among the liberal departures, Shirley Brice Heath's pathbreaking *Ways with Words* (1983) offered a nontraditional ethnographic model of teaching and learning that unfortunately had no impact on state legislation or on district-wide curricular policies. Another pedagogical challenge was offered by Richard Richardson, *Literacy in the Open-Access College* (1983). Richardson did not blame working students for their learning deficits; instead, he pointed to mechanical teaching, which ladled knowledge out as "bits" of information, to state under-funding of mass higher education, and to the vocational bias of the community college as obstacles to the "critical literacy" needed by students.

Other meagerly discussed reports in this dissenting group were the NIE's *Involvement in Learning* (1984), the New World Foundation's *Choosing Equality* (1985), the Association of American College's *Integrity in the College Curriculum* (1985), and John Goodlad's monumental *A Place Called School* (1983). These substantial documents presented alternate policy and pedagogy against the conservative tide of the 1980s. *Choosing Equality* boldly recommended egalitarian federal funding, public economic development to create jobs, and student/teacher/parent "empowerment" as the foundations for educational reform. It was one "grass-roots" correction to an "excellence" mystique launched by *A Nation at Risk* and *Action for Excellence*, and promoted by "excellence" networkers like Diane Ravitch and Chester Finn.[12]

From the egalitarian side, policy issues were matched by presentations of alternate pedagogy. Heath's work in the Carolina Piedmont demonstrated the power of student-centered teaching that broke the traditional separation of school and community. The NIE and AAC reports took stands for interactive, interdisciplinary curriculum. Goodlad supported experimental, participatory pedagogy against the traditional teacher-talk dominating the thousand classrooms his researchers visited. Sizer, Boyer, and Goodlad all acknowledged the failure of the regular school syllabus to address the needs and themes of adolescents. Darling-Hammond discussed the unequal curriculum offered to black students. The NIE and AAC reports acknowledged the failure of traditional curricula to serve the educational needs of college students, whose learning was hindered by the academy's departmental sectarianism, preference for lecture methods, and rewarding of professors for narrow research instead of teaching.[13] This dissenting body of literature did not support "get-tough" programs for the school malaise.

The Heart in the Dissenting Body: An Egalitarian Synthesis

The liberal dissents in this antiliberal period occupied marginal ground. Their defense of student-centered, egalitarian, and interactive values was a heroic holding action. In this dissenting margin, though, one undeveloped value was education as a *change-agent*. The New World Foundation report, *Choosing Equality* (1985), stands out here for its advocacy of community empowerment and community-based school reform. It called for including parents in school policy-making. This was a *change-agency* egalitarianism missing in the other documents. The issue here is linking education to local leadership and existing community organizations. A vision of the educator participating in social change was developed even farther out in the margins, in energetic networks of "participatory researchers" and adult or community educators.[14]

In addition to the idea of change-agency, the heart in this dissenting body needed an egalitarian overview that it did not articulate. Such a synthesis is too important to leave implicit or unrecognized.

I propose the following framework as one way to view egalitarianism and change-agency in education: *equality is excellence because inequality leads to alienation.* Excellence without equality only produces more inequality. Inequality leads to learning deficits and to alienation in the great mass of students. Alienation in school is the number one learning problem, depressing academic performance and elevating student resistance. Student resistance to intellectual life is socially produced by inequality and by authoritarian pedagogy in school, worsening the literacy problem and the crisis in teacher burnout.[15] Teacher burnout and student resistance are social problems of an unequal system and cannot be *fully* addressed by teacher-education reforms or by classroom remedies *alone.* Participatory and critical pedagogy coupled with egalitarian policies in school and society can *holistically* address the education crisis.

I am suggesting that the education crisis is thus an expression of the social crisis of inequality. As one solution, equality empowers people and raises aspirations in school and society. Power and hope are sources of motivation to learn and to do. Motivation produces student involvement and involvement produces learning and literacy. Student participation also supports teacher morale, making the hard work of teaching attractive and rewarding, lessening burnout. Teacher and student morale from the joy of learning will inspire more people to choose teaching as a career, and to stay in teaching once there, easing the teacher shortage. Inspiring classrooms can also encourage more teachers and students to take themselves seriously as intellectuals who can critically grasp any issue, technical process, body of knowledge, moment in history, or political condition in society. Teachers and students oriented to debate and critical study will be better able to act as citizens democratically transforming society. Democratic participation in society may include action against the arms race and budget cuts, potentially shifting wealth from guns to learning, improving the quality and appeal of intellectual life in schools.

The above synthesis recognizes that the fate of education is grossly influenced by economics, by community life and literacy, by commercial mass culture, and by political action outside the classroom. Besides the billions spent on weapons, the most glaring social inequity is the greater money invested in the education of richer students at all levels. Years after California's landmark Serrano decision (1971) against unequal school funding, children of poor and working families still have much less invested in their educations, according to a New York State Court finding in 1981 and to Sizer's assessment after touring high schools around the nation in 1984.[16] This inequality is only the tip of the iceberg, because the daily lives, the ways of using language, and the job futures of poor or working students provide other realities dysfunctional to success in traditional classrooms.[17] This "inequality" (and "arms race") explanation of the school crisis did not appear in the official reports because it blames the economic system rather than pointing a haughty finger at student-teacher "mediocrity," at "spongy" courses in high school, at open admission to college, or at the alleged breakdown of discipline in the family. Economic and social policy gutted mass education, inviting students and teachers to go on a *performance strike.*

Performance Anxiety: Why Teaching Matters

While factors beyond the classroom grossly affect education, what goes on in school makes an important difference, not only in the quality of a student's life and learning, but also in the possible transformation of students, teachers, and of the society setting the curriculum. The strongest potential of education lies in studying the politics and student cultures affecting the classroom. It is politically naive or simply "technocratic" to see the classroom as a world apart where inequality, ideology, and economic policy don't affect learning. It is just as damaging to think pessimistically that nothing good can be achieved in the classroom until the economic system and society are changed. It is also mistaken to believe euphorically that education can change society one classroom at a time.

Lone classrooms cannot change a social system. Only political movements can transform inequality. Egalitarian pedagogy can interfere with the *disabling socialization* of students. School is one large agency among several that socializes students. One way to touch the real potential of teaching is to see that education can either confirm or challenge socialization into inequality. Classrooms can confirm student rejection of critical thinking, that is, confirm the *curricular* disempowerment of their intelligence; or teachers can employ an egalitarian pedagogy to counter their students' disabling education. School is a dependent sector of society that plays a role in reproducing alienated consciousness; it is also an arena of contention where critical teachers can search for openings to challenge inequality, through a critical curriculum in a democratic learning process, to study the culture offering a mass disabling education.

When pedagogy and curricular policy reflect egalitarian goals, they do what education can do: *oppose socialization with desocialization*; choose critical consciousness over commercial consciousness, transformation of society over reproduction of inequality; promote democracy by practicing it and by studying authoritarianism; challenge student withdrawal through participatory courses; illuminate the myths supporting the elite hierarchy of society; interfere with the scholastic disabling of students through a critical literacy program; raise awareness about the thought and language expressed in daily life; distribute research skills and censored information useful for investigating power and policy in society; and invite students to reflect socially on their conditions, to consider overcoming the limits.

Such a critical pedagogy reinvents education in opposition to the traditional purpose of curriculum, which is the reproduction of inequality, a function studied handsomely by Jencks, Bowles and Gintis, Carnoy and Levin, Willis, Apple, Giroux, and others.[18] In opposing the reproduction of subordinate consciousness, there are several roads to critical learning. I and others have experimented with Paulo Freire methods.[19] Shirley Heath tested an ethnographic model. Herb Kohl offered a student-centered language program similar to Stephen Judy's (1980) proposals. Robert Pattison (1982) suggested a "bi-idiomatic" approach to teaching colloquial and formal discourse simultaneously. Jonathan Kozol (1985) proposed a national literacy campaign aimed at adults.

We can pose the question of critical pedagogy (desocialization) when we discuss teacher education programs or curriculum at any level of schooling. Once we accept education's role as challenging inequality and dominant myths rather than as socializing students into the status quo, we have a foundation needed to invent practical methods. Desocialization itself, as a curricular goal, builds on the dissenting terrain already staked out by the liberal departures. Pattison, for example, refused to enthrone correct usage as a universal standard of excellence, referring to it simply as the idiom of the triumphant middle classes, useful for supporting authoritarian societies as easily as democratic ones.[20] Boyer (1983) asserted equality as an unfinished agenda for education. Darling-Hammond (1984b) repeated Boyer's thought in her study of schooling for black students, whose egalitarian gains from the 1960s have eroded since 1975. Further, she saw the micro-management of the classroom by state-mandated testing and syllabi as depressing the performance of teachers (Darling-Hammond, 1984a).[21] Sizer (1984) acknowledged the great impact *social class* has on education while *class* as a theme was not included in the syllabus. Heath (1983) suggested reaching out into everyday life to build on the existing literacy of any school population. Her work was a refreshing break with routine assertions that students were "illiterate." Goodlad (1983) offered the most systematic critique of traditional teaching, including the racial inequities of tracking. Lastly, the Association of American Colleges's *Integrity in the College Curriculum* (1985) strongly criticized the remoteness of college professors from teaching.

The liberal dissents and desocialization may yet make the more important history if only because the authoritarian approach—memorization, mechanical testing, teacher-talk and student silence, abstract subjects remote from student interest, standardized syllabi, balkanized faculties, byzantine administrations—cannot solve the current school crisis. This is the regime that produced student alienation and teacher burnout in the first place. By proposing solutions that caused the problem, the commissions and legislatures offer water to a drowning school system. Conservative nonanswers will only worsen the dilemmas faced by teachers and students in school. The authorities are inviting a more severe crisis down the road.[22] At that moment, liberal humanists may find their program an idea whose time has come, in the vacuum of Reagan-era reforms.

Cleaner Vacuums: The Reform Wave Washes Over Teacher Education

The second-wave debate on reforming teacher education included again some liberal departures overshadowed by traditional policy. Goodlad's (1983) comments on teacher education and Heath's (1983) teaching model stand out from the dominant business as usual. Goodlad recommended experimental schools in each district, where future teachers would train to enter the profession. Teacher-apprentices would spend two years as interns in these experimental schools, learning their craft in settings that model student-centered pedagogy. This would induct them into teaching through an interactive approach rather than a passive one. The influential Holmes Group (1986) proposed a similar idea, converting Goodlad's idea into a graduate degree program and a managerial restructuring of the teaching hierarchy. Holmes called for designating some public schools as "Professional Development Schools" for the training of new teachers. The Professional Development School would promote open-minded, experimental, and interactive pedagogy instead of the "dreary dullness" of both the high school and undergraduate curricula. Going farther, the Holmes Group strenuously urged the abolition of undergraduate education programs, the transfer of teacher education to an exclusive graduate enterprise, and the reform of undergraduate pedagogy to active methods instead of lecture-based models.

Besides the Holmes critique of passive pedagogy, a third dissenting option is Shirley Heath's model of ethnographic research as a method for teacher-training. Teachers would be ethnographers of their students' communities, researching the literacy and lives in student culture. This ethnographic model uses the same study process for students, who would be trained to be local ethnographers, studying scientifically the language and habits they had previously only experienced. Through such a pedagogy, students teach themselves and the teacher while the teacher learns from the very students she or he is also teaching. This mutual education also offers students distance on reality, modeling the critical habit of mind. Heath's program collapsed the wall between classroom and community, between research and teaching, and between research and living. It is an example of the experiential/conceptual approach to learning Dewey proposed.[23]

However, the trend of curricular reform after 1983 was not towards participatory pedagogy, experimental training units, or liberal educational policy. The debate defined teaching and learning in conservative ways that evaded the real needs of the classroom. One evasion focused on managing the profession—teacher testing, certification requirements, differential pay, competitive career ladders—while skirting the three big-ticket items that most concerned teachers: higher wages across the board, smaller class size, and lighter course loads. A second evasion concerned the learning process. Teaching and learning were defined primarily in terms of traditional values and the Great Books, as fixed authority based in standard reading lists, with the teacher as a delivery system in a one-way transfer of information and skills to students. This mechanical notion of education sought traditional material as its core curriculum: the American Heritage and Western Civilization.[24] Such rejections of the multicultural diversity emerging from the 1960s can be read ideally in E. D. Hirsch's definition of "cultural literacy" as a 130-page reading list of Eurocentric works.[25] Hirsch assured us that this list could be reduced for curriculum purposes to a more manageable size, but without such an excursion through a canon dominated by white, male, Western authors, a person could not be considered culturally literate. Another canonical thrust was Mortimer Adler's bookish "paideia" program, which endorsed the knowledge of "classics," in a lecture-dominated pedagogy.[26]

The notion of a core curriculum based in traditional values and classical texts appealed also to Chester Finn, when as Assistant Secretary of Education in the Reagan Administration he prepared *What Works: Research About Teaching and Learning* (1986). This angelic tome began by exhorting the family to do more at home for education and by insisting that hard work and self-reliance (not social policy or school funding) are at the heart of student failure or success.[27] The traditional bent of Finn, a key "excellence" spokesperson, was demonstrated by the many quotes from ancient and pre-1800 sources sprinkling the text, as well as by recommendations to teach a "shared" heritage to students that would instill national pride. This myth of a neutral, shared, national history reduces the critical and multicultural potentials of education. The models proposed by Finn, Adler, and Hirsch were the kind that informed legislative action. They denied the student-centered and experiential values of Goodlad and Heath, and of Charles Silberman during the upheavals of the 1960s, when Silberman (1971) defined a community "paideia."[28] Goodlad (1983) also referred to "paideia" as education in a whole community, not as a school-bound event alone. But, the house of authority heard only Adler.

One lesson here is that the reading list and the learning process are forms of politics and ideology, not neutral terrains. Another lesson is that the learning process you set for the schools is the model socializing future teachers in how to teach. By reasserting an elite canon, in a mechanical menu of testing and teacher-talk, the official commissions and legislative bodies after 1983 were also reimposing a model of teaching. In-service teachers feel great pressure to teach to the tests, while future teachers receive passive canonical instruction in high school, in collegiate liberal arts, and in their academic majors. A passive pedagogy married to dismal texts and traditional reading lists is the curriculum modeled to students, including that fraction who will one day be teachers. This is why *all* of school is actually "teacher education," a *paideia* socializing teachers in how to teach and what to learn. To segregate "pedagogy" courses as *the* place to study teaching is one way to hide the authoritarian, mechanical training embedded in the standard curriculum.

Cannons Aimed at Canons: The Culture War over Learning Process

For over a century, mechanical, factory models of teaching and learning have been at war with critical, interactive education.[29] The quality of the learning process was an issue to liberal dissenters after 1983, heirs as they are to the Deweyan side in the long culture war over curriculum. In one more liberal departure from the dominant trend, the Academy for Educational Development's report *Teacher Development in Schools* (1985) suggested that the *teacher's* learning process required far more than information skills or mechanical grasp of subject matter. The document pointed towards the pre-service teacher's need to study the cultural influences surrounding an individual school, and how teachers and students actually learn in real classrooms.[30]

On the managerial side of this debate, some samples of silence on the learning process can be found in reports from the Southern Regional Education Board, *Improving Teacher Education* (1985a) and *Teacher Preparation: The Anatomy of a Degree* (1985b);

from Oregon's *Quality Assurance: Teacher Education in the Oregon State System of Higher Education* (1984); from the California Commission on the Teaching Profession's policy study *Who Will Teach Our Children?* (1985); from the State University of New York's *Report of the Chancellor's Task Force on Teacher Education* (1985) and the New York State Education Department's *Strengthening Teaching in New York State* (1985); from the Washington-based National Center for Education Information's *The Making of a Teacher: A Report on Teacher Education and Certification* (1984); and from the most prominent of all, the National Commission for Excellence in Teacher Education's *A Call for Change in Teacher Education* (1985).

Instead of a critical discussion of a future teacher's learning process, the reports focus on managing the profession, on admissions and graduation standards to programs, on certification of teachers, on differential pay schemes, and on time spent by students in collegiate courses. The mechanical pedagogy modeled to students at all levels does not surface as a serious concern. Thus, while the reports differ in style and emphases, they show compatibility and consensus. A consensual policy agenda from this group could be synthesized as follows:

- The teaching profession needs higher standards for training and licensure. Teacher education programs are not selective enough, while in-service teachers need to meet more rigorous standards. Admissions and graduation standards in college programs should be raised.
- Teachers need more in-service development. Veteran classroom teachers can train new ones in school and future teachers in campus programs.
- Salaries need improvement, especially at entry-level, and career ladders should be instituted to give teachers incentives.
- Assign teachers fewer noninstructional duties, offer teachers more autonomy in their classroom, and include them more in administrative and policy decisions.
- More care and funds should be given to student teaching in college programs. Teacher preparation should include at least a one-year student-teaching internship.
- The training of teachers should remain primarily on college campuses at the undergraduate level with some alternate, off-campus routes into the profession (a choice made by a number of states, including New Jersey and its alternate certification plan).[31]
- Education majors need more liberal arts courses in college.
- For certification, new teachers should have to pass exams in subject matter, basic skills, and knowledge of pedagogy, in addition to successfully completing a one-year internship in student teaching.

- Efforts should be made to attract the brightest students, especially high-achieving minority candidates, to teaching.
- Research on teaching needs to be more widely disseminated in education courses and in public schools.
- A *five-year* undergraduate teacher education program is needed, requiring liberal arts, concentration in an academic major, education courses, and an internship in student teaching, all of which cannot be completed within the current four-year degree.

A five-year undergraduate program was suggested by the National Commission and by the California Commission in their documents, but it also appeared in the NIE statement *Involvement in Learning* (1984). The New York State Chancellor's Task Force was evenly split between the four- and five-year degree program. The heads of both teacher unions, Albert Shanker of the AFT and Mary Hatwood Futrell of the NEA, served on the National Commission and strongly endorsed the recommendation for a five-year baccalaureate program. Shanker later gave full support to the Carnegie report *A Nation Prepared* (1986), which joined the Holmes Group in urging the *abolition* of the undergraduate degree in education, in favor of graduate programs only. Holmes called for an end to all undergraduate education programs while favoring most of the above consensual agenda. I will come back to this undergraduate-graduate dispute shortly to discuss *"time"* fallacies in mechanical approaches to learning. The five-year baccalaureate and the undergraduate-graduate debate are two ways to paint yourself into a corner if you lose sight of the *quality* of a learning process. Pedagogy took a back seat in this dispute between two wings of the academy—the graduate research universities that want to offer and to "professionalize" the teaching degree versus the established undergraduate teacher programs. This dispute suggested a "trade war" in higher education over who will control the huge teacher-training market. Trade war aside, the above consensual agenda did suggest items beneficial to the teaching profession: higher pay, more classroom autonomy for teachers, carefully mentored internships, in-service development, veteran schoolteachers serving as adjunct faculty in college programs (suggested also by Holmes and by Shanker).[32] The California Commission even recommended the teacher's nightly wish: reduce class size. The agenda, however, was undemocratically developed and imposed with little or no input from teachers. Class size and course load have not come down, while salaries have made some selective gains. The high-profile reforms first pushed through have been more testing of teachers and of students in information and in basic skills, and more required courses in the syllabus, without debate on the learning process in teacher education or in the schools and colleges.

The Proof of the Pudding Is in the Process: If More Liberal Arts Is the Answer, What Is the Question?

One repeated claim in the major reports is that education courses are soft on content while liberal arts courses are hard. Therefore, future teachers who need a better grasp of the canon should study more academic subjects. Future secondary teachers already spend the largest part of their credits in liberal arts and only about 20 percent of their baccalaureate hours in education courses.[33] Still, the information mystique of the liberal arts (social science, natural science, literature, the arts) reappears at a time when mechanical pedagogy fits the needs of top-down reform. The mechanical model offers quantitative and pointless answers to the education crisis: require teachers to take more academic courses, require students to take more information courses, and test both students and teachers on how much they memorized. The grave error is to define memorization as education. The grave disservice to the liberal arts is to define them as information centers.

The humanities curriculum should be admired when it generates critical thought in students and inspires them to interactive learning. Academic studies should not be bodies-of-knowledge eaten in gulps by "information-poor" students. Liberal courses should develop conceptual habits of mind, critical methods of inquiry, in-depth scrutiny, by displaying the relationship between intellect, politics, values, and society. To send future teachers to liberal arts courses to be lectured at and made passive recipients of information is to socialize them further in the wrong model of learning and teaching. This is a point raised in the Holmes Report, and suggested in the earlier AAC and NIE documents, *Integrity in the College Curriculum* (1985) and *Involvement in Learning* (1984). The challenge to every liberal arts course is how much critical thinking does it generate and how much participation does it mobilize, how does it relate its body-of-knowledge to other disciplines, to the communities and literacies of the students, and to the larger conditions of society. These are the pedagogical responsibilities of any course, it should be said, not merely liberal arts. We've come to expect career, business, tech, and science courses to be trade-school arenas that don't provoke spacious understanding or critical thinking around values. This is as bad as expecting liberal arts to be the *sole repository* of historical thinking, values analysis, and comprehensive knowledge.

Soul Repository: The Spirit of Freirean Learning

In proposing a quality process instead of mechanical learning, I suggest here a Freirean pedagogy that is *participatory, critical, values-oriented, multicultural, student-centered, experiential, research-minded, and interdisciplinary*. Such pedagogy focuses on the quality of the activity, not on the quantity of skills or facts memorized, or on the quantity of hours or credits spent on a task. Further, the quality-approach answers two major myths in the recent discussion of teacher education, that undergraduate preparation of teachers requires *five* years instead of *four*, or that teacher education must be done at the graduate level only. These are mechanical fallacies in reports that can be credited for speaking of the need to make teacher education more clinical, more in touch with research, and more open to minorities (even though the new teacher tests are producing high minority failure rates).

Because one side favors a year-long internship in student-teaching at the end of the baccalaureate, it runs into a time problem in the four-year degree, not to mention a money problem in the limited budgets usually allocated to education schools. A seriously mentored internship requires more money and more faculty attention on campus and in the cooperating school than is likely to be invested. Clinical settings in real schools are the best places to learn a teacher's craft. However, when the reports line up in favor of *more* subject-matter specialization and *more* academic courses at the undergraduate level, they wind up having to opt for a *fifth* year to squeeze in a baccalaureate with a teacher-internship. For the other side of the debate, the claim that teaching cannot be a "true" profession until it becomes a graduate enterprise means once again extending teacher preparation to six or seven years of college work. This is the sad fate of the quantitative approach to learning. If you measure knowledge by minutes, hours, courses, credits, semesters, and years, you are ruled by the clock instead of by the intellect. You strain to cover the syllabus. If a passive model of pedagogy dominates all levels of school and college classrooms, what good is it for future teachers to spend an extra year socialized in the worst model of teaching? Four years of bad models will not be remedied by adding a fifth. The Holmes Group understood this, but it did not allow that four years of *good* models—critical, participatory learning—will make the need for graduate teacher-training far less urgent. The challenge here is the same as it was in the information myth of the liberal arts. What kind of learning and teaching is modeled at every year and level of education? If the learning process is interactive and critical, then four years is enough to prepare future teachers. If the learning process models equality and critical thought on school and society, then teacher-education will be a serious enterprise at the graduate or undergraduate level. If curriculum at any degree level for any number of years is dominated by teacher-talk, didactic lectures, canonical reading lists, commercial textbooks, and standardized testing, then five or six years of undergraduate work or two years of graduate study will not develop the teachers needed to inspire learning. Further, even the best teacher education will have limited results as long as low pay, large classes, heavy work loads, administrative oversupervision, standardized testing, and shabby conditions dominate the classroom.

It will be useful for teacher-education reform to confront the time fallacy. More time in liberal arts, a five-year baccalaureate, or a two-year M.A.T. pale in comparison to the question of the learning process. The socializing power of any experience is more in its quality than in its quantity, more in the quality of social relations than in the quantity of statements or rules. A desocializing, egalitarian, and critical pedagogy is a quality process that can invite teachers and students to take their educations seriously. It is one not being modeled now.

Modeling New Fashions: Freirean Themes for Teacher Education

To help define a desocializing model for teacher education, I want to offer a Freirean agenda for the learning process:

1. *Dialogue Teaching.* The dialogue-method discussed by Paulo Freire (1970, 1973, 1987) is one way to reduce student withdrawal and teacher-talk in the classroom. A dialogic class begins with problem-posing discussion and sends powerful signals to students that their participation is expected and needed. It will not be easy to learn the arts of dialogue because education now offers so little critical discussion and so few constructive peer-exchanges. Dialogue calls for a teacher's art of intervention and art of restraint, so that the verbal density of a trained intellectual does not silence the verbal styles of unscholastic students.

   Practice in leading dialogic inquiries in class will require making the teacher-education curriculum itself dialogic. It also suggests study in group dynamics, the social relations of discourse, and the linguistic habits of students in their communities, in relation to their sex, class, race, region, age, and ethnic origin.

2. *Critical Literacy.* Literacy that provokes critical awareness and desocialization will mean more than basic competency. It will be critical literacy across the curriculum, asking all courses to develop reading, writing, thinking, speaking, and listening habits,

to provoke conceptual inquiry into self and society and into the very discipline under study. This means that future teachers in every subject, from biology to architecture, can study how their special competence can generally develop thinking and language skills.

Critical literacy invites teachers and students to *problematize* all subjects of study, that is, to understand existing knowledge as a historical product deeply invested with the values of those who developed such knowledge. A critically literate person does not stay at the empirical level of memorizing data, or at the impressionistic level of opinion, or at the level of dominant myths in society, but goes beneath the surface to understand the origin, structure, and consequences of any body of knowledge, technical process, or object under study. This model of literacy establishes teaching and learning as forms of research and experimentation, testing hypotheses, examining items, questioning what we know. In addition, teaching/learning as research suggests that teachers constantly observe students' learning, to make pedagogical decisions, while students are also researching their language, their society, and their own learning.

3. *Situated Pedagogy.* This goal asks teachers to situate learning in the students' cultures—their literacy, their themes, their present cognitive and affective levels, their aspirations, their daily lives. The goal is to integrate experiential materials with conceptual methods and academic subjects. Grounding economics or nursing or engineering or mathematics or biology in student life and literacy will insert these courses in the *subjectivity* of the learners.

Subjectivity is a synonym for motivation. Material that is of subjective concern is by definition important to those studying it. By turning to subjectivity, the situated course will not only connect experience with critical thought, but will also demonstrate that intellectual work has a tangible purpose in our lives, in discourse connected to student habits of communication. Further, only a situated pedagogy can bring critical study to bear on the concrete circumstances of living, the immediate conditions of life that critical learning may help recreate.

4. *Ethnography and Cross-Cultural Communications.* A teacher's academic program needs components in ethnography and cultural anthropology. To situate critical literacy and dialogue inside the language, themes, and cognitive levels of the students, a teacher needs to study the population he or she is teaching for. This study can be carried out using the ethnographic methods described by Heath, the sociolinguistics demonstrated by Richard Hoggart and by Noelle Bisseret, and the grounded theory approach to research discussed by Glaser and Strauss.[34]

Further, experience in cross-cultural communications will be valuable for teachers who are likely to lead classrooms with diverse student populations. In this regard, the functions of bidialectalism and bilingualism in schools are other academic themes that can address the communications problems of teaching in a multicultural society. A final anthropological feature of teacher education is the need to study nontraditional literatures outside the official canon, from labor culture, ethnic groups, and women's writings.

5. *Change-Agency.* To be egalitarian change-agents, teachers need to study community analysis and models of community change.[35] How do communities structure themselves? How do they change? How do outsiders identify and work with local leaders? How can classroom instruction model itself on key issues of community life?

The teacher will also need to study school organization, school-based curriculum design, the legislative environment for education, and professional politics. Inside the institution of a school or college, political methods for change can include staff development seminars, community-school linkages, faculty committees and assemblies, internal publications, political lobbying, and union organization. Future teachers can benefit from studying histories of organizing change in the classroom, in schools or colleges, and in communities.

6. *Inequality in School and Society.* This academic interest can be studied through sociology, economics, history, and psychology courses. How do inequalities of race, sex, and class influence school outcomes and expenditures? How did the current school system emerge in relation to the politics of each preceding age? What impact have egalitarian movements had on school and social policy? How have nontraditional, egalitarian programs affected student performance?[36]

7. *Performing Skills.* Teachers can benefit from voice and drama training to enhance their skills of presentation and discussion-leading. To be a creative problem-poser in the classroom, drama and voice skills are helpful. The teacher needs to think of herself or himself as a creative artist whose craft is instruction. An exciting instructor is a communications artist who can engage students in provocative dialogue. Also, performing skills can habituate new teachers to the intimidating challenge of standing up each hour in front of a large group and taking charge of the session. Lastly, a dramatic teacher models the aesthetic joy of dialogue, the pleasure of thinking out loud with others.

This agenda of themes is meant to be suggestive rather than exhaustive. Each study item does not require a separate course. Several themes can be integrated into the same course; for example, an ethnography class can also demonstrate dialogue methods of teaching as well as provide background on literacy situated in student culture, which can be studied for the impact of social inequality on daily life and learning. The above program can be coordinated with student teaching. Further, there are other subjects worthy of study: child psychology and adolescent development, the history of pedagogical thought, international education, immigrant patterns of assimilation, a second language (preferably Spanish for U.S. teachers), and how to survive the first year in the classroom. The most important value is participatory learning that mobilizes critical thought and democratic debate.

Class Dismissed

In conclusion, I would emphasize that learning is not the transfer of skills or information from a talking teacher to a passive student. Education is different from narrow training in business careers. These are the negative recipes for even more student alienation and teacher burnout.

A teacher must grow from the spacious hope of being much more than a talking textbook, more than a mere functionary who implements tests and mandated syllabi. Teaching should offer an illumination of reality that helps us and the students examine the social limits constraining us. Spacious learning does not define students as empty vessels to be filled with packaged information on a thin path of facts and figures. This means opposing the mechanical pedagogy and the unequal tracking that take some to success and most others to cheap labor and underemployment, to despair and anti-intellectualism.

Learning which is more than job training and more than socialization into subordinate lives seeks the critical study of society. Such education is a charmingly utopian challenge to inequality and to authoritarian methods, through a humorous, rigorous, and humanizing dialogue, with the April hope of lowering student resistance and teacher burnout, with the August desire of reknowing ourselves and history, in that vast arena of culture war called education.

Notes

1. See Ronald Gross and Beatrice Gross, *The Great School Debate: Which Way for American Education?* (New York: Simon and Schuster, 1985); A. Harry Passow, "Tackling the Reform Reports of the 1980s," *Phi Delta Kappan*, June, 1984, 674-683; Education Commission of the States, *A Summary of Major Reports on Education*, Denver, November, 1983, and *Action in the States*, Task Force on Education for Economic Growth, Denver, 1984. For a summation that includes some critique, see K. Patricia Cross, "The Rising Tide of School Reform Reports," *Phi Delta Kappan*, November, 1984, 167-172.
2. See the National Commission on Excellence in Education, *A Nation at Risk* (Washington, DC, 1983), 9-10; Task Force on Education for Economic Growth, Education Commission of the States, *Action for Excellence* (Denver, 1983), 17-19; and Panel on Secondary School Education for the Changing Workplace, *Schools and the Changing Workplace: The Employers' View*, (Washington, DC: National Academy Press, 1984), 17-19, xi-xii, for commentary on the business-military perception of literacy and work discipline in young graduates.
3. C. Emily Feistrizer, *The Making of a Teacher: A Report on Teacher Education and Certification* (Washington, DC: National Center for Education Information, 1984), 30.
4. One exception to the routine assertions of the 1983 reform wave is *High Schools and the Changing Workplace, op. cit.*, which did not wax grandiloquent on high-tech and computers, as did the other reports. Stanford economist Henry Levin was on the panel producing this report, and its cool assessment of high-tech may reflect his research into the marginal impact computers would have on wages, opportunities, and employment in the future job market. Another exceptional moment is the "Background Paper" by Paul E. Peterson attached to the Twentieth Century Fund report, *Making the Grade* (1983). Peterson's research found no educational crisis or collapse to justify the official claims of 1983. His lengthy study showed the positive outcomes from federal equity programs in the 1960s, thus reversing the report's majority statement in favor of more emphasis on "excellence" and less on equality. A third exception is the California Commission on the Teaching Profession's report, *Who Will Teach Our Children?* (1985), which recommended ending state regulation of teacher education programs, thus allowing each campus to experiment. John Goodlad was on this Commission and this unusual recommendation reflected at least one concern in his study, *A Place Called School* (1983).
5. See Ira Shor, *Culture Wars: School and Society in the Conservative Restoration, 1969-1984* (New York: Routledge and Kegan Paul, 1986), Chapter 2, on career education, and Chapter 3, on the literacy crisis. For more background on the depressant political effects of vocationalism in the 1970s, see Jerome Karabel, "Community Colleges and Social Stratification," *Harvard Educational Review*, Vol. 42, No. 4, November, 1972, 521-562; W. Norton Grubb and Marvin Lazerson, "Rally Round the Workplace: Continuities and Fallacies in Career Education," *Harvard Educational Review*, Vol. 45, November, 1975, 451-474; and Fred Pincus, "The False Promises of Community Colleges: Class Conflict and Vocational Education," *Harvard Educational Review*, Vol. 50, August, 1980, 332-361. An illuminating study of the economics of the 1970s and 1980s can be found in Samuel Bowles, David Gordon, and Thomas Weiskopf, *Beyond the Wasteland: A Democratic Alternative to Economic Decline* (New York: Anchor, 1983). Another spacious survey is in Samuel Bowles and Herbert Gintis, "The Crisis of Liberal Democratic Capitalism in the Case of the United States," *Politics and Society*, Vol. 2, No. 2, 1982, 51-93. The aggressive, conservative politics of this

age were studied in Piven and Cloward, *The New Class War: Reagan's Attack on the Welfare State* (New York: Pantheon, 1982).

6. For some analysis of the domestic brain drain, see Henry Levin, "Solving the Shortage of Mathematics and Science Teachers," *Education Evaluation and Policy Analysis*, Vol. 7, No. 4, Winter, 1985, 371-382. Levin's research points out that from 15 to 50 percent of all scientific personnel are employed directly or indirectly by the Defense Department.

7. For a discussion of the job market's impact on school performance, see the National Coalition of Advocates for Children, *Barriers to Excellence: Our Children at Risk* (Boston, 1985). Another consideration of how economic decline after the 1960s affected student learning is Henry Levin's "Back-to-Basics and the Economy," *Radical Teacher*, Number 20, 1981, 8-10. For a discussion of business' tilting of curriculum in the 1980s, see Joel Spring's "From Study Hall to Hiring Hall," *The Progressive*, April, 1984, 30-31.

8. Richard Freeman, *The Overeducated American* (New York: Academic, 1976); Ivar Berg, *Education and Jobs: The Great Training Robbery* (New York: Praeger, 1970); Department of Health, Education and Welfare, *Work in America* (panel chaired by James O'Toole, Washington, DC, 1983); Harry Braverman, *Labor and Monopoly Capital* (New York: Monthly Review, 1974); Henry Levin and Russell Rumberger, "The Educational Implications of High Technology," Institute for Research on Educational Finance and Governance, Stanford University, 1983.

9. For a sample of the restricted debate in the mass media, see the following cover stories on the education crisis: "Saving Our Schools," *Newsweek*, May 9, 1983; "Shaping Up: America's Schools Are Getting Better," *Time*, October 10, 1983; "What Makes Great Schools Great," *U.S. News and World Report*, August 27, 1984; and "Why Teachers Fail: How to Make Them Better," *Newsweek*, September 24, 1984.

10. For Boyer's dismay on the reform wave, see his 1983 Carnegie study, *High School* (p. 5 and following), and his essay, "Reflections on the Great Debate of '83," *New York Teacher*, June 11, 1984, 9-11 (reprinted from the *Phi Delta Kappan*, April, 1984). Sizer's remarks on compassion and reform appeared in *Time* magazine's cover story on the 1983 crisis, October 10, 1983, p. 66.

11. See John Goodlad, *A Place Called School* (1983), Chapter One especially, for his dismay at the educational programs of the period. Harold Howe II's reservations can be read in "Education Moves to Center Stage: An Overview of Recent Studies," *Phi Delta Kappan*, November, 1983, 167-172, and in his "Let's Have Another SAT Score Decline," *Phi Delta Kappan*, May, 1985, 599-602. Less visible critiques of the reforms can be found in George Leonard, "The Great School Reform Hoax," *Esquire*, April, 1984, 47-56; Andrew Hacker, "The Schools Flunk Out," *New York Review*, April 12, 1984, 35-40; Walter Karp, "Why Johnny Can't Think: The Politics of Bad Schooling," *Harper's*, June, 1985, 69-73.

12. Ravitch and Finn set up the National Network for Excellence in Education in 1984. They edited a compendium with Robert T. Fancher called *Against Mediocrity: The Humanities in America's High Schools* (New York: Holmes and Meier, 1984), which includes their "Conclusions and Recommendations: High Expectations and Disciplined Effort," a traditional curricular position in the great debate. For Finn's conservative view on educational policy, see his "Moving Toward a Public Consensus," *Change*, April, 1983, 15-22, and his "Why Public and Private Schools Matter," *Harvard Educational Review*, November, 1981, 510-514. A liberal response to the elite impact of the "excellence" reforms can be read in Thomas Toch's "The Dark Side of the Excellence Movement," *Phi Delta Kappan*, November, 1984, 173-176.

13. The NIE report, *Involvement in Learning* (1984), deals more with learning process than does the AAC report, *Integrity in the College Curriculum* (1985). AAC focused on curricular policy for higher education, promoting interdisciplinary and critical themes, in a desire to reorient a research professoriat back toward teaching.

14. Some networks supporting community-based, participatory, or change-agency education include the Institute for Responsive Education (Boston), the Public Education Information Network (St. Louis), the Association for Community-Based Education (Washington, DC), Basic Choices (Madison, WI), the Participatory Research Group (Toronto), the Center for Popular Economics (Amherst), the Lindeman Center (Chicago), the Highlander Center (Newmarket, TN), and the Labor Institute (New York). See, for example, Frank Adams's and Myles Horton's *Unearthing Seeds of Fire: The Idea of Highlander* (Blair, NC, 1975); the Labor Institute's *What's Wrong with the U.S. Economy? A Popular Guide for the Rest of Us* (Southend, Boston, 1982); and the Institute for Responsive Education's study, *Action for Educational Equity: A Guide for Parents and Members of Community Groups* (Boston, 1984, Order No. 16C). For one experience in community-based, change-oriented education, see Meredith Minkler and Kathleen Cox, "Creating Critical Consciousness in Health," *International Journal of Health Services*, Vol. 10, No. 2, 1980, 311-322.

15. In *The 1984 Metropolitan Life Survey of the American Teacher* (New York: Louis Harris and Associates), teachers ranked lack of student interest as the most serious problem in the classroom, with budget cuts running a close second.

16. See Edward B. Fiske, "Court Invalidates School Financing in New York State," *The New York Times*, October 27, 1981; Theodore Sizer, *Horace's Compromise* (Boston: Houghton Mifflin, 1984, p. 36). The 1972 study by Christopher Jencks, *Inequality* (New York: Basic), is still the watershed document on this issue. See also Samuel Bowles's and Herbert Gintis's *Schooling in Capitalist America* (New York: Basic, 1976, pp. 4, 33, 133 especially).

17. Shirley Brice Heath's *Ways with Words* (New York: McGraw-Hill, 1983) is an illuminating study of how community literacy and school literacy conflict. The idioms of black and white non-elite schoolkids in the Piedmont clashed with the elite usage favored by the schools. Another excellent study of the clash between language and culture in the schools is Paul Willis's *Learning to Labor: How Working Class Kids Get Working Class Jobs* (New York: Columbia University Press, 1981).

18. Christopher Jencks, et al., *Inequality, op. cit.;* Samuel Bowles and Herbert Gintis, *Schooling in Capitalist America, op. cit.;* Martin Carnoy and Henry Levin, *Schooling and Work in the Democratic State* (Stanford: Stanford University Press, 1985); Paul Willis, *Learning to Labor, op. cit.;* Michael Apple, *Cultural and Economic Reproduction in Education* (London: Routledge and Kegan Paul, 1982); Henry Giroux, *Theory and Resistance in Education* (South Hadley, MA: Bergin and Garvey, 1983). Giroux went on to discuss an "emancipatory" pedagogy and "critical literacy" from a Freire perspective.

19. See Ira Shor, *Critical Teaching and Everyday Life* (Chicago: University of Chicago Press, 1987). Other educators are experimenting with Freire approaches. See Marilyn Frankenstein, "Critical Mathematics Education: An Application of Paulo Freire's Epistemology," *Journal of Education*, Vol. 165, No. 4, 1983, 315-339; Kyle Fiore and Nan Elsasser, " 'Strangers No More': A Liberatory Literacy Curriculum," *College English*, Vol. 44, No. 2, February, 1982, 115-128; Linda Shaw Finlay and Valerie Faith, "Illiteracy and Alienation in American Colleges: Is Paulo Freire's Pedagogy Relevant?" *Radical Teacher*, No. 16, December 1979,

28–40; and Nina Wallerstein, *Language and Culture in Conflict: Problem-Posing in the ESL Classroom* (Reading, MA: Addison-Wesley, 1983).

20. See Chapters 5, 6, and 7 especially in Robert Pattison's *On Literacy: The Politics of the Word from Homer to the Age of Rock* (New York: Oxford, 1982).

21. See also Linda Darling-Hammond's critique of the testing craze in the 1983 reform wave, "Mad-Hatter Tests of Good Teaching," *The New York Times*, January 8, 1984. Her 1984 study of black students was carried out for the College Board.

22. Larry Cuban wisely assessed the potential for failure in a mechanical reform program in "School Reform by Remote Control: SB 813 in California," *Phi Delta Kappan*, November, 1984, 213–215.

23. John Dewey, *The Child and the Curriculum* (Chicago: University of Chicago Press, [1902] 1956) and *The School and Society* (Chicago: University of Chicago Press, [1900] 1956), and *Experience and Education* (New York: Collier, [1938] 1963).

24. These were the curricular emphases in California's reform legislation Senate Bill 813 and in New York's Regents Action Plan with its Part 100 Regulations. Secretary of Education William Bennett took up these themes also in *To Reclaim a Legacy: A Report on the Humanities in Higher Education* (Washington, DC: U.S. Government Printing Office, 1984).

25. E. D. Hirsch's quantitative canon was discussed in his essay "Cultural Literacy," *The American Scholar*, Vol. 52, Spring, 1983, 159–169, and in his "Cultural Literacy and the Schools," *American Educator*, Summer, 1985, 8–15. Larry Cuban's "School Reform by Remote Control: SB 813 in California," *op. cit.*, offers also a concise critique of the mechanical approach to learning. For some historical perspective on the politics of literacy, see James Donald, "How Illiteracy Became a Problem (And Literacy Stopped Being One)," *Journal of Education*, Vol. 165, No. 1, Winter, 1983, 35–52. Donald offers an illuminating look at the literacy debate in nineteenth-century Britain, when state-sponsored literacy in official schools helped reduce popular dissent. Another fine discussion of literacy is Richard Ohmann's "Literacy, Technology, and Monopoly Capital," *College English*, Vol. 47, No. 7, November, 1985, 675–689.

26. See Mortimer Adler's *The Paideia Proposal* (New York: Macmillan, 1982), and his follow-up "how-to" book, *Paideia: Problems and Possibilities* (New York: Macmillan, 1983).

27. *What Works: Research About Teaching and Learning* (Washington, DC: Department of Education, 1986). The politics of this document are largely denied by Secretary Bennett and Assistant Secretary Finn, who refer to its recommendations as "common sense," a "useful distillation," and "true opinion." While there are enlightened moments in the text, such as its endorsement of a writing process for composition classes, the burden of the report repeats the traditional homilies of the earlier *A Nation at Risk*.

28. Charles Silberman, *Crisis in the Classroom* (New York: Vintage, 1971). In discussing a progressive, community-oriented, social learning, Silberman refers to "paideia" twice, pp. 5 and 49.

29. In the heated reform year 1983, the *Phi Delta Kappan* published a cheerful counter to the conservative agendas and a pointed reminder of the long debate over curriculum, in an essay by Richard A. Gibboney, "Learning: A Process Approach from Francis Parker," September, 1983, 55–56. This article discussed Colonel Parker's reversal of educational decline in the Quincy schools in the 1870s through "progressive" pedagogy. A substantial history of the progressive movement can be found in Lawrence Cremin's *The Transformation of the School* (New York: Vintage, 1964).

30. See *Teacher Development in Schools* (New York: Academy for Educational Development, 1985), pp. 17–31 especially on learning process.

31. A report on New Jersey's alternate certification program can be found in Gene Maeroff, "Alternate Route Leads Teachers to the Classroom," *The New York Times*, August 13, 1985. See also Jonathan Friendly, "Jersey Hires Teachers Without Education Courses," *The New York Times*, August 15, 1985.

32. Albert Shanker proposed hiring veteran teachers as mentors and adjunct faculty in teacher education programs in *The Making of a Profession* (Washington, DC: American Federation of Teachers, 1985). He also confirmed his support of a national teacher-testing program and career ladders, including a category of "transient" teacher at the entry-level position. The "transient" teacher idea reappeared in the Holmes Group report (1986) as the job of "instructor," basically the same nontenure track, subordinate position outlined by Shanker.

33. In the National Commission on Excellence in Teacher Education's report, *A Call for Change in Teacher Education* (Washington, DC: 1985), how an education major spends her or his credits at the undergraduate level is discussed on p. 13. The Holmes Group report made the same emphatic point about teacher-preparation already being a liberal arts enterprise.

34. Shirley Brice Heath, *Ways with Words, op. cit.*, Richard Hoggart, *The Uses of Literacy* (London: Chatto Windus, 1957); Noelle Bisseret, *Education, Class Language, and Ideology* (London: Routledge and Kegan Paul, 1979); Barney G. Glaser and Anselm L. Straus, *The Discovery of Grounded Theory: Strategies for Qualitative Research* (Chicago: Aldine, 1967).

35. For one well-defined program in community education, see Ian M. Harris, "An Undergraduate Community Education Curriculum for Community Development," *Journal of the Community Development Society*, Vol. 13, No. 1, 1982, 69-82.

36. An informative survey of the unknown successes in nontraditional programs can be found in Wayne Jennings' and Joe Nathan's essay "Startling/Disturbing Research on School Program Effectiveness," *Phi Delta Kappan*, March, 1977, 568-572. On this issue of nontraditional education, see also Nathan's *Free to Teach: Equity and Excellence in Schools* (New York: Pilgrim, 1983).

References

Academic preparation for college: What students need to know and be able to do. (1983). New York: College Board.

Action for excellence. (1983). Denver: Education Commission of the States (Task Force on Education for Economic Growth).

Adler, M. (1982). *The Paideia proposal.* New York: Macmillan.

Adler, M. (1983). *Paideia: Problems and possibilities.* New York: Macmillan.

America's competitive challenge. (1983). Washington, DC: The Business-Higher Education Forum.

Bastian, A., Fruchter, N., Gittell, M., Greer, C., & Haskins, K. (1985). *Choosing equality: The case for democratic schooling.* New York: New World Foundation.

Boyer, E. L. (1983). *High school.* New York: Harper & Row.

A call for change in teacher education. (1985). Washington, DC: National Commission for Excellence in Teacher Education.

Darling-Hammond, L. (1984a). *Beyond the commission reports: The coming crisis in teaching.* Santa Monica: Rand Corporation.

Darling-Hammond, L. (1984b). *Equality and excellence: The educational status of black Americans.* New York: The College Board.

Educating Americans for the twenty-first century. (1983). Washington, DC: National Science Board.

Feistritzer, C. E. (1984). *The making of a teacher: A report on teacher education and certification.* Washington, DC: National Center for Education Information.

Freire, P. (1970). *Pedagogy of the oppressed.* New York: Seabury.

Freire, P. (1973). *Education for critical consciousness.* New York: Seabury.

Goodlad, J. (1983). *A place called school.* New York: McGraw-Hill.

Heath, S. B. (1983). *Ways with words.* New York: McGraw-Hill.

High schools and the changing workplace: The employer's view. (1984). Washington, DC: National Academy Press.

Improving teacher education: An agenda for higher education and the schools. (1985). Atlanta: Southern Regional Education Board.

Integrity in the college curriculum. (1985). Washington, DC: Association of American Colleges.

Involvement in learning: Realizing the potential of American higher education. (1984). Washington, DC: National Institute of Education.

Judy, S. (1980). *The ABCs of literacy.* New York: Oxford University Press.

Kohl, H. (1984). *Basic skills.* New York: Bantam.

Kozol, J. (1985). *Illiterate America.* New York: Doubleday.

Maeroff, G. (1982). *Don't blame the kids: The trouble with America's schools.* New York: McGraw-Hill.

Making the grade. (1983). New York: The Twentieth Century Fund.

A nation at risk. (1983). Washington, DC: National Commission on Excellence in Education.

A nation prepared: Teachers for the 21st century. (1986). New York: Carnegie Forum on Education and the Economy (Task Force on Teaching as a Profession).

Pattison, R. (1982). *On literacy: The politics of the word from Homer to the age of rock.* New York: Oxford University Press.

Quality assurance: Teacher education in the Oregon State System of Higher Education. (1984). Eugene, OR: Oregon State System of Higher Education.

Report of the chancellor's task force on teacher education. (1985). Albany: State University of New York.

Richardson, R. C., Fisk, E. C., & Okun, M. K. (1983). *Literacy in the open-access college.* San Francisco: Jossey Bass.

Shor, I., & Freire, P. (1987). *A pedagogy for liberation: Dialogues on transforming education.* South Hadley, MA: Bergin and Garvey.

Silberman, C. (1971). *Crisis in the classroom.* New York: Vintage.

Sizer, T. (1984). *Horace's compromise.* Boston: Houghton Mifflin.

Strengthening teaching in New York State. (1985). Albany: New York State Education Department.

Teacher development in schools: A report to the Ford Foundation. (1985). New York: Academy for Educational Development.

Teacher preparation: The anatomy of a college degree. (1985). Atlanta: Southern Region Education Board.

Tomorrow's teachers: A report of the Holmes Group. (1986). East Lansing, MI: Holmes Group.

What works: Research about teaching and learning. (1986). Washington, DC: Department of Education.

Who will teach our children? A strategy for improving California's schools. (1985). Sacramento: California Commission on the Teaching Profession.

2.

Problem-Posing Education: Freire's Method for Transformation

NINA WALLERSTEIN

The problem-posing approach described here originated with the work of Brazilian educator Paulo Freire. In the late 1950s, Freire initiated a highly successful literacy program for slum dwellers and peasants in Brazil. Concerned with his students' fatalistic outlook, he started "culture circles" that used pictures to challenge students to think critically about their lives and begin to control their own destinies. Culture circles evolved into literacy classes with carefully chosen words that represented the emotionally and socially problematic issues in participants' lives. The dialogue about each "generative" word stimulated their understanding of the social root causes of problems and how they could effect change. Freire's programs empowered students with the reading and writing skills necessary to gain the vote and participate in the political process. His work was so successful that he was forced into exile by the Brazilian military in 1964.

Over the last two decades, Freire's ideas and vision of "education for transformation" have been a catalyst for literacy, English as a Second Language, labor, peace and health education, and community development worldwide. Freire has worked for the World Council of Churches, consulted for Third World countries in adult education, and given conferences in many U.S. universities, returning to Brazil in 1980. An increasing number of educators are adapting his ideas in the United States, Canada, and Europe.

Freire's central premise is that education is not neutral; whether it occurs in a classroom or in a community setting, the interaction of teacher and student does not take place in a vacuum. People bring with them their cultural expectations, their experiences of social discrimination and life pressures, and their strengths in surviving. Education starts from the experiences of people, and either reinforces or challenges the existing social forces that keep them passive.

In Freire's terms, the purpose of education should be human liberation, which "takes place to the extent that people reflect upon . . . the relationship to the world in which they live. And . . . in conscientizing themselves, they insert themselves in history as subjects (Freire, 1971). This goal of education is based on Freire's view of the learner and of knowledge: the learner is not an empty vessel to be filled by the teacher, nor an object of education. "Studying is a form of re-inventing, re-creating, re-writing, and this is a subject's, not an object's task" (Freire, 1985, p. 2). Learners enter into the process of learning not by acquiring facts, but by constructing their reality in social exchange with others.

To achieve this education, Freire proposes a dialogical approach in which everyone—teacher/student, administrator/teacher, health educator/community member—participates as colearners. The goal of dialogue is critical thinking (or "conscientization" from the Portuguese) and action. Critical thinking starts from perceiving the root causes of one's place in society—the socioeconomic, political, cultural, and historical context of our personal lives. But critical thinking continues beyond perception—toward the actions and decisions people make to shape and gain control over their lives. True knowledge evolves from the interaction of reflection and action (or praxis) and occurs "when human beings participate in a transforming act" (Freire, 1985, p. 106).

Problem-posing is a group process that draws on personal experience to create social connectedness and mutual responsibility. Because students' confidence has been undermined by societal pressures, empowerment must therefore be social (Shor, 1987).

Problem-posing is particularly applicable to immigrant and refugee English as a Second Language (ESL) students, or workers with little control over their lives. The majority of ESL students come from low socioeconomic backgrounds with restricted access to education in their home countries. In the United States, they work primarily in unskilled or low-skilled jobs; they often experience social or emotional barriers to learning English, cultural conflicts, lack of self-esteem and a feeling of vulnerability in their new society. In the workplace, they may experience distance or discomfort from fellow American workers.

Yet, a curriculum centered on the shared nature of these conflicts and problematic interactions (similar to Freire's "generative words") enables students to envision different working conditions and to fashion an individual or community response to the problem. Unlike other methods where the teacher creates both the content and structure of learning, in problem-posing much of the content comes from students' lives. Because of its societal and emotional affect, problem-posing becomes a powerful motivating factor in language acquisition. As students learn the methodology, they also begin to assume responsibility for the structure of learning.

A problem-posing methodology involves three phases: listening (or investigating the issues or generative themes of the community), dialogue (or codifying issues into discussion starters for critical thinking), and action (or strategizing the changes students envision following their reflections).

Listening

There are many ways to discover students' generative themes. We all listen to our students in class or during breaks. But which issues are important and how do we listen for deeper understanding?

For example, in typical classroom interactions, we often ask about our students' families. The simple question "Where do you live?" may unwittingly send an undocumented worker into a panic. Or, we may discuss a work accident that kept a student home for a week. We may ask how and why the accident happened. Yet, what if she was afraid she would be fired? What if her manager did not tell her about Workers' Compensation and she could not afford her medical bills? How sympathetic or devastating were her encounters with clinic staff, with her boss, with her family during the time she lost at work?

Such encounters and underlying issues certainly affect her view of herself in the United States, her view of English, and possibly her view of the teacher.

These emotions or "hidden voices" that students bring with them are essential for educators to uncover, as they have the power to block learning. The blocks can be emotional (such as low self-esteem), structural (such as lack of contact with English speakers), or socioeconomic (such as job instability or prejudice). Yet, the emotional power behind these hidden voices can also inspire learning. By helping students articulate their concerns in the classroom, teachers help students understand the blocks and move beyond them.

How do we listen for students' hidden voices? In problem-posing, unlike other competency-based approaches, the "needs assessment" is not completed before the beginning of class, nor is the listening effort undertaken by the teacher alone. As content is drawn from learners' daily lives, listening becomes an ongoing process involving both teachers and students as colearners and coexplorers.

Listening in Class

Usually, at the beginning you do not know exactly what you are looking for. Start therefore with a learner's stance, listening for themes or content areas that have high emotional impact. What are students worried about? What makes them sad, happy, or angry? General categories include the work process, relationships at work, decision-making structures, monetary problems, values and beliefs associated with work, interaction of family and worklife, cultural differences, historical trends, and future directions for students.

Often students voice their concerns in informal conversations during breaks, before or after class. These concerns can be elaborated in class as a lesson. Sometimes discussion in students' first language (or phrases that require translation) helps students initially explore the issue. With follow-up in English, the use of first language deepens students' critical analysis and may facilitate more sophisticated use of the English language.

Listening Outside Class

Problem-posing fosters a conscious team effort for out-of-class listening. Student participation expands your eyes and ears, especially if you do not have access to their work sites. Have students consider themselves observers and reporters of their workplaces and communities.

Three tools of anthropological research are helpful for teachers and students: observation, interviews, and document analysis. Observing suggests a reawakening of wonder and of watching a situation with new eyes. Students who have worked in a company for a long period of time may be desensitized to their surroundings. More often, students have never questioned the reasons behind the structure or relations at work. Invite students to imagine they are entering their workplace for the first time. What do they notice about work speed, people's interactions, length of time people stand or sit in the same position, level of noise, differences between shifts? As a teacher, take any opportunity to visit work sites or student neighborhoods at different times of day and occasions.

To observe more closely, use tools to record what you see: photographs, drawings of dynamics between people, written notes of conversations or descriptions of place. Students can generate their own visual aids or role-plays for futher listening and discussion: charts, collages, and artwork. Photographs, taken by teachers or students, may give a new perspective on the ordinary, such as a juxtaposition of events, previously unnoticed.

Another tool for listening is the "found" or familiar object that students use daily at home or at work. These can be cultural artifacts, work tools, chemical labels—anything that facilitates understanding students' environment. For instance, ask students to bring something from work they are proud of or concerned about (if possible). Found objects encourage students to get to know each other better and to value each other's life and work.

Encourage students to observe co-workers' conversations. Do conversations change when supervisors leave the work area? From their listening, what do students begin to wonder about their own workplaces? Systematic note-taking about who students talk to, how often, in what language, and about what topics can be part of students' own needs assessments.

The second strategy of interviews calls for direct interaction with others. What do students want to ask their fellow immigrants, American workers or supervisors? Students can ask questions during everyday conversation or through formal interviews. Informally, students can ask for more information or clarification of an issue being discussed. Formal interviews require planning. Students can write a list of questions or topics that they've decided to pursue after their conversations. Each student then interviews one or two people and brings back responses for a class discussion.

The third strategy is making lesson plans out of documents brought into class. Documents, such as company policies, union contracts, health and safety injury logs may uncover new issues, provide a historical context or give supporting evidence for a problem students are discussing.

These participatory research strategies provide a structure for students to be coequals in their learning. Through investigation, students develop critical thinking tools of analysis, use their English outside the classroom, and realize their potential for participating in decision-making.

Dialogue

After identifying the issues, how do we bring them into the classroom for discussion? These issues by definition are emotional and offer no immediate solutions. For instance, how easily can students resolve their conflicts with American workers when their supervisors demand faster work? Our students often comply to get a good work record. American workers, on the other hand, will resent the increased pressure after they've worked to stabilize the job at a slower pace. We need a structure for positive group dialogue, so students don't give up in frustration or only articulate their resentments. By using discussion objects called "codes" ("codification" in Freire's terms) followed by an inductive questioning strategy, students can ground their discussion in personal experience, integrate that experience into the broad social context, and together evolve alternatives.

A code is a concrete physical representation of a particularly critical issue that has come up during the listening phase. Developed by teachers initially or by students as they learn the process, codes can take many forms: a written dialogue, a story, a photograph, a skit, a collage, or a song. No matter what the form, a code re-presents the students' reality back to the class and allows them to project their emotional and social responses in a focused fashion. An effective code should have the following characteristics:

- It should represent a familiar problem situation immediately recognized by the group
- It should be presented as a problem with many sides or contradictions to avoid conveying a good or bad point of view
- It should focus on one concern at a time, but not in a fragmented way; the historical, cultural, and social connections in students lives should be suggested
- It should be open-ended and not provide solutions; any resolution or strategies should emerge from the group discussion
- The problem should not be overwhelming, but should offer possibilities for group affirmation and small actions toward change

Why is it important to have an object to mediate discussion? By our process of listening; we are dealing with loaded issues that may be too threatening to approach directly or too overwhelming or embarrassing to confront individually. A code on sexual harrassment, for example, allows people as a group to project their concerns into the problem, one step removed from personal incidents. Students can offer similar experiences of friends or their own as they feel comfortable. If the discussion becomes too personal, you, as teacher, can redirect attention back to the code and the neutral object. Because no solution is offered, participants suggest their own options for action.

In sum, a code "codifies" into one depersonalized representation, a conflict or problem that carries emotional or social impact in people's lives. It is more than a visual aid or a structured language exercise, as its purpose is to promote critical thinking and action.

Questions for Discussion

Although codes present open-ended situations, critical thinking does not occur spontaneously. Problem-posing with a code uses a five-step questioning strategy that moved the discussion from the concrete to the analytic level. Students are asked to

1. Describe what they see
2. Define the problem(s)

3. Share similar experiences
4. Question why there's a problem
5. Strategize what they can do about the problem

By starting with the concrete descriptive level, participating is encouraged with the maximum number of people. Students who answer the simple identification questions and share experiences first are more likely to be willing and prepared to answer the probing questions later. Jumping too quickly to generalizations or "why" questions inhibits the thinking process.

For example, let's look at a health and safety code with questions for discussion from the student units:

ROBERT: The report from the health and safety inspector is in.
MARY: What does it say?
GEORGE: It says there's no problem! The chemicals in the new paint finish are safe.
JOHN: But we know there's a problem! We all have the skin rash on our hands.
GEORGE: The report says there's nothing wrong.
MARY: Well, we should know. We work here.

Questions for Discussion

1. Have students describe or name what they see in the code. Do they understand all the vocabulary: "What health problems do workers have? Who is the health and safety inspector? What does he or she do?"
2. Ask students to define the problem. What's really happening? The question "How does each person in the code feel?" often gets to the heart of the problem through different people's perceptions: "How do John and Mary feel about the health report? About their rashes? Do you think there is a health problem?"
3. Ask if students have experienced this problem before. How is it similar or different from our class? How do they feel about it? It may be safer to ask if they know anyone else with this problem. As students share experiences, they begin to "own" the issue in its social context and feel less isolated: "Do any substances bother you or your fellow employees at work? Have you ever had a problem that someone said was not a problem? How did you feel? What happened?
4. Direct students to fit their personal stories into the larger socioeconomic, cultural or political context, to ask why there's a problem. In this step, students generalize and project their

opinions. It may help to ask who benefits and who loses from this problem: "Why do you think the report says there's no problem? Who do you think is right? Who benefits from this report? Who is the expert about health problems at work?"

5. Discuss strategies for solutions. What can the people in the code do about the problem? What can students do in their lives? Encourage sharing of success stories from the past and any ideas for small action steps: "What do you think the workers should do? Should they stop worrying about the skin rash? Do they have a right to know about the health problems? Who should they talk to? What would you do? What have you done in the past?"

The final questioning stage takes students into positive action, though solutions may take a long time, trial and error, and different strategies. This process is therefore called problem-posing, not problem-solving, recognizing the need for continuous actions and the complexity of solutions for students in their workplaces. Although change may evolve slowly, problem-posing can and should be a nurturing process. It is important to explore the problem and its causes, but also the visions and ideals people have for their work, communities, families, and themselves.

These five stages of problem-posing questions may be easily remembered through the acronym, SHOWeD, formed by the words: See, Happening, Our (lives), Why, and Do (Shaffer, 1983). The specific questions in any text should be seen as suggestions or guidelines, not rigid prescriptions. Teachers or students can ask their own questions depending on class interest. The beauty of codes is that each new group develops its own open-ended dialogue from the individual realities that form the group analysis.

Other discussion techniques can supplement this questioning sequence to uncover root causes. The "But why?" method starts with a problem situation, asking what causes it (Werner, 1977). After each student response, the question "But why?" elicits deeper or different reasons. For example, if a student reports he has headaches at work, the teacher may ask why. He may say because he's working too hard.

But why are you working too hard?
I want a promotion to another department.

But why do you want a promotion?
I need more money for my family.

But why don't you have enough money?
I only get minimum wage and I also have my brother's family at home, etc.

Root causes often have many dimensions: cultural, socioeconomic, political, historical. Sometimes it helps to separate them in chart form and address each problem separately. Students may handle cultural issues by acquiring communication skills. Social problems may require group interventions, such as having all employees in a work group deal with a discriminatory statement. Political reasons behind a problem demand more student confidence and organizational skills, such as challenging the company to alter their pay inequities. Historical dimensions give the long-range perspective; students can gain hope from knowing about past working conditions or gains.

Role of the Teacher in Group Dialogue

"A cultural circle is a live and creative dialogue in which everyone knows some things and does not know others, in which all seek together to know more. This is why you, as the coordinator of a cultural circle, must be humble, so that you can grow with the group instead of losing your humility and claiming to direct the group, once it is animated" (Freire, 1971).

Our students have few opportunities in their lives to take charge of their learning. They have often been conditioned in school or jobs to respond to orders or to other people's initiatives. Students may initially feel uncomfortable with dialogue and peer teaching/learning. In the beginning, teachers should meet student expectations by providing structure and asking questions. As students become comfortable with sharing experiences through codes, the classroom environment will change. They will begin to ask each other questions, give helpful ideas on a problem, and develop their own codes. The physical arrangement of the room, placing students in a circle or in small groups, reinforces students' self-image as colearners and coteachers. Group listening, trust exercises, and cooperative language or action activities further bond and encourage people to rely on each other for learning, and for effecting change.

The use of a code allows genuine peer interaction among students; the teacher can step back from the discussion as students project their experiences into the code and ask each other for more information. The role of the teacher is to ask questions but also to provide necessary information that promotes critical thinking. For example, in a code on pay issues, students may need information on the local employment market to understand prevailing wages. Teachers however should not impose their own answers or solutions to the questions. Strategies emerge from the group as students analyze their reality and come up with new ideas.

Action

Action, or following through to the consequences of reflection, is essential for learning. As students test out their analyses in the real world, they begin a deeper cycle of reflection that includes input from their new experiential base. This recurrent cycle of reflection and action is the praxis of knowing. As students understand this cycle, they can celebrate successes, analyze mistakes or failures, and formulate other approaches to the problem.

Action for students means learning to see themselves as social and political beings, with rights to access to the political systems in their workplaces or their cities. Plans for action evolve from students understanding the immediate and root causes of problems, as well as having visions of better conditions. Individual or group actions from a class, therefore, depend on many factors (Moriarty & Wallerstein, 1983):

- Internal class dynamics—the length of time students have been together in class; whether they come from one or many worksites; whether they are from the same or different linguistic and cultural backgrounds; their level of trust and participation in positive dialogue
- External societal factors—students' understanding of the barriers to change; the possibility of actions through worksites, i.e., union vs. nonunion settings, through the law or political action
- Internal feelings—the level of self-confidence created through learning English and problem-posing in class; through other life settings; and through prior roles and experiences in their own culture
- Other support mechanisms—students' family, community, and work environments that provide support and hope for change

Potential actions vary considerably. In class, students have a safe environment to stumble with English, test out ideas, and successfully communicate. Actions in class revolve around building a community of support through dialogue. Students can write life stories, develop individual or group codes, and plan classroom projects. Group visual codes can be constructed, such as students drawing images of their lives on newsprint: their factories, their schools, their transportation to work, their breaks at work—anything to stimulate critical discussion. Group projects over time foster collaborative learning and can make the bridge between class and the outside world: letters to the editor, radio public service spots, videotapes, oral histories of workers, or articles for a union newspaper.

Students can practice taking action at work through in-class roleplays and action competencies, such as reporting a problem or filing a complaint. Action competencies are tools for students to take out of the classroom into their daily work lives. The language practice becomes a means to action, not only to learn English.

Actions outside of class also vary: from interviewing a co-worker or a resource agency about legal rights to actually taking action to rectify a problem—by themselves, with co-workers, with the union, through the law, or through lobbying and community organizing. Actions can involve fighting for funding to continue the English class, or adopting an outside issue, such as toxic emissions in a neighboring factory.

Regardless of the level of action taken, students learn through the experience of action itself, that people can effectively interact in the U.S. political system to transform their reality. If actions are unsuccessful, students will gain new knowledge and perspectives to try another strategy. Historically, immigrant workers have participated in and led many successful movements in the workplace. Unions have lobbied for and won changes in the law, such as the Occupational Safety and Health Act (OSHA). Historical and current events are important for students to gain a larger vision than what can be immediately possible in their daily lives.

One method to determine smaller possibilities of action within a larger vision is to conduct a brainstorming session on the problem the class is studying. Make four columns on the board with the following headings: problem(s), barriers to change, larger vision, and immediate plans. The lists under these columns will shift as students explore the problems and try out some of their small steps. The key is to reinforce the possibilities for vision in a new land and to build on students' dreams they have already demonstrated by coming to the United States.

Evaluation

Evaluation of students' progress with a problem-posing curriculum demands a different approach than other teaching methods. Because the curriculum constantly evolves from student issues, teachers can't measure fulfillment of predetermined objectives or test outcomes. Problem-posing evaluation concerns a broad spectrum of students' abilities to articulate their issues in English, generate their own learning materials, redefine their views of the world, and take the risks to act in their daily lives. Because students' abilities change over time, problem-posing requires a process evaluation of both the expected and unexpected changes.

In concert with the entire approach, evaluation can be an empowering tool. Students can learn to evaluate their own learning and to reflect as a group about the actions they have taken. To start the evaluation process, look at the effects of codes on student learning, and on promoting discussion and action. Did the code tap a generative familiar theme? Did the room come to life with students' emotions, laughter, and stories? Did it foster student understanding of root causes of the problem and was action taken? What did students learn about themselves or about their collective work as a group? What was the result of the action, and how would they do it differently next time? Finally, what new problems did it uncover to pursue in the curriculum (Moriarity, 1984)?

Evaluation about actions reinforces the purpose of education as personal and social change so students can become actors in their own worlds. The problem-posing approach of listening, dialogue, and action together comprise an education that is based on students' needs for language, self-expression, and control over their own lives.

References

Freire, P. (1971). To the coordinator of a cultural circle. *Convergence, 4*(1), 61–62.
Freire, P. (1973). *Education for critical consciousness.* New York: Seabury.
Freire, P. (1985). *Politics of education.* South Hadley, MA: Bergin and Garvey.
Moriarty, P. (1984). *Codifications in Freire's pedagogy: A North American application.* Unpublished master's thesis, San Francisco State University, San Francisco.
Moriarty, P., & Wallerstein, N. (1983). *Teaching about nuclear war: A positive problem-posing strategy.* San Francisco: Catholic Archdiocese (Commission on Social Justice).
Shaffer, R. (1983). *Beyond the dispensary.* Nairobi, Kenya: AMREF.
Shor, I. (1987). *Critical teaching and everyday life.* Chicago: University of Chicago Press.
Werner, D. (1977). *Where there is no doctor.* Palo Alto, CA: Hesperian Foundation.

3.

An Interactionist Approach to Advancing Literacy

NAN ELSASSER and
VERA JOHN-STEINER

Today millions of people throughout the world who have historically been excluded from institutions that control their lives are claiming their right to an education. Central to their assertion is the recognition that oral communication is inadequate to meet the requirements of the modern world and that written communication is necessary for social and economic well-being. Because of their demands, teachers are now more frequently confronted with students who demonstrate competence in oral communication but who produce written work that is often incoherent. The history of the last decades shows that traditional approaches to teaching writing do not work. As a result educators are being forced to look beyond the age-old debates centered on motor skills and "good" grammar and to raise more significant questions concerning literacy. For example, the first issue of *Basic Writing*, a journal devoted to developing theory and strategies to help students master basic writing skills, addressed itself to these questions: "How do we teach [the student] to judge the degree of common ground he can assume? how far he must go in spelling out his meanings in detail? how many cues of place, sequence and reference he must build in?" (D'Eloia, 1975, p. 11).

Answers to these questions are basic to a theory of written speech, but another set of questions must be answered first—questions regarding the cognitive and social dynamics that produce incoherent writing. In the works of L. S. Vygotsky and Paulo Freire we have found a set of theoretical assumptions from which to develop an analysis of these issues. We believe these works are critical to an understanding of the mental and social processes involved in producing accomplished writing. In addition, they provide the bases of strategies designed to aid learners by expanding their awareness and control of these processes.

45

Each of these theorists conceived of the use of words both as an historically shaped process and as one that in this century has become increasingly necessary for more and more people. Vygotsky ([1934] 1962) described the developmental course of language and the different phases in the interweaving of language and thought. A central theme of his analysis is the concept of internalization: children engaged in the process of acquiring language are viewed as active learners able to unite the diverse strands of their experience to form critical, human consciousnesses. Vygotsky's theory is interactionist in its assumptions and relies upon dialectical concepts as essential tools for analysis of human development. Particularly significant for our theory of the advancement of literacy is Vygotsky's concept of the multiple transformations required to "unfold" inner speech. In the course of their development, young speakers engage in meaningful interactions with members of their community; through this interaction, telegrammatic inner language unfolds to become the basis of competent oral communication.

As we will describe later, a different and more complex set of transformations is necessary to attain competence in written communication. Yet most people have very limited opportunities to develop personally and socially relevant written communication skills. Lacking these opportunities, it is unrealistic to expect that learners will be motivated to perfect their skills beyond the most elementary levels of literacy. However, rapid social changes during the twentieth century, including the rise of technology and an urban style of life, have created a need for more widespread literacy. This combination of social need and lack of individual motivation calls for the development of powerful teaching strategies to advance the rudimentary writing skills of students who spend a limited time in the classroom.

Although many attempts have been made to provide literacy programs for populations previously excluded from their countries' economic and educational institutions, most of these attempts have failed. In our opinion, the lack of success has been due in part to the absence of a meaningful analysis of the social realities of poverty and rural life.[1] To meet this need, Freire has developed programs based upon his political understanding of and sensitivity to living conditions that give individuals a profound sense of powerlessness.

In many oppressive societies poor people respond to their feeling of powerlessness through silent forms of resistance (Freire, 1973).[2] One commentator has noted that poor people practice silence "because they have been forced by circumstances to reject as dangerous a 'thrusting' orientation to life" (Greenberg, 1969, p. 79). Children are taught that "silence is safest, so volunteer nothing; that the teacher is the state and tell them only what they want to hear; that the law and learning are white man's law and learning" (Cobb, 1965, p. 106). This silent opposition, the result of their apparent inability to intervene and transform their reality, is often misinterpreted by people who have not been subjected to such oppression. Frustrated, impatient educators who observe this silence often conclude that poor people do not care about the education of their children. Educators and social scientists fail to consider that oppressed peoples have developed their stances toward dominant social groups in response to particular historical experiences.

The silence through which poor people communicate with strangers and officials contrasts sharply with the intensity of daily verbal communication among community people. Labov, in particular, has described this contrast and its educational implication for young black children in urban ghettoes (Labov, 1972, pp. 201–240). These latter exchanges take place within a shared life context that makes certain kinds of verbal elaborations and written explanations unnecessary. Anyone who has ever asked for directions in an isolated rural community has probably experienced bewilderment similar to that of Polly Greenberg, an activist educator working in Mississippi. Greenberg recounts her misadventures in trying for the third time to locate a day-care center of the Child Development Group of Mississippi.

> The directions were "turn right at the puddle"—but it had dried up—"turn left at the dairy farm"—it was a weathered heap of grayboards without visible cows and I didn't know it was a dairy farm—"go a ways"—it was ten miles—"and left at the high embankment where the hogs are"—the whole road was beautiful, high, wild, vine-swarming embankments and the hogs weren't there that day (Greenberg, 1969, p. 241).

According to Freire's analysis, it is very difficult to sustain dialogues with people who are not members of one's own social and economic community. True communication demands equality between speakers, and this often requires an alteration in current social relationships. Similarly, the increasing urgency with which oppressed people are now claiming the right and the need to be taught more complex literacy skills reflects a change in their perception, if not the reality, of their social roles and status. Educators genuinely interested in making communication skills available to all members of a society must understand the educational impact of such social transformations.

Turning Thoughts Inside Out

Mastery of written communication requires a difficult but critical shift in the consciousness of the learner, a shift of attention from an immediate audience that shares the learner's experiences and frame of reference to a larger, abstract, and unfamiliar audience. This necessary change in perspective is illustrated by the Schoolboys of Barbiana (1970). The authors decided to footnote all references to people, places, and institutions that might be unfamiliar to readers. However, they did not supply a footnote for Don Borghi, a local priest. When one of the English translators asked the young men why, they replied, "But everyone knows Don Borghi!" (p. 86).

We have found in Vygotsky's theory of thought and language, specifically in his examination of inner speech and its elaboration into written speech, a powerful explanation of why students' writings are often context-bound. He argues that to communicate well in writing a person must unfold and elaborate for an unknown audience an idea that may very well be represented in her or his mind by a single word or short phrase. To write, one must proceed from the "maximally compact inner speech through which experiences are stored to the maximally detailed written speech requiring what might be called deliberate semantics—deliberate structuring of the web of meaning" (Vygotsky, [1934] 1962, p. 100). The mastery of such transformations is determined by the internal cognitive processes from which writing derived and the social context in which it is produced.

Vygotsky recognizes written speech as "a separate linguistic function, differing from oral speech in both structure and mode of functioning" (Vygotsky, [1934] 1962, p. 98). The key difference between these two forms of communication is the high level of abstraction and elaboration required for minimally comprehensible written speech. The audience for writing most likely does not share the writer's physical or emotional context and, therefore, cannot provide any immediate feedback about the success of the communication effort. The writer lacks the immediate clues of audience response—facial expressions, sounds, pitch, and intonation—all of which are characteristic of oral dialogue. Furthermore, written communication is a system of second-order symbolism: signs replace the sounds of words, which, in turn, are signs for objects and relations present in the real world (Vygotsky, 1978). In oral speech every sentence is prompted by an immediate, obvious motive; in the written monologue "the motives are more abstract, more intellectualized, further removed from immediate needs" (Vygotsky, [1934] 1962, p. 99).

For our purpose the most exciting and significant part of Vygotsky's theory of writing is his description of the internal processes that characterize the production of the written word. Vygotsky says that the original mental source of writing is "inner speech," which evolved from a child's egocentric speech and is further abbreviated and personalized. Vygotsky distinguishes four features of inner speech, which is the language of self-direction and intrapersonal communication. One feature is *heavy predication*. Because the speaker always knows the subject of thought, the referent is likely to be either missing completely or vaguely developed. In the following description of a movie, a junior-high-school student has directly transferred inner speech to paper: "He was talking trash. Boy was triing to tell him to get away from her. He said do you want a knuckles sandwich. He say I am waiting for a chile burger. Then he wint to a liquor store. . . . "[3] *Semantic shortcuts* appear because "a single word is so saturated with sense that many words would be required to explain it in external speech" (Vygotsky, [1934] 1962, p. 148). Effective written communication requires the transformation of the predicative idiomatic structure of inner speech into syntactically and semantically elaborated forms.[4] When this cognitive act fails to occur, writing may look like the two student samples below:

> The many advantages and disadvantages of inflation and desire to see some of the Northern Colorado, the rush hour, Nursing School at UNM, and tutoring is a big step to want a student to attend UNM to try a smaller college where the population is lower in New Mexico, or a college with more educational advancement.

> Well, I agree with the electricity that people are using more of it. But I think people are overdoing how they should use less energy. They don't think electric is just for fun using it but it's hard to get it.

In *agglutination*, according to Vygotsky, "several words are merged into one word, and the new word not only expresses a rather complex idea but designates all the separate elements contained in that idea." This may be what is occurring when words like *importation, undevplored* (underdeveloped and explored) or *bass* (band and jazz)[5] appear in students' writing. The final feature, *the combination and unity of the senses of different words*, is " a process governed by different laws from those governing combinations of meanings. . . . The senses of different words flow into one another—literally 'influence' one another—so that the earlier ones are contained in, and modify, the later one" (Vygotsky, [1934] 1962, p. 147).

In his description of inner speech, Vygotsky recognizes that, as in all aspects of human cognition, an individual changes and develops with age and experience. Language is extraordinarly important in the growing cognitive sophistication of children, as well as in their increasing social affectiveness, because language is the means by which children (and adults) systematize their perceptions. Through words human beings formulate generalizations, abstractions, and other forms of mediated thinking. Yet these words, the fragile bridges upon which our thoughts must travel, are sociohistorically determined and therefore shaped, limited, or expanded through individual and collective experience.

For educators the challenge, then, is to develop a teaching methodology that expands this experience, that allows people previously excluded to master the written word. As we have shown, Vygotsky and Freire provide a reasonable and fecund explanation of why millions of people have difficulty in learning to write organized prose. But their theories not only provide explanation, they also suggest strategies through which silent speakers can become potent writers. Through Vygotsky's work we can begin to appreciate the nature and complexity of the cognitive changes that are required to expand basic literacy to advanced literacy. And Freire leads us to further understand the dynamics of this intellectual process:

> Knowing, whatever its level, is not the act by which a Subject transformed into an object docilely and passively accepts the contents other give or impose on him or her. Knowledge, on the contrary, necessitates the curious presence of Subjects confronted with the world. It requires their transforming action on reality. It demands a constant searching. It implies invention and reinvention. . . . In the learning process the only person who really *learns* is s/he who appropriates what is learned, who apprehends and thereby reinvents that learning; s/he who is able to apply the appropriate learning to concrete existential situations. On the other hand, the person who is filled by another with "content" whose meaning s/he is not aware of, which contradicts his or her way of being in the world, cannot learn because s/he is not challenged (Freire, 1973, p. 101).

The Historical Basis of Cognitive Change

No one has yet scientifically documented the specific relationship between historical change and the expansion of intellectual and cognitive skills among oppressed peoples. The full analysis of this relationship is a challenge beyond the scope of this essay. However, in the absence of systematic data we have drawn upon the anecdotal accounts of observers in very diverse social settings to examine the historical basis of cognitive change. In addition, we have relied upon Alexander R. Luria (1976), who detailed some of the psychological changes that took place in the Soviet Union during thirty years of profound social and economic transformation.

Shortly after the Russian Revolution, Vygotsky and his student, Luria, visited remote rural areas of Uzbekistan and Kirghizia. They were impressed by the difference in attitudes between those individuals still personally untouched by the social transformations under way and those who, as a result of experiences on collective farms and in literacy courses, were already becoming "Subjects" in Freire's sense. The people lacking new social and educational experiences were reluctant to enter into dialogue, to participate in discussion as critical beings. When invited to ask the visitors questions about life beyond the village, they responded:

> I can't imagine what to ask about . . . to ask you need knowledge and all we do is hoe weeds in the field.

> I don't know how to obtain knowledge . . . where would I find the questions. For questions you need knowledge. You can ask questions when you have understanding but my head is empty (Luria, 1976, pp. 137–138).

But the peasants who had participated in the transforming process of the revolution had many questions about their collective lives:

> How can life be made better? Why is the life of a worker better than that of a peasant? How can I acquire knowledge more readily? Also: Why are city workers more skilled than peasants?

> Well, what could I do to make our kolkhozniks [members of collective farms] better people? . . . And then I'm interested in how the world exists, where things come from, how the rich become rich and why the poor are poor (Luria, 1976, pp. 141–142).

This type of change has been observed in varied contexts where people have begun to transform their sociolinguistic reality—in Chile, Brazil, Guinea-Bissau, Cuba, Mississippi, and the Navajo Nation.[6] When people are convinced that they can shape their social reality and that they are no longer isolated and powerless, they begin to participate in dialogue with a larger world, first orally and then through writing.

This development is not linear; it involves multiple transformations that are complex and dialectical. One transformation brings to individuals a growing sense of control as they change from "objects" into "Subjects." A peasant who had always toiled in the fields expressed the significance of this realization by stating, "I work and in

working I transform the world" (Freire, 1973, p. 48). A second transformation reflects the consequences of these altered relationships that
are of particular significance in people's cognitive and motivational
approaches. Instead of denying their right to engage in dialogue with
others as equals, they affirm their responsibility as creators and trans-
formers of their culture: "Every people has its own culture, and no
people has less than others. Our culture is a gift that we bring to you"
(Schoolboys of Barbiana, 1970, p. 109). Third, the desire and need
for educationally transmitted knowledge become of vital concern as
a result of social and personal changes. Although in many instances
schools and educational institutions have failed to meet the legitimate
aspirations of oppressed groups, parents and students alike recognize
that formal education offers skills that they need to transform themselves and their relationships with the dominant society:

> I would like to see the younger Indian people to get a good edu-
> cation so they can compete against the palefaces. . . . I don't
> want my kids to go far away to take up a career which won't be
> of benefit to the Navajos. I prefer that they stay around here . . .
> and become the Indian leaders of tomorrow (Norris, 1970, p. 18).

Or, as a young woman replied when asked why she spent her summer
vacation attending a "freedom school," "I want to become a part of
history also" (Holt, 1963, p. 322).

In spite of the belief, widely held in America, that education in
and of itself can transform both people's sense of power and the existing social and economic hierarchies, educational intervention without
actual social change is, in fact, ineffective. This is particularly true in
poor and Third World communities where parents and children have
traditionally felt marginal or excluded. Testimonies by a Mississippi
subsistence farmer and a Navajo parent illustrate some reactions to
such programs:

> They [the school] leaves me out; so I stay out, all the way out.
> They got no use for me cause they says I ain't got sense. I got
> no use fer them, neither, cause they ain't got sense enough to
> treat peoples human (Greenberg, 1969, p. 100).

> If a student learns in school, then he grows away from what he
> had learned to value at home. I don't know what parents think
> about these problems. They're bewildered (Norris, 1970, p. 15).

As long as children sense the powerlessness of their community,
the impact of educators' best efforts lasts but a short time. Effective
education requires the recognition and utilization of the potential in
all human beings to participate actively in their own learning. There-

fore educational success depends upon a change in the social environment—a break with the past alienation and marginality. Thus educational reform is an essential component but not in and of itself a cause of changes in educational engagement.

Although they lived in different times and worked in different hemispheres, Vygotsky and Freire shared approaches that emphasized the crucial intertwining of social and educational change. While Vygotsky focused on the psychological dynamics, Freire concentrated on developing appropriate pedagogical strategies.

The Dialogue in Education

During periods of rapid social change many individuals envision new futures for themselves. However, for people to benefit fully from new possibilities, meaningful educational programs must be created. The ultimate success of these programs depends on two factors. First, mutual respect and understanding must flow between educators and students—between representatives of the larger outside world and the poor with whom they are working. Second, the curriculum must be built upon the "here and now" of the learners (Freire, 1970b). Educational programs that are directed by distant bureaucracies without regard for local interests, resources, or needs produce boredom, frustration, and apathy. In Chile, for example, literacy workers using Freire's methods found that "the peasants became interested in the discussion only when the codification related directly to their felt needs. Any deviation . . . produced silence and indifference" (Freire, 1970b, p. 109).

Freire explains such silence and indifference in this way: "For the act of communication to be successful, there must be accord between the reciprocally communicating Subjects. That is, the verbal expressions of one of the Subjects must be perceptible within a frame of reference that is meaningful to the other Subject" (Freire, 1973, p. 138). This entails more than avoiding or explaining "big" words; often the same word or sign has entirely different meanings to different peoples in different contexts. This type of semantic confusion is illustrated by Greenberg's account, described earlier in this essay, of her attempt to locate an isolated day-care center in Mississippi.

Even in classes grounded in the here and now, where there is mutual respect between teachers and students, academic progress is not guaranteed. Chilean educators, for example, found that their adult students were sometimes unable to perceive relationships between their felt needs and the causes of those needs (Freire, 1970b). One explanation for these learning difficulties is found in Luria's work in Uzbekistan and Kirghizia. The tasks Luria and Vygotsky presented included defining abstract concepts—What is the sun? How would you explain it to a blind man? What is freedom?—and generic classification. Nonliterate adults in these communities had great difficulty handling some of these tasks. For example, under the category "tool," peasants often grouped such diverse possessions as a donkey, firewood, an axe, cocoons, and a skull cap. When asked to solve problems requiring logical reasoning skills, individuals had to go beyond the insights gained from practical experience. Decontextualized thought is required to solve such problems and to recognize the connections between felt needs and external conditions. The necessary cognitive operations function within a closed system of logical formulation and are detached from the here and now. But it was just such a mode of cognition with which the peasants Luria studied and many other peoples were unfamiliar.

These kinds of cognitive skills are often both acquired and required in school. From their work in West Africa, Cole and Scribner (1974) have documented the cumulative effects of schooling on the acquisition of logical forms of thought. To interpret their findings, they use Luria's argument that "higher mental functions are complex, organized, *functional* systems" triggered by the task at hand (Luria, 1976, pp. 23 ff.). As Vygotsky originally described these functional learning systems, both the elements in these systems and their working relationships are formed during the course of an individual's development and are dependent upon the child's social experiences.

Most contemporary education, however, fails to trigger the growth of new functional systems because it follows what Freire has called "the banking concept," which "anesthetizes and inhibits creative power" (Freire, 1970b). The student is only expected to internalize existing knowledge; frequently this means internalizing the objectives of the dominant groups in society. By contrast, meaningful knowledge builds upon the human potential for active learning and is linked to praxis. When teachers and learners are partners in dialogue, a different conception of the processes of knowledge acquisition emerges:

> Insofar as language is impossible without thought and language and thought are impossible without the word to which they refer, the human word is more than vocabulary—it is word-and-action. The cognitive dimensions of the literacy process must include the relationships of men with their world. These relationships are the source of the dialectic between the products men achieve in transforming the words and the conditioning which these products in turn exercise on men (Freire, 1970a, p. 12).

In no intellectual endeavor are these skills more essential than in the acquisition of mastery of written speech. To move beyond oral speech to writing, students must make an additional leap: they have to acquire a new code that demands further abstraction, semantic expansion, and syntactic elaboration.

Many literacy workers have emphasized the complexities of learning to communicate through an abstract sign system that lacks the cues of oral speech. Freire, however, has demonstrated that literacy can itself be the focal point for transformations of consciousness. When socially significant, "generative" words are employed in literacy programs, they permit learners to reflect on their experiences, to critically examine it. In this way teaching adults to read and write is no longer an inconsequential matter of *ba, be, bi, bo, bu* or of memorizing alienated words, but a difficult apprenticeship in "naming the world" (Freire, 1970a, p. 11). And such naming is liberating:

> In some areas of Chile undergoing agrarian reform the peasants participating in the literacy programs wrote words with their tools on the dirt roads where they were working . . . "These men are sowers of the word," said a sociologist. . . . Indeed, they were not only sowing words, but discussing ideas, and coming to understand their role in the world better and better (Freire, 1970a, p. 22).

Through this type of education, learners and educators participate together in an ever-widening context; no longer are students limited to their immediate experience. As the circle of communication expands both for teachers and students, the role and structure of the linguistic sign are stretched and transformed. In this process, "it is not merely the content of a word that changes, but the way in which reality is generalized and reflected in a word" (Vygotsky, [1934] 1962, pp. 121–122). This transformation, however, does not take place in isolation; as Freire insightfully reminds us: "Just as there is no such thing as an isolated human being there is also no such thing as isolated thinking. Any act of thinking requires a Subject who thinks, an object thought about which mediates the thinking Subjects and the communication between the latter, manifested by linguistic signs" (Freire, 1973, pp. 136–137).

From Literacy to Writing: A Pilot Study

Literacy is valued as a source of other skills and strategies necessary to achieve critical reconstruction of social and personal realities. The aim of the best literacy programs has been "to challenge the myths of our society, to perceive more clearly its realities and to find alternatives, and, ultimately, new directions for action" (Holt, 1965, p. 103). Basic literacy, however, is not sufficient to achieve these far-reaching ends. People must reach a level of mastery of language skills from which they can critically examine and theoretically elaborate their political and cultural experiences. Simultaneously literacy must be adequately developed so as to provide increasing numbers of women and men with access to technological and vocational skills and information (Darcy de Oliveira & Darcy de Oliveira, 1976).

To date, many advanced-literacy programs have lacked the coherence and direction that only a clearly defined and articulated theoretical framework can provide. Some basic-literacy programs, both in the United States and abroad, have been constructed implicitly or explicitly on some of the principles of Vygotsky and Freire. We believe that Freire's methods and Vygotsky's hypotheses concerning the transformation of inner speech to written speech can be not only powerful tools in basic-literacy programs, but also a framework for promoting more advanced writing skills.

Using the theories of Freire and Vygotsky, Elsasser, Behling, and others developed a pilot program for advanced literacy within the context of an open-admissions policy at two New Mexico universities.[7] Compared to more usual methods, the results of this approach have been impressive (Behling & Elsasser, 1976; Elsasser, 1976). The commonly used anthology-based curricula assume that students' cognitive structures are such that mere exposure to well-formulated literary models is contagious and effective. The behavioristically-based curricula, on the other hand, assume that writing skills should be broken down into specialized tasks to be taught individually and sequentially. In contrast to these two approaches, the experimental courses of the Elsasser-Behling pilot study assume an intricate interaction among teachers, learners, and social change, which in turn provides a dynamic of continuity and change that enhances the development of written communication. At the beginning of the course, teachers explain this interaction to the students in detail. They also discuss Vygotsky's analysis of the elaboration of thoughts to increasingly more decontextualized forms of communication—from intimate verbal speech through more formal verbal communication to fully elaborated written speech. Thus, the learners gain an appreciation of both the difficulties and the advantages of expressing their thoughts through the written word. Several specific exercises that built upon the original explanation demonstrate the process of decontextualizing and elaborating one's thoughts. Before students attempt written exposition, Behling and Elsasser's initial exercises offer them an opportunity to become aware of the skills required in writing for an audience that does not share the writer's frame of reference.

The need for one such skill, elaboration, can be illustrated by displaying several pictures that express a similar theme, each with some markedly distinguishable features. The pictures should depict familiar aspects of the learner's environment, such as local landscapes; those used at the University of Albuquerque showed mountains and mesas. Each learner is asked to select one picture and to list a series of words that describes the picture in such a way that other members of the class can easily identify it. In his work, Freire observed that simply projecting familiar representations on a board or slide aids learners to "effect an operation basic to the act of knowing: they gain distance from the knowable object . . . the aim of decodification is to arrive at the critical level of knowledge, beginning with the learner's experience of the situation in the 'real' context" (Freire, 1970a, p. 15).

When learners at the University of Albuquerque shared their lists and attempted to find each other's choices, everyone became more aware of differences among kinds of words. Some words denoting objective, physical attributes (crags, shadows, peaks) were immediately mutually descriptive; other words indicating subjective reactions to the visual stimulus (spacious, inviolate, freedom, proud) were personally descriptive. Through dialogue, especially when different individuals had divergent reactions to the same representation, participants learned what types of further explanation would allow another to comprehend personally descriptive attributes. The need for elaboration in all forms of communication, particularly in writing, thus became apparent.

A second method demonstrates to learners the abbreviated nature of intrapersonal communication and the amount of detail required to flesh it out. This method relies on a common, everyday task like grocery shopping. Each learner is asked to prepare two sets of instructions—one for himself or herself and one for an unknown other person. One's personal set is usually a cryptic, minimal reminder, as these lists from three students demonstrate:

Student A	Student B	Student C
milk	soap	milk
eggs	meat	meat
bread	chips	eggs
soap	beer	potatoes
T.P.	bread	ice cream
		vitamins

The participants discussed what additional kinds of information might be helpful if the task were assigned to someone else: for instance, size, grade, brand, type, price limitations. After the discussion some students immediately prepared elaborated shopping lists which would have been sufficient for any surrogate shopper:

Student A	*Student B*
Cream and homogenized milk, one-half gallon	2 bars of soap
1 dozen grade A large eggs	1 package of hamburger meat
Roman Meal bread—large loaf	1 package of potato chips
Toni soap	2 six-packs of Budweiser
Toilet tissue—individually wrapped Scott	1 loaf of bread

Some simply repeated the lists written for themselves.

In the ensuing conversation students added other hints, including explanations of what foods could be purchased with food stamps and which store was closest to the buyer's home. These comments, in turn, provided the basis for further elaboration suited to an even more removed audience. What if the buyer didn't know about food stamps? Was not familiar with supermarkets? Did not know your neighborhood? In this process students gained a heightened awareness of the need for full description and explanation. Thus an initially simple task stimulated the kind of dialogue that Freire considers crucial to the transformation of the individual's understanding of communicative exchanges. The assignment following this discussion was to write an essay on grocery shopping, incorporating the material discussed.

A third type of exercise used in this program emphasized our everyday reliance in oral speech on verbal and visual cues and aided learners in decontextualizing their explanations. Each member of the class received a geometric design and attempted to give other members of the group verbal instructions for reproducing the design. The instructions had to be sufficiently clear so that, without seeing the original, the listeners could construct reasonable facsimiles of the design. Some students performed facing the class, interacting verbally and visually; others transmitted the instructions with their backs to the group, forfeiting all verbal and visual response. The other students' reproductions immediately indicated the relative adequacy of the explanations. Initially the learners who interacted with their audience performed significantly better than those denied any response, but variations of the task were repeated until every member of the group was cognizant of the audience's needs and what information had to be provided to meet those needs.

This theoretically based program for advanced literacy proceeds sequentially to encourage and guide the unfolding of conceptual knowledge. Through a process of oral discussion in which ideas are continually broadened and fleshed out, constant attention to the types of elaboration required for an unknown other are emphasized. Immediate feedback from both the instructor and the students' peers indicates the success or failure of the written effort. This methodological continuity can lead from the initial tasks to more extended forms of writing traditionally required in composition courses. Among the communicative efforts emphasized within this theoretical framework are definition of an abstract concept, persuasion based on an imagined audience's values, narration of a personal experience, and a letter to an editor. Exercises in written communication can require increasing decontextualization for a removed and impersonal audience. Each assignment can be preceded by a discussion of several topics: what is or is not shared knowledge; the information needs of the intended audience; the particularities of the writer's experience; and the linguistic prejudices of the projected audience. Group discussion of these facts helps learners make their thoughts explicit. It also produces an understanding of the sources of thoughts and the ways in which thoughts change in the process of critical examination and analysis.

Cognitive and Social Dynamics of Writing

The literacy programs we are advocating differ fundamentally from remedial instruction based on behaviorism or nativism. We believe that a more effective approach uses as its basis Vygotsky's interactionist assumption relating the biological substrata of behavior to changing social conditions. He wrote:

> In order to study development in children, one must begin with an understanding of the dialectical unity of two principally different lines (the biological and the cultural); to adequately study this process, then, an experimenter must study both components and the laws which govern their *interlacement* at each stage of the child's development (Vygotsky, 1978, p. 5).

Vygotsky's "exploration of these interactions is based on a view that regards the human organism as one of great plasticity and the environment as historically and culturally shifting contexts into which children are born and which they, too, eventually will come to change" (John-Steiner & Souberman, 1978, p. 5).

The model we have presented and are committed to developing further evolves from the theories of both Freire and Vygotsky. They argue that language is developed, extended, and modified through the constant interaction of individuals and their social context. Written speech is an act of knowing "the existence of two interrelated contexts. One is the context of authentic dialogue between learners and educators as equally knowing subjects . . . the second is the real, concrete context of facts, the social reality in which men exist" (Freire, 1970a, p. 14). Education designed for active, engaged learners provides an opportunity to understand the nature of the written word, the possibilities for its effective communication, and the difficulties in its production. Above all, such education offers learners a range of strategies that enables them to externalize their thoughts through writing. To develop these strategies we must direct our attention not only to written products but to the cognitive underpinnings of those products. Vygotsky's theory of the structure of language and its transformation into communicatively effective written and oral speech suggests many programmatic possibilities. Short-term improvement in literacy skills can be achieved by motivating students and by reinforcing their written work. But only programs that build upon cognitive processes can help individuals meet the long-term objective of using their literacy as a tool of personal growth and social transformation.

Although most educators now acknowledge the social nature of language, they do not recognize it in their programs. The critical role of dialogue, highlighted by both Freire and Vygotsky, can be put into effect by the conscious and productive reliance upon groups in which learners confront and work through—orally and in writing—issues of significance to their lives.

Notes

1. The failure of such programs also stems from their sociohistorical contexts. A student's sense of personal power and control emerges largely as a result of the increasing movement of his or her social group towards self-determination. In the absence of such movement, educational intervention is most often futile.
2. Freire calls this resistance "the culture of silence" by which he means the form of passive protest used by the oppressed when confronting individuals of the oppressing classes. Freire's sense of the term is not to be confused with the idea as it is used by verbal deprivationists who believe that oppressed peoples, owing to some inner shortcomings—either cultural or psychological or genetic—do not possess linguistic skills at any but the most minimal level.
3. Courtesy of Dean Brodkey, Director, English Tutorial Program, University of New Mexico. This example and the two following are from students enrolled in his program.

4. Throughout this essay we are using the term *elaborated* in Vygotsky's sense as a form of speech (usually written) that is fully deployed and maximally decontextualized because it does not rely on the more usual verbal and visual communicative cues.
5. These examples are from: The English Tutorial Program, University of New Mexico; D'Eloia, 1975, p. 11; and courtesy of Chris Behling (Behling & Elsasser, 1976), respectively.
6. For information on these programs see: Freire, 1970b and 1973 (Brazil and Chile); Darcy de Oliveira and Darcy de Oliveira, 1976 (Guinea-Bissau); Holt, 1965 and Greenberg, 1969 (Mississippi); and Norris, 1970 (Ramah, Navajo Nation).
7. The students involved were predominantly Chicano and Native American. Their communities' powerlessness vis-à-vis the institutions of the larger society is parallel in many ways to the oppression of peasants and workers in other nations.

References

Behling, C., & Elsasser, N. (March 1976). *Role taking in writing.* Workshop conducted at the TESOL Convention, New York.
Cobb, C. (1965). Notes on teaching in Mississippi. In L. Holt (Ed.), *The summer that didn't end.* New York: Morrow.
Cole, M., & Scribner, S. (1974). *Culture and thought.* New York: Wiley.
Darcy de Oliveira, R., & Darcy de Oliveira, M. (1976). *Guinea-Bissau: Reinventing education* (Document 11/12). Geneva: Institute of Cultural Action.
D'Eloia, S. (1975). Teaching standard written English. *Basic Writing, 1*, 5-14.
Elsasser, N. (1976). *Turning our thoughts inside out.* Unpublished manuscript, University of New Mexico, Albuquerque, N.M.
Freire, P. (1970a). *Cultural action for freedom* (Monograph Series No. 1). Cambridge, MA: Harvard Educational Review & Center for Study of Development and Social Change.
Freire, P. (1970b). *Pedagogy of the oppressed.* New York: Seabury.
Freire, P. (1973). *Education for critical consciousness.* New York: Seabury.
Greenberg, P. (1969). *The devil has slippery shoes.* London: Macmillan.
Holt, L. (Ed.), (1965). *The summer that didn't end.* New York: Morrow.
John-Steiner, V., & Leacock, L. (1978). The structure of failure. In D. Wilkerson (Ed.), *Educating children of the poor.* Westport, CT: Mediax.
John-Steiner, V., & Souberman, E. (1978). The dialectic of cognitive growth (Introductory Essay). In L. S. Vygotsky, *Mind in society: The development of higher psychological processes* (M. Cole, V. John-Steiner, S. Scribner, & E. Souberman, Eds.). Cambridge, MA: Harvard University Press.
Labov, W. (1972). The logic of nonstandard English. In *Language in the inner city.* Philadelphia: University of Pennsylvania Press.
Laurence, P. (1975). Error's endless train: Why students don't perceive errors. *Basic Writing, 1*, 23-42.
Luria, A. R. (1976). *Cognitive development: Its cultural and social foundations.* Cambridge, MA: Harvard University Press.
Norris, R. (1970). *A Navajo community develops its own high school curriculum.* Unpublished manuscript, University of New Mexico, Albuquerque, NM.
Schoolboys of Barbiana. (1970). *Letter to a teacher.* New York: Random House.

Vygotsky, L. S. (1962). *Language and thought.* (Originally published, 1934). Cambridge, MA: MIT Press.
Vygotsky, L. S. (1978). *Mind in society: The development of higher psychological processes.* (M. Cole, V. John-Steiner, S. Scribner, & E. Souberman, Eds.). Cambridge, MA: Harvard University Press.

4.

Illiteracy and Alienation in American Colleges: Is Paulo Freire's Pedagogy Relevant?

LINDA SHAW FINLAY and VALERIE FAITH

This essay describes a course we taught that attempted to improve the language skills of upper-middle-class American college students, based on the philosophy and methodology of Paulo Freire.[1] Though our immediate goal was improving communication skills, what we discovered has broad implications for adult education. Our students, like so many others in the United States, manifested various weaknesses in reading and writing and appeared to lack intellectual curiosity. Since Freire addresses problems of motivation in language learning, we designed a course embodying and presenting Freire's principles and theory, even though we recognized that our students' problems might be only superficially similar to those of Freire's Third World students.

Initially, we feared the inappropriateness of applying a Third World pedagogy to the education of upper-middle-class students in American colleges; our doubts were both political and pedagogical. First, we did not want to reduce the educational process described by Freire to a mechanical technique, thereby dulling its cutting edge, the moral/political awakening concomitant with emerging literacy. Second, we wondered if Freire's method could help students who were already functionally literate but whose writing lacked the clarity and coherence of active thinkers. In spite of these hesitations we were encouraged to proceed in part by reading a paper that suggested the possibility of combining the pedagogical principles of Freire with the developmental psychology of Lev Vygotsky (1962), the Russian cognitive psychologist whose work in the twenties and thirties is only now receiving the recognition it merits.

According to Vygotsky, good writing is related to abstract thinking. What Vygotsky means by "abstract thinking" can be understood

63

in his account of the cognitive processes required for successful oral and written communication. Oral communication ordinarily takes place in a context that supplies a number of external clues to the speaker's intended meaning (i.e., facial expression, common social background, life patterns, geography, etc.). But written communication requires the writer to shift attention from an immediate audience with whom much is shared to a more unfamiliar audience with whom less common ground can be assumed, one for which no clues to meaning other than those given in the text can be provided. The successful accomplishment of this shift from an oral to a written form of communication is a developmental process by which the writer moves from maximally compact "inner speech" (in which many related associations and meanings may be signified by one term or phrase) to maximally elaborated written speech (in which implicit inner speech must be pulled apart and made explicit to express the writer's meaning). Communication depends on the writer's awareness of what is shared with the intended audience and what must be explained. Thus, to write well, a social as well as a linguistic analysis is necessary; one must master linguistic forms and understand the relation of one's own perspective to that of others. The latter requirement is often omitted in discussions of literacy, but it is vital. What a Russian or Brazilian peasant and a middle-class college student may have in common, in spite of their very different circumstances and opportunities, is an inability to relate their personal perspective to that of others within their culture. When this failure occurs, it is a barrier to literacy.

Freire's pedagogy, which respects the connection between the critical use of language and an awareness of oneself in social relations, dovetails with Vygotsky's developmental psychology. Both emphasize the importance of the interaction between persons and cultural elements in moving from inner speech to written language. So, relying on Freire and Vygotsky, we decided to approach language teaching through our students' understanding of the relationship between language and society, between the use of words and the structure of their reality.

The 27 students who took part in this experiment were a self-selected group representing all classes and a wide variety of majors. Nineteen had signed up because they or their teachers perceived linguistic inadequacies. Several students were, or had been, on academic probation because they were either unwilling or unable to complete acceptable written course work. Moreover, from previous class experience with some of these students, we knew that they had difficulty following logical chains of reasoning and had used language as if words had no objective relationship to particular ideas, objects, or experiences.

Consciousness and Language

By abstracting the crucial elements of the educational process from Freire's descriptions (1970, 1972), we devised a structure for the course. According to Freire, education is a three-phase process:

1. *Investigation.* Investigation is the examination and discovery of human consciousness as naive, superstitious, or critical.
2. *Thematization.* Thematization includes (a) examination of the thematic universe by reduction, coding, decodification; (b) the learners' discovery of new generative themes suggested by earlier themes.
3. *Problematization.* Problematization includes (a) discovery of limit situations and (b) their corresponding limit acts leading to *authentic praxis:* permanent cultural action for liberation (Collins, 1977, p. 83).

The first phase, investigation of consciousness, is referred to by Freire as the "archeology of consciousness." Like many of Freire's key terms, its meaning is best understood by looking at its etymology. *Arche* comes from the Greek; it means "principal" or "that which is fundamental and primary." The archeology of consciousness is a study of the fundamental *form* of consciousness. The purpose of the investigative stage is to discover a spontaneous prereflective attitude that most accurately characterizes a person's consciousness of the world, in order to uncover the relationship of people to the ideas upon which they act. Are these ideas held naively, superstitiously, or critically?

In determining the form of consciousness, the pivotal question is: Do people recognize how human action and language create their world? In Freire's terms, do they distinguish between what is natural and what is cultural? Nature, after all, offers laws that are given, not options. Culture, the sphere of human institutions, is governed by choices that are historically and materially conditioned. When culture masquerades as nature, it appears impervious to human effort, or, as Freire quoting Pierre Furter notes, it appears as a "massive presence to which I can but adapt," rather than "as a scope, a domain which takes shape as I act upon it" (Freire, 1970, p. 81). The failure to distinguish culture (the product of human action) from nature impairs the ability to use language critically as well as the ability to act. In the archeology of consciousness, students and teachers focus on language-use as the most accessible mirror of naive, superstitious, or critical consciousness. Students who see themselves as makers of culture experience their relation to reality and their powers to change reality. This challenges their alienation.

The chief characteristic of naive consciousness is an unreflecting acceptance of the solidity and inevitability of the world and one's own views. Naive thinkers cannot conceive of a basic perspective different from their own. The thought of naive persons shapes their behavior precisely because concepts and values are held unreflectively. On the level of language, habit dominates word choice, and ideas and values are expressed as unqualified generalizations.

Even when persons no longer take cultural institutions, systems, and beliefs for granted, their attitudes may well be superstitious rather than critical. People with a superstitious consciousness may consciously recognize that there are cultural options but feel powerless to realize them. They regard their culture as inherited, ready-made, and do not perceive how they participate in sustaining and making it. To the degree to which social institutions and forms remain mysteries, they are endowed with magical status: their effects seem independent of known causes, and therefore, as uncontrollable. The linguistic expression of the superstitious consciousness is a jargon replete with vague phrases and passive constructions, and marked by the absence of detailed analysis. They repeat formulas that they cannot explain, and account for social structures by referring to a vague and powerful "they."

In contrast, critical consciousness is characterized, according to Freire, by two active recognitions: cultural institutions are created and sustained by human purpose and action, and language both shapes and reflects people's perceptions of cultural institutions. Since all of the elements that make up the human "world" (i.e., the social forms that govern human interactions: institutions, beliefs, laws, customs, religion, language) were given their initial form by people, they are susceptible to reformation. With critical consciousness, social institutions can be analyzed, understood, and therefore—in principle— shaped, modified, and controlled by members of the community. In practice, the shaping or modifying of institutions requires collective action. The language of the critically conscious person reflects the understanding that since language-use shapes people's perceptions of their culture as well as reflects them, the naming of cultural elements is of fundamental social significance. Reflection on language-use is the primary means of transforming habitual thought into critical consciousness. Because of its centrality, this point requires elaboration.

Verbal Thought

Language is a critical part of social life because the relation between the individual and the social world is mediated by what Freire calls "thought-language." Vygotsky's comment on words as "the units of verbal thought" clarifies the principle behind Freire's method in the investigation of consciousness. Vygotsky states that thought and language coincide in "word meaning":

> There is every reason to suppose that the qualitative distinction between sensation and thought is the presence in the latter of a *generalized* reflection of reality, which is also the essence of word meaning; and consequently, that meaning is an act of thought in the full sense of the term. But at the same time meaning is an inalienable part of words as such, and thus it belongs in the realm of language as much as in the realm of thought. A word without meaning is an empty sound, no longer a part of human speech. Since word meaning is both thought and speech, we find in it the unit of verbal thought we are looking for. Clearly, then, the method to follow in our exploration of the nature of verbal thought is semantic analysis—the study of the development, the functioning, and the structure of this unit, which contains thought and speech interrelated (Vygotsky, 1962, p. 5).

These ideas were assumed but not fully explained by Freire.

In brief, Freire went about discovering students' forms of consciousness by showing them pictures of their everyday activities, and then reflecting with them on the "thought-language" they used in describing the image to reveal the level (form) of their prereflective consciousness. The pictures enabled Freire's students to focus on their oral and written language as the object of study. In addition, the images demonstrated the difference between nature and culture. The crucial transition from perception to reflection on it was achieved by decoding the pictorial symbol whose linguistic representation, as the locus of meaning, was seen to be a "microcosm of human consciousness" (Vygotsky, 1962, p. 153). Decoding is the process by which implicit ideas are made explicit and then considered in relation to the social and political context. We wanted to follow the same general plan, but with our post-literate students it was possible to begin immediately with a linguistic object to study and decode.

Key Words: Beginning the Course

In order to find a linguistic object for reflection that accurately mirrors precritical perspectives and is as untainted as possible by self-conscious desires to please the teachers, we gave the students the following assignment: "Please bring a list of words that seem to you to be keys to areas of knowledge or life that you want to open up; then, group these words in any way they seem to fit together to you."[2] Each student's list of "key" words was gathered and the lists were typed on one page in the sequence in which they had been collected. Then we returned this page to the students who were asked to arrange these words in whatever groups seemed appropriate to them.

One point Freire emphasizes is that no matter how well the teachers imagine that they know the students and their concerns, the themes can only be elicited from the students by an archeology of consciousness. This key-word exercise and what followed convinced us of the indispensability of generating with the students the themes to be studied in the course. This pedagogy thus departs from an expert teacher lecturing on grammar and rhetoric, or the study of short stories in a standard text. Themes are considered not in the abstract but in the *students' relation to those themes.*

The key-word assignment provided the generative themes for our class. It is true, as both Freire and Vygotsky see, that "a word is a microcosm of human consciousness," but a word can be used without a self-conscious understanding of that microcosm. The generative themes are the buried assumptions, unspoken and, at first, unspeakable; they make their appearance as surprising byproducts of the effort to perform some superficially unrelated task. When the grouped key words were returned, they revealed a clear dichotomy between two basic mutually exclusive groups of words. In all but five papers, the following groups of words appeared with only minor variations:[3]

Left Group	*Right Group*
injustice	emotion
power	happiness
systems	belief
they	buddhism
government	energy
education	art
mind	wholeness
order-organize	faith
conceptualize	freedom
environment	music
oppression	love
world-economics	friendship
	God

After the grouped words had been returned to us but before we first discussed them in class, we had one class meeting. To provide a common ground for discussion, we presented a stipulative definition

of the word "language": "Language is an arbitrary culturally-histori-
cally inherited symbol system of a group." The students responded in
anger to this definition. They rejected not only this particular definition, for reasons that they could not articulate, but also the very effort
to define. This emotional rejection astonished us, so we invited the
students to make their own definition by completing the following
sentence: "Language is. . . ." All of the students defined language in
terms of its desired effects, communication or self-expression, rather
than in terms of its structure. They thought of language as a kind of
magic that, somehow, achieves linking between people. But they
judged its power to be unreliable, perhaps because it is so often un-
available to them. A deep mistrust of words as carriers of meaning,
understandable in the light of their poor verbal skills, manifested itself as an insistence that body "language"—motion, hitting, touching—
was more communicative than verbal expressions. And their most
emotional rejection was reserved for the notion of language as "an
organized system of signs."

Dialogue on Oppression

Through the discussion of the grouped key words, we came to
understand the emotional response to the definition of language and
in the context of this discussion we saw, though only partially, the
significance of having defined language as a "system."

ESME: The ones in the left-hand group are things we don't have
power over.
JONATHAN: We control the things in the right-hand group.
LAUREL: Yeah, they are personal things, emotional. You have to
analyze, intellectualize to understand the ones on the left. But
you can't define the words on the right; they have a personal
meaning.
ELLEN: That list tells about our resentment.
ANN: See, education is there on the left. It has a bad connotation.
I felt hostility to those words [on the left]. The right-hand words
aroused good feelings.
TONY: Those on the right are personal, emotional, not analytical. We
distrust public life, want noninvolvement, but that has a negative
result.
PAT: Yeah, now we are easier to control.

This rebellion of the private against the public life (apparent
freedom from domination by institutions as opposed to apparent
domination by institutions) was made explicit by a student who said

she grouped the words alphabetically for the class, but "really grouped them" secretly for herself. The themes sounded in this initial discussion were reiterated, deepened, and gradually connected to the idea that emerged as *the* generative theme of our class to which all others were related. This theme was given its first clear, though incomplete, articulation by a student who pointed out that education was in the left-handed group because it was to "prepare us for" the anonymous cultural institutions for which the word "they" stood, which "they" ran.

The word "oppression" was the focus of much discussion during this period. The students saw clearly that they were not victims of oppression in economic terms, and that in fact, their education would, as one student said, "enable us to take our places as oppressors." But they identified emotionally with the oppressed peasants described by Freire rather than with people of their own economically privileged class. It took many weeks for the students to be able to state precisely the reason for their identification with victims of oppression: their sense of powerlessness with respect to social institutions. Initially, they could speak only vaguely of their burdens. They realized that the feeling of oppression was incongruous with their economically privileged position. As Charlotte wrote:

> I wonder if the fact that we (the class) cannot call ourselves "oppressed" also means we cannot become angry about the situation that we find ourselves in. Firstly, what is the situation? The way I view it is that we are products of an educational system that has neglected the needs of our changing culture. We have all suffered to a greater or lesser degree.
>
> The people in our class are not economically marginalized and oppressed (we have never felt hunger or gone without medical attention); yet we feel the effects of another oppression. The dictionary states that "oppress" means "to weigh down or burden." Are we not weighed down (emotionally and actively) by the limit-situations of the educational system?

The clarification finally came as a result of a class exchange between two students in which one pointed out that "God" appeared on the right-hand, "good" list, and the other countered that "Church" could not have appeared there. The remainder of the class described above was an intense discussion in which the students expressed a profound distrust of all major cultural institutions. They believed that their education was designed to channel them unthinkingly into those institutions rather than to enable them to understand and direct either the course of those institutions or of their own lives. Their response to this unarticulated perception had been to treat school and all school-related topics as an irrelevance to be endured. Their "real" lives were lived in other places and their "real" voices were exercised elsewhere. As an example, they pointed out that in school they had not been encouraged to develop what we came to call "an authentic voice," but rather had learned to write "what teachers want" in order to "pass." The result was that the language they used for school-related projects was often a patchwork of words whose meaning was inappropriate for the context. When this was pointed out to the students, they often responded in a way that indicated that they did not think of words essentially in terms of their meanings, as this very common exchange shows: "You mean that if I used x instead of y, the answer would be right?" "Yes." "Then it's *just* a matter of words. Why should you give me a bad grade just because I used one word instead of another? *I meant y.*" They showed us that what we had interpreted as carelessness or lack of experience with written language was something deeper; it was a deep mistrust of language as a bearer of meaning, and by extension, of the possibility of objective knowledge and linguistic communication.

The fully articulated, central theme that emerged from the class's investigation of their thought-language was this: their profound distrust of and alienation from major cultural institutions, coupled with the passive, fatalistic acquiescence to eventually participating in these institutions, which attitude was symbolized in their own thought by their continued attendance in school.[4] Until this theme was articulated and acknowledged, the energy that could have been expressed in effective actions had been turned inward and experienced as depression. What had appeared on the surface to be laziness, apathy, or a lack of motivation was this depression marked by silent passive resistance with a potential for anger. Theirs is the state of students who are unwilling or half-hearted participants in an educational system serving purposes that are not theirs and even seem antithetical to their own real needs.

The students' view of language mirrored their view of other social institutions: they both acknowledged and denied its power. And neither the acknowledgment nor the denial was based on a critical analysis. It is just this lack of a critical response that Freire described as characteristic of members of "the culture of silence": "Silence does not signify an absence of response but rather a response which lacks a critical quality (Freire, 1973, p. 24). Their acknowledgment took the form of tacitly granting magical power or "natural" status to social institutions toward which they were passive. And their denial took the form of asserting the value of the private over the public life. The issue for us as teachers was how to enable students to see their relations to both society and language as dynamic.

Voice and Awareness

The students perceived the educational process as training their voices out of them. Their lives were dichotomized: there was the realm of "success" presented by school to whose code they sullenly complied, and there was the realm of "truth" that was private and beyond words. So far they seemed mutually exclusive. In a journal entry, one student who had early on expressed the most distrust of language and who used neither standardized spelling nor grammar, clearly expressed his perceptions and the way he dealt with these issues:

> If course you have to beware there are traps and districtions all along the way to make you seak, warre they are presented in such a nice way you don't even realize.
>
> Televisun
>
> electric heat   cars
>
> dishwashers
>
> all these impliments of man, are beutifull they make existence easier, not as rough, but I fear that the truth isn't easy, the answer is not to participate in the *Mass Mushing of the Mind.*[5]

The first assignments were attempts to help the students to clarify the meaning of naive, superstitious, and critical states of consciousness. The students were asked, after reading passages from several of Freire's books, to write a definition of each level of consciousness, and then to describe the thought process of a person at each level. This proved to be difficult. The students associated definition with objectivity and description with subjectivity, and the latter term of each pair had important emotional connotations for many of them. Objectivity, like definitions, had the connotation of public standards arbitrarily imposed on them, in contrast to description, in which it was "all right to be subjective" because one's own private perceptions of the world cannot be disputed. Our class discussion showed that the students did not understand any of these terms clearly. Thus, both intellectually and emotionally the assignment presented difficulties. A thorough discussion of the relation of objectivity and subjectivity was necessary.

From Freire's point of view, the reaction of the students to the concepts of subjectivity and objectivity was understandable as a deceptive, but very common, conception of the nature of knowledge. According to this conception, knowledge is, ideally, completely determined by the features of the object that are independent of the knower, who observes what is there but contributes nothing to the content of knowledge. The objective world is presumed to exist independently of the meaning-endowing activity of human consciousness (subjectivity). Features designated as linguistically significant are assumed to be structural parts of reality, existing separately from the historically conditioned perspectives of humans by whom reality is represented in speech. This conception of knowledge assumes a neutral observation language that can be used to represent objects as thought without contributing anything to their image. Freire terms this the "objectivist" notion of knowledge, and terms its opposite, which ultimately reduces to solipsism, the "subjectivist" view. The "objectivist" conception denies that meaning comes into the human world through human agency and consciousness (subjectivity); the "subjectivist" stance denies there are limits on the activity of consciousness in constituting meaning. What our students took to be objectivity was the "objectivist" ideal of knowledge. In rejecting it, they turned, predictably, to "subjectivist" stances. Naively, they identified "being subjective" with "being themselves," with the personal experience and attitudes that school seemed to dismiss or exclude. They identified "being objective" with knowledge that excluded the concerns of the knower and that rested on the possibility of common concepts whose existence they doubted. Freire's insistence on "the indisputable unity between subjectivity and objectivity in the act of knowing" (Freire, 1972, pp. 13–14) surprised and puzzled them.

Prior to the class discussions of subjectivity and objectivity, the students were often literally unable to understand each other or us because they responded to words not in terms of their common meanings, but as stimuli that triggered a chain of emotional associations rooted in personal psychology and experience. Gradually they learned to distinguish between the "subjectivist" stance implicit in this response, and an idea of knowledge that, while respecting the role of human consciousness (subjectivity) in the constitution of meaning, is not subjectivist. According to this notion, all knowledge is necessarily subjective; that is, knowledge is of concepts, features of thought. As such, concepts are not given as nature is but are human constructions of meaning. Meaning is a function of human consciousness. As human beings transform nature they establish objective meanings through dialogue. Generalization, symbolization, and dialogue are the conditions for objective knowledge. The most important correlate of this position is that all knowledge is partial, since the perspective (e.g., cultural, ideological, temporal, spatial, etc.) of the knower necessarily defines, and therefore limits, the view of the object. In establishing meaning, dialogue is necessary for people to compensate for the limitations imposed by any single perspective, to establish the recognizable features of reality.

For to know is not to guess, as Freire writes. Although all knowledge, as a feature of human thought, is subjective and partial, it is also, by contrast to fantasy, objective. Objective features are those features of reality that are recognizable by multiple subjects; they are established by people in dialogue, a linguistic intersubjective sharing of perspectives. This is certainly not to say that reality is created by human consciousness, but rather that human beings collectively establish its knowable features. When subjectivity and objectivity are properly understood it is clear that they cannot, in fact, be separated. As Freire explains,

> One cannot conceive of objectivity without subjectivity. Neither can exist without the other, nor can they be dichotomized. The separation of objectivity from subjectivity, the denial of the latter when analyzing reality or acting upon it, is objectivism. On the other hand the denial of objectivity in analysis or action, resulting in a subjectivism which leads to solipsistic positions, denies action itself by denying objective reality. . . .
> To deny the importance of subjectivity . . . is to admit the impossible: a world without human beings. This objectivist position is as ingenuous as that of subjectivism which postulates human beings without a world (Freire, 1970, pp. 35–36).

To say that knowledge is objective is to say that reality can be represented in significations that are recognizable by many subjects. To say that it is necessarily subjective, as Freire does, is to see that meaning comes into being through human consciousness and to recognize dialogue, an intersubjective linguistic relation, as the foundation of objective meaning. Our students eventually acknowledged, as Freire does, that knowledge requires both something that is given and something that is constructed—an object and a recognizable interpretation of that object by multiple subjects.

Not only did this discussion clear the intellectual air, it created a new willingness to pursue objectivity, which was of immediate practical use to our students in their efforts to define and describe. They could see how every good description is objective in the sense that it is the sign of careful observation and not of free association. They could also see the sense in which every definition is subjective: since there is no "neutral observation language," concepts defined in language reflect a personal and cultural perspective. Every word is a generalization and an interpretation, as Vygotsky saw, and not a mirror, replica, or repetition of an object. And every (personal or cultural) interpretation is the interpretation of an object by a subject (thinker) who contributes *the context of meaning* in which the object (thing or concept) is set. Critical consciousness was born as students began to understand that to use language unreflectively is to accept cultural definitions and perspectives unreflectively, and to use language critically is to begin to analyze the cultural definitions and perspectives. When our students finally understood this clearly, they linked the critical use of language to the development of their own views and voices. The major discovery of the course was that the students' inability to read and write was connected to their sense that language, like other cultural institutions they distrusted, belonged on the left-hand list of key words. Cultural alienation can take a linguistic form. When they saw clearly how their attitude made them complicit in what they perceived as their personal destruction, they began to struggle to gain control of language.

A Struggle for Language and Reality

In our students' struggle for the control of language, they began distinguishing in themselves and in the comments of other students, subjectivist positions from genuine, though often partial, knowledge. They also realized that though they had a strong emotional reaction to American institutions, rooted in their sense of powerlessness, their level of social understanding was superstitious rather than critical. To help them understand cultural institutions, we read and discussed Berger and Luckmann (1966), which presents an analysis consistent with Freire's assumptions.

In all his writing, Freire cites the central importance of distinguishing natural from cultural elements, for intellectual and moral development. Our experience supports this distinction as a prerequisite for the emergence of critical consciousness. In the absence of this distinction, language can function as myth rather than as an instrument of critical thought. The essential feature of the mythic form of speech is that it makes a human construction appear as a natural fact, and this transforms history into nature. A certain adaptive behavior to the *status quo* is its real intention. Mythic speech masks the relation of human agency to human institutions, thereby making an adequate analysis of social forms impossible.[6]

Berger and Luckmann, like Freire, recognize that cultural institutions, laws, customs, etc. have a reality and structure that are independent of the volition and purposes of individual persons; yet these structures are cultural, not natural. They are social constructions reflecting human perceptions and human needs and culturally acknowledged as "real." But cultural institutions originate in "subjective relations between people (Skiner, 1978, p. 28), and therefore, "the institutional world is objectivated human activity, and so is every single institution (Berger & Luckmann, 1966, p. 60). To document the above argument is not within the scope of this essay, but we must record the importance of the analysis for our students. Reading Berger and Luckmann, they saw how socially defined roles sustain institutions and how language legitimates the reifications of social institutions, which reinforce the confusion of nature with culture. This recognition made them less superstitious and more hopeful that they could understand their world, and perhaps even influence it.

The theoretical truth of this brought elation and a sense of control. Because institutions were made by human acts, theoretically our students could act to reform them to accord to their needs and beliefs. But when this theoretical truth was brought to bear on their own concrete, specific personal worlds, the elation turned to anxiety. The focus of this anxiety was the writing section of the course.

When they first began to voice their alienation and consequent hypocrisy in tacitly working for success in systems they found to be antithetical to their human needs, they acknowledged no responsibility for this situation. As the term progressed, however, students became increasingly conscious of their responsibility for their situation. Knowing that institutions were human constructions meant that they had to acknowledge their human responsibility to shape them, not merely acquiesce to errors and injustices they perceived in their political, social and (more immediately) educational institutions. Assenting to this knowledge on a theoretical level was one thing; acting on it was another. Acting would require uniting the "real" (private) world with the "school" (public) world, worlds that had been more or less mutually exclusive; it would also mean taking responsibility not only for their own lives but for their culture as well. Ultimately, as the intellectual grasp of the concepts began to illuminate the contradiction between their insights and their actions, a shift, described below, occurred in their attitude toward language, writing and education. When the crisis came, in the form of anger and a refusal to write, the understanding necessary for its resolution was already there. Comparing this course to another one in which the students arrived at the same impasse and were not able to get beyond it, we were forced to recognize the value of the theoretical framework in enabling the students to *confront themselves and act* to improve their skills. They were able to act because they tied gaining control of their language to assuming responsible control of their lives. As a result, they experienced a dramatic improvement in the quality of their thought, and especially of their writing.

It was in the students' writing that they felt and saw for themselves their lack of critical skills, and more frightening still, their failure to develop an authentic voice. Yet they were afraid of taking the steps to develop their own voices, think their own thoughts, and take the responsibility for acting in accordance with their own beliefs. They eventually recognized and stated that for them the writing assignments presented, in Freire's terms, the "limit situation." Writing was their limit task. Freire's analysis fully describes our experience with them:

> People . . . because they are conscious beings—exist in a dialectical relationship between the determination of limits and their own freedom. As they separate themselves from the world, which they objectify, as they separate themselves from their own activity, as they locate the seat of their decisions in themselves and in their relations with the world and others, they overcome the situations which limit them: the "limit-situations." . . . It is not the limit-situations in and of themselves which create a climate of hopelessness, but rather how they are perceived by people at a given historical moment; whether they appear as fetters or an insurmountable barrier. As critical perception is embodied in action, a climate of hope and confidence develops which leads humans to attempt to overcome the limit-situations (Freire, 1970, p. 89).

Writing became their limit task because it was there they confronted their own inability to express their thoughts in a free, authentic voice. It was in writing, not in some general discussion about their place in society, that the students—especially the most philosophically aware students—sensed the gulf between their own thought and the language taught them by their culture, especially the academic jargon they learned to produce for success in school.

Self-Knowledge, Language, and Community

At the beginning of the course, some of our students were characteristically naive about writing. For these students, facility with language was just something you had been given, a "natural" talent that gave some people an edge in school. But most of our students—especially the most vocal about their alienation—had a superstitious rather than a naive consciousness regarding language. They viewed language as an instrument for coercive social control. They did not believe that language might be the primary means for examining their own thoughts, that it might be a tool for self-knowledge and a way of sharing thoughts and feelings for building a community. Language had been mystified for them. They had learned to recognize and use certain terms and forms appropriate to the academic level they were expected to have reached (and so they tested out on standardized tests at or above their grade levels), but they did not understand the principles behind their language use or the purposes of the structures they had learned to mimic. They had learned *the spell*: a jargon made up of vague terms and mysterious syntactic structures that gave them some measure of power within certain specific situations—particularly situations relating to institutions. Early in the journal of one of our students, we found a clear discussion of how jargon was the means of her "initiation" into the club, and the consequent awareness that she had paid a stiff price—the ability to think her own thoughts and express them to others in her own voice. In class, she stated that she always could whip off a paper in a "gut" course and get an A, but she found herself unable to write when a course interested her enough to think deeply on the subject or stimulated her to express her own ideas and feelings. Consequently, she did not write papers for these courses at all, and had accrued a long list of incompletes. She seemed like many of the bright but puzzling students in our experience, whose journals and verbal discussions of the course were deep and alive, but whose papers were superficial, inaccurate, vague—and nearly devoid of a living voice.

Gradually, it became clear to all of us why the writing sections had so angered and frustrated the students. For some, their reluctance to write directly, in their own voices, was related to their reluctance to give up the little control they imagined they had over their "public" life. This, in turn, showed them how much they desired the power of the very institutions they had earlier in the course designated as "oppressive." In the context of Freire's philosophy and the aims of our own class, the students had admitted theoretically that a responsible, conscious use of language required a willingness to know what you know and to share that knowledge with others. But at the same time, their growing sense of the oppressiveness of the cultural institutions—to which their written language was so closely related—made it a frightening thing to admit either that you were a victim of that system, or worse yet, an aspiring participant in it.

In this setting, we had two main objectives. The first was to stimulate the students' thinking and discussion of language; this was approached primarily through a discussion of Vygotsky's ideas. We wanted the students to understand how word meaning is, in Vygotsky's language, the place where "thoughts and speech unite." We hoped that as they valued their own thought they would begin to value words as well, and that this would enable them to engage in the writing exercises and discussions devised to bridge the gap between prereflective and reflective language. We expected that presenting the concept of what Vygotsky called inner speech, which many of them demonstrated (e.g., agglutination, heavy predication, semantic shortcuts), and explaining how you can learn to translate your inner speech, which is maximally compact, into written speech, which is maximally developed, would generate satisfaction and self-confidence. Their resistance to writing surprised us because we were not sensitive enough to their distress in finding out that their speech and their thought did not unite. We did not understand how frightening it must have been for them to have to confront, or suppress, this question: If my writing does not reflect my thought, what *does* it reflect? Thus, it was not until after the class had defined writing as *the* limiting task that the students vigorously engaged in discussion of Vygotsky's analysis of the development of thought-language.

The second main objective of the writing classes was to identify and analyze some of the structures most commonly used without critical understanding. We first explored how jargon language tends to eliminate simple verbs in a number of ways. For instance, academic jargon overuses the passive voice ("It may be found that . . ." instead of "I saw . . ."); also, it uses noun constructions instead of gerunds ("by reflection upon" instead of "reflecting on"). We noted how these and other structures of jargon language tended to cut down on the dynamic nature of thought and action by treating elements of human life and ideas as things, obscuring, rather than clarifying, the relationship between the subject and the action.

As we reflect on the students' comments and performance regarding the active/passive voice and use of noun constructions in their own writing, the students started seeing how the form of their thought was reflected in the form of their language constructions. They began to discover that jargon techniques enabled the writer to avoid definite, complete judgments on the idea in the sentence.

The students habitually discussed their ideas in the passive voice, bringing themselves into the grammatical position of the object ("It has been demonstrated to me," rather than "I learned"; "It has been noted to me," instead of "I saw"). They did not fully perceive themselves as subjects, either in the grammatical way or in the way that Freire uses the term, as free human beings who are capable of taking action on their world, and their writing reflected this subconscious judgment.

In doing the passive/active voice analysis, we began to understand why these students found it hard to understand what seemed to be a very simple concept—the sentence. We had noticed that our students often wrote in sentence fragments or run-on sentences, although they could easily recognize and correct these errors when they were presented abstractly in classroom exercises. Run-on sentences usually have a number of subjects and predicates that are somehow related, but there is no way a reader can tell for certain what specific relationship the writer means them to have. A sentence fragment presents a subject, but doesn't say anything about it; or presents a predicate without specifically tying it to a subject. By writing in sentence fragments and run-on sentences, they were, in effect, presenting topics for consideration, relieving themselves of the responsibility for asserting their own judgments on those topics. They lacked the confidence that they were qualified, or allowed, to make the judgments that active, declarative sentences required. So they didn't write them. Their *psychological grammar* was quite accurate. They did not believe it to be within their power to make judgments, statements, decisions, and to act on them. Before they could begin to find their own natural voices, they needed to see themselves as subjects, as knowers, as persons responsible for taking action in creating their world.

The reasons for the students' early resentment of the writing assignments were now clear. In the writing classes, the jargon had been exposed, analyzed, seen as a tool not for associating persons, and illuminating thoughts, but as a means for obfuscating thoughts or purposes in order to control others. No longer permitted to write with jargon, they found that they were unable to write without it. Moreover, our students were increasingly disturbed by their own use of jargon, for they saw and taught us that their jargon-laden language was bad ethically as well as rhetorically. It fostered hypocrisy, it made you one of "them" and it served the powers of the left-hand list of the key words. The consequent truth of this analysis was borne out not only by the group's consensus that it was so, but by the way it illuminated so many of the puzzling earlier experiences of the class, regenerated our abilities to find fruitful activities and situations for learning, made possible the community of shared teacher-student responsibility emerging in the final month of the course, and, most of all, evoked a dramatic change in the quality of the students' writing.

Final Reflections

We ended this course with more respect for our students, and heightened awareness of our students' deep alienation from major cultural institutions. The central insight to emerge from the class is that one form this alienation takes is a kind of illiteracy. Language deficiency is greater than anticipated and the current mechanical remediation of what some educators call "higher illiteracy" (Shapiro and Kriftcher,

1976, pp. 381–386) does not address the problem. We believe that no amount of training in the mechanics of language use will work because the problem is rooted in alienation: the students' accurate perception of the gulf between the use to which language is commonly put in our society and the ideal of language as a means of analysis, illumination, self-expression, and communication.[7] The illiteracy of our students is not a symptom of individual failure alone, but of cultural disintegration. A sense of powerlessness in the face of cultural institutions permits our students to identify with other powerless peoples.

The discussion of the key words showed us that what concerned our students above all was their relationship to their world as they conceived it. The question they asked, which their education was not helping them to answer, was "How do I fit into the world?" The academic subjects of our course—educational philosophy, sociology of knowledge, epistemology, and language skills—ultimately could give them tools to address this question, but first the question had to be made explicit, and our students had to examine the value of social actions whose worth they have assumed. Moreover, from reading our students' journals, we learned that in order to begin to acquire these tools they had to "feel safe" in class. They needed the safety of a community in order to set aside their defenses and explore their ideas and level of skills honestly; to join with instead of being set against their teachers and the institution for which the teacher is the representative. Not until they experienced a sense of community and understood their participation in the "social construction of reality" would they risk exposing their own written thought to each other for analysis and criticism. It was not the *discussion* of "community" that our students needed, but the experience of a way of relating that makes learning possible. By the final third of the course they were able to risk both judging and being judged. A dramatic change occurred when they saw the relevance of language skills to discovering their own voices and their places in the world.

Trusting student concerns to guide the course's thematic content, and recognizing that they need the safety of a community to set aside their defenses in order to learn, are obvious principles for teaching children, but they are generally neglected or simply given lip service when teaching adults. It was Freire's philosophy that led us to understand why it is that you cannot expect to teach adults to read and write using mechanical techniques. For adults, the question is always there, either explicit or lurking, "What does this *mean*?" As Freire discovered, adults learn to read and write only when they are simultaneously learning the skill and reflecting on its personal and social significance; every human occupation must also be a preoccupation. We found that before our students would give their energy over to learning technical and rational skills, they needed to understand not only the nature of the technical and rational flaws exhibited by their writing, but also the personal and social significance of their inability to write clearly.

It was our students, through the key-word discussions, who made us understand the necessity for explicitly studying epistemology. They taught us how Freire's criticism of American education's superstitious fascination with method corresponded to the students' superstitious attitude toward education and writing. They taught us by concrete experience that we had until then only partially understood that "knowing is a teleological activity; it is impossible to know without ends."[8]

In her book, Sylvia Ashton-Warner says that she developed her key-word method of teaching reading to Maori children particularly to counteract "an aversion to the written word . . . a habit I have seen born under my own eyes" (1963, p. 34). This same observation was part of our motivation in trying this course. Talking specifically of Maori children who must suddenly move, at a very formative age, into a foreign (European) culture, she states:

> It's not beauty to abruptly halt the growth of a young mind and to overlay it with the frame of an imposed culture. There are ways of training and grafting young growth. The true conception of beauty is the shape of organic life and that is the very thing at stake in the transition from one culture to another (1963, p. 34).

Like the Maori, our students fear and distrust the culture that runs the schools, a culture that they perceive as subordinating individual activity to the needs of a consumer economy. Since our students are not children, however, their education is complicated by their awareness that they have become accomplices in maintaining this culture and its values. They want those consumer goods, they want the college degree for earning power, political power, social power of many kinds. We and our students had to face the contradiction between the values of the consumer society—the products of which they enjoy—and their "childlike" instinct for personal determination that made them want to turn away from the institutions of this society. Our class could not resolve this society-wide contradiction, but it could raise it to a level where reflection can begin and conscious choices can be made. Our students' writing, the habit of aversion born under the eyes of their teachers, was where this struggle between the philosophical and ethical perspectives of their human selves and their social selves emerged.

Before closing, we must add a brief note about the dialogue process. We realized at the end of the course that had we not begun the class with consideration of student attitudes secured through dialogue, it would have been a very different and much less fruitful experience. Dialogue is the indispensable condition of the formation of objective meaning. Like the goal we aimed at—the students' realization of the dynamic quality of their relation to both language and society—dialogue unites the epistemological and political dimensions. In dialogue, both objective meaning and direction emerge.

We needed the philosophy drawn from experience of the Third World to teach us what we needed to know. Freire's philosophy is not simply specialized to teaching Third World people how to read and write, but also is helpful for examining particular cultures, our common human purpose, and how these two are related. We must bring these philosophical concerns into the forefront and into focus, reminding ourselves of their central importance in education at all levels. These concerns must be embodied in the attitudes of teachers and students to inform the methods we use, not vice versa. We need to develop curricula that will address themselves to the serious study of the nature of cultural institutions, to the epistemological dimensions of language, and the ethical dimensions of vocabulary, grammar, syntax and rhetoric. The control of the mechanical and technical skills follows with incredible speed and accuracy once these fundamental concerns of students are met.

All of this seems to go far afield from the study of remedial language arts in American colleges. Thus, it is crucial to find out whether the knowledge we have gained from this experience can be duplicated by the experience of other groups of teachers and students. The pattern of increasing adult "illiteracy" is pervasive. So far, educators have generally assumed that the cause is an inadequate grasp of the mechanics of reading and writing. Courses have been structured to remedy these ills, but studies indicate that they have been generally ineffective. Our study suggests that the problems are not rooted in mechanical deficiencies. Students in the best universities in the country are displaying the same patterns as students attending less prestigious schools. The fact that students at many levels of intellectual and skills development have this problem suggests that its roots are attitudinal and cultural rather than mechanical and individual. It was our effort to trace these problems to the roots that led us, implausible as it may seem, to questions of values, meaning, and human purpose. Freire is, of course, aware that because of the unorthodoxy of his views and pedagogy, some people will regard his position

> as purely idealistic, or may even consider discussion of ontological vocation, love, dialogue, hope, humility, and sympathy as so much reactionary "blah" (Freire, 1970, p. 21).

But the response of our students affirms the value of Freire's approach.

The final statement of this essay is not ours, but is one of our students'. It is an accurate, concise, and beautiful statement of our class's experience and hopes:

> The Philosophy of Education course meant a great deal to me. I found a way to overcome a growing feeling of alienation from my fellow men and women, my cultural relatives. Before I studied the work of Freire, Vygotsky, and Berger and Luckmann, I'd have been at a loss to explain the isolation I was feeling. This shows that I was suffering not only a lack of cultural awareness but also a lack of self-awareness. I feel now that developing one's understanding of self and developing one's understanding of culture go hand-in-hand. I further feel that the means of this development is an ability to use language, to communicate, clearly, and from a position of self-worth. With this understanding I can begin the task of understanding the world and constructing a place in if for myself. I no longer feel alone or afraid. Not long ago I felt that my die had been cast. I was fatalistic and hopeless. This has passed. I have a goal now, understanding the world, and a tool, language. I can go to work.

Appendix

Raw key-word list (prior to student grouping into opposing columns)

Philosophy of Education

death	oppression
music	injustice
emotion	idealism
introspection	society
belief	change
reality	why
human nature	values
humility	energy
communication	awareness
compassion	consideration
media	friendship
creativity	dependability
growth	faith
honesty	patience
mediation	life
buddhism	world-people
running	nature

perception
perspectives
realize
mind
organize-order
universe
autonomy
education
independence
literature
love
science
subjective
freedom
God
cultures
relative (everything is relative)
forms (all forms)
peace
curiosity
appreciation
discipline
listening
inventions
innovations
discovery
motivation
government
alcohol
body chemistry
space
time

foreign policy
art
crafts-making
dance
theory of relativity
world economics
photography
environment
conceptualize
integrate
experience
variety
wholeness
maleness
care
important
they
anticipation
goals
happiness
systems
power
course
consciousness
myth
alternatives
energy-information-matter
skills
objective
woman

Notes

1. A detailed explanation of the chronology and structure of this course is available from the authors.
    The course texts were Paulo Freire's *Pedagogy of the Oppressed; Cultural Action for Freedom;* and *Education for Critical Consciousness;* Dennis Collins's *Paulo Freire: His Life and His Works;* Lev Vygotsky's *Thought and Language;* and Peter Berger and Thomas Luckmann's *The Social Construction of Reality.*
2. The genesis of the key-word assignment was a result of our reflection on two books: Sylvia Ashton-Warner's *Teacher,* and Raymond Williams's *Keywords.*
3. See the Appendix for a complete list of words from which these groups were formed.

4. These themes are those of *our* class, particular students in a particular setting. They may not be the generative themes for other students, even those in similar situations. Although the principles that define the process of the class can be generalized, the content cannot.
5. This student's views are clear enough. The writing sample is interesting because it contains the characteristics of "inner speech" as described by Vygotsky.
6. For a useful amplification of Freire's reasoning, see Roland Barthes (19xx, pp. 109-159).
7. They had no trouble in bringing in examples to show how well their jargon language had been rewarded, and they showed us an article from the magazine *Nutshell*, which recently had been distributed on campus, titled "Flowery Term Papers Win Teachers' Accolades":

> Professor Joseph Williams of the University of Chicago and Rosemary Hake of Chicago State University took a well-written paper on the difference in values between today's generations and changed the language a bit. They kept the ideas and concepts similar but wrote two different versions. One contained simplified, straightforward language; the second was written with verbose, flowery language.
>
> Both papers were first submitted to nine high school teachers who ultimately graded the verbose papers with nearly perfect scores but downgraded the straightforward essay as being too simple and shallow.
>
> The two papers were then submitted to 90 more teachers, and again the flowery language received the better grades. Three out of four high school teachers and two out of three college professors consistently gave higher marks to the pompous writing.
>
> "Verbose language is so deeply ingrained that it becomes a subconscious thing," said Williams (*Nutshell*, 1977/78, published by 13-30 Corporation, 505 Market St., Knoxville, TN 37902).

8. Notes by Linda Finlay to record a conversation with Freire in July 1974.

References

Ashton-Warner, S. (1979). *Teacher* (First Edition 1963). New York: Bantam.
Barthes, R. (1972). *Mythologies*. New York: Hill and Wang.
Berger, P., & Luckmann, T. (1966). *The social construction of reality*. Garden City, NY: Doubleday.
Collins, D. (1977). *Paulo Freire: His life, thought and work*. New York: Paulist Press.
Elsasser, N., & John-Steiner, V. (August 1977). An interactionist approach to advancing literacy. *Harvard Educational Review*, *XLVII*(3), 355-369.
Freire, P. (1970). *Pedagogy of the oppressed*. New York: Continuum.
Freire, P. (1972). *Cultural action for freedom*. Baltimore: Penguin.
Freire, P. (1973). *Education for critical consciousness*. New York: Continuum.
Shapiro, N., & Kriftcher, N. (February 1976). Combatting the lower and higher illiteracies. *Journal of Reading*, pp. 381-386.
Skiner, Q. (June 15, 1978). The flight from positivism. *New York Review of Books*, p. 28.
Vygotsky, L. (1962). *Thought and language* (E. Hanfmann & G. Vaker, Trans.). Cambridge, MA: MIT Press.
Williams, R. (1976). *Keywords*. New York: Oxford University Press.

5.

"Strangers No More": A Liberatory Literacy Curriculum

KYLE FIORE and NAN ELSASSER

College of the Bahamas
November 17, 1979

Dear Kyle, Pat and Larry,

I think our basic writing curriculum works! After ten weeks
of discussing reading and writing about the generative theme
of marriage, students have actually begun to use their newly
won knowledge and skills for their own purposes. Last night
we were reviewing for the final—a test designed, administered, and graded by the College English Department—when
Louise, one of my students, broke in to say that no test
could measure what she had learned over the semester! Another student nodded in agreement. She said, "We've learned
to write. We've learned about ourselves." Perfect Freirean
synthesis! As if that weren't reward enough for one night,
Eurena suggested that the class—all women—summarize and
publish their knowledge. Then everyone jumped in. Our
review of dashes and semicolons was forgotten as the class
designed its first publication. It's hard to believe that in September these women had difficulty thinking in terms of a
paragraph—now they want a manifesto! I'll keep you posted.

Love, Nan

Nan Elsasser's letter elated us. That semester she had been experimenting with a remedial English program we had designed in the spring
of 1978.[1] We had first come together just after Christmas, drawn to

87

each other by the desire to share our classroom frustrations, our successes, our gripes, over a common pitcher of beer. Trading stories with
one another, we discovered we were four teachers in search of a curriculum. Standard English textbooks and traditional curricula did not
fit our students at the University of Albuquerque and the University
of New Mexico. Chicanos, Blacks, Anglos, and Native Americans, they
had enrolled in our courses to gain writing skills that would help them
succeed in college and carve a place for themselves in society. Once
they arrived, however, our students found themselves strangers in a
strange world. A wide gulf stretched between the classroom curriculum
and their own knowledge gained in the barrios of Albuquerque and the
rural towns and pueblos of New Mexico. Confronted by a course that
negated their culture, many failed to master the skills they sought.
Others succeeded by developing a second skin. Leaving their own customs, habits, and skills behind, they participated in school and in the
world by adapting themselves to fit the existing order. Their acquisition of literacy left them not in control of their social context, but
controlled by it.

We were troubled. We wanted our students to be able to bring
their culture, their knowledge, into the classroom. We wanted them
to understand and master the intricacies of the writing process. And
we wanted them to be able to use writing as a means of intervening in
their own social environment. Sparked by our common concerns, we
decided to create a curriculum that would meet our goals. As we cast
about for theories and pedagogies, we discovered the works of Lev
Vygotsky and Paulo Freire. These scholars intrigued us because they
believe writing involves both cognitive skills and social learnings. Their
approaches parallel and complement each other. Vygotsky explores
students' internal learning processes. Freire emphasizes the impact of
external social reality.

Vygotsky's work clarifies the complex process of writing. He pos-
tulates that learning to write involves the mastery of cognitive skills
and the development of new social understandings. According to
Vygotsky, we categorize and synthesize our lives through inner speech,
the language of thought. In inner speech, a single word or phrase is em-
broidered with variegated threads of ideas, experiences, and emotions.
The multileveled, personal nature of inner speech is illustrated by a
woman student's response to a word association exercise: *sex*: home,
time, never, rough, sleep.

Vygotsky explains that to transform the inner speech symbols
to written text, this woman must consciously step outside the short-
hand of her thoughts and mentally enter the social context she shares
with her reader. Only from this common perspective can she begin to
unfold the mystery of her thoughts to create written prose.

Focusing on the learner's environment, Freire discusses the social and political aspects of writing. A designer of liberatory or revolutionary literacy programs, Freire maintains that the goal of a literacy program is to help students become critically conscious of the connection between their own lives and the larger society and to empower them to use literacy as a means of changing their own environment. Like Vygotsky, Freire believes the transformation of thought to text requires the conscious consideration of one's social context. Often, Freire says, students unaware of the connections between their own lives and society personalize their problems. To encourage students to understand the impact of society on their lives, Freire proposes students and teachers talk about generative themes drawn from the students' everyday world. Investigating issues such as work or family life from an individual and a sociohistorical perspective, students bring their own knowledge into the classroom and broaden their sense of social context.

For example, one woman beaten by her husband may think she has simply made a bad choice and must bear her lot with dignity. Another woman may think her husband would stop if she could live up to his expectations. When they talk with each other and other women, these two discover that brutality is a social phenomenon; it is widespread in the community. As they read, they learn that many aspects of their problem are rooted in the social realm and can best be attacked by pressing for legal changes, battered women's shelters, more responsive attitudes on the part of the police. Through continued discussion, these women realize how they can use literacy to win those changes by swearing out complaints in court, sending petitions to public officials, or writing newspaper articles and letters to the editor.

We decided to base our curriculum on Vygotsky's theory and Freire's pedagogy. Vygotsky's theory of inner speech would enable students to understand the writing process. Freire's pedagogy would encourage them to bring their culture and personal knowledge into the classroom, help them understand the connections between their own lives and society, and empower them to use writing to control their environment.

As advanced literacy teachers in traditional universities, we realized we could not use a pure Freirean approach. Designed for teachers in revolutionary settings, Freire's basic literacy programs do not consider the time constraint of semesters or the academic pressure of preparing students to meet English department standards. However, we thought it would be possible to combine Freire's goal of increasing students' critical consciousness with the teaching of advanced literacy skills. As Freire wrote, "The best way to accomplish those things that are impossible today is to do today whatever is possible" (Freire, 1978, p. 64).

That spring we met every Saturday at each other's houses. Spurred on by coffee and raised glazed doughnuts, we talked about the advanced literacy techniques we were using and explored ways to link those techniques with Vygotsky's and Freire's works. We designed word association exercises to Vygotsky's theory of inner speech. We charted ways to fit rhetorical forms in a Freirean investigation. We finished in May. That same month Nan Elsasser kept us abreast of her experiment by mail. In the pages that follow, we have summarized her letters and combined them with copies of student papers to create a first-person account of our curriculum in process.

The College of the Bahamas: An Experiment in Possibilities

Arriving in the Bahamas before the semester begins, I have a few days to learn about the college.

Located on the island of New Providence, the College of the Bahamas is a two-year community college offering daytime and evening classes. Over ninety percent of the students at the college are black Bahamians. Many work by day, attend school by night. Two-thirds of these students are women.

The language skills class I am to teach is the first in a series of four English courses offered by the college prep program. All of these courses are taught along traditional lines. To practice grammar, students change tenses, add punctuation, or fill in blank spaces in assigned sentences. To demonstrate reading ability they answer multiple choice or true-false questions on short paragraphs. A colleague tells me that the year before, forty-five to sixty percent of the students failed to meet English Department standards. She also shows me a College of the Bahamas study demonstrating no significant correlation between grades in English and grades in other academic subjects. Her revelations strengthened my determination to try out our curriculum.

I get to class early on the first night, worried that my students' traditional expectations will make them leery of a new approach. Checking my roster, I discover all my students are women (later, I learn women make up two-thirds of the college's student body). I start class by introducing myself and describing the problems I've encountered teaching English traditionally. Telling the women we'll be using an experimental approach, I stress this experiment will succeed only if we can pick topics, discuss material, and evaluate results together. I admit the class will lack coherency at times, and one student asks if they will be able to pass the standardized English exam given at the end of the semester. I say I think so, but that she is free to transfer if she wants a more traditional approach. She leaves; but the rest stay.

To establish a sense of common ground, I ask my students about their work and former schooling. Half of them clerk in banks. The others type or run computers. Collectively, these women represent the first generation of Bahamian women to enter the business world and go to college. They have an average of six years of education behind them. Recalling her early school days, one woman speaks of days spent copying poems from a colonial primer. Another recounts the times she stayed home to care for the younger ones while her mother went to sell her wares at the straw market. They all remember problems with writing.

So they can begin to understand the cause of their problems, we spend the next three weeks investigating the complexities of going from inner speech to finished written product. We begin with a series of word association exercises designed to illustrate Vygotsky's theory. Comparing their responses to trigger words such as *sex, home, work*, the women start to see that even at this most basic level they categorize and store information in various ways. Some students list contrasting affective responses. Others jot down visual images. One woman divides the inner speech word into subtopics, like an outline: *"job*: where you would like to work, type boss, what specific field." Contrasting their different ways of organizing and listing thoughts, students gain a strong sense of why they need to elaborate their thoughts in writing. To end the session, we each transform our private lists to public prose.

To continue our study of the transformations involved in writing clear, explicit prose, I look for a topic that will stress the value of personal knowledge, break down the dichotomy between personal and classroom knowledge, and require explicit elaboration. As a newcomer to the island, I ask them to advise me as to "What You Need to Know to Live in the Bahamas." I introduce this assignment by talking about writing as an interaction between process and product, personal and social points of view, concrete and abstract knowledge. A student writing a recipe for conch salad needs concrete knowledge about preparing conch combined with the abstract knowledge of an audience as people with some shared assumptions as well as some lack of common ground.

The women have a number of problems with this assignment, evidencing what Freire calls the inability to step outside immediate contextual realities and incorporate broader points of view. Some students write very brief suggestions. Others write in the first person or list topics of interest, but don't include concrete information. Still others complain they are stymied trying to figure out what I'd like to do. Though she knows I am a stranger to the island, the woman writing me a recipe for conch salad assumed conch is a familiar food.

Yet another woman constructs an imaginary audience to help herself focus on the assignment: "What You Need to Know to Live in the Bahamas. A Young married couple on Vacation. Leisure Activities. Whatever your taste in holiday diversion you'll never be at loss for something to do in the Bahamas. . . ."

This assignment extends over several sessions. Students write and rewrite their essays. During this time we develop the basic procedure we'll use to investigate a generative theme. First, we discuss the topic at hand (e.g., "What You Need to Know to Live in the Bahamas"). Then one student volunteers a thesis statement related to the topic. Other women help narrow and sharpen this statement and develop an essay outline. Students use these as guidelines for their drafts. I reproduce the drafts, and we read and comment on them. After prolonged discussion, each woman rewrites her draft to meet the questions we've raised.

In moving from the discussion of inner speech to writing about the Bahamas, students take on more and more responsibility for the class. While in writing they are still trapped by their personal perspectives, in discussions they begin to critique and respond to one another's views. Gradually they start to investigate their environment. Before, they passively received knowledge. Now, they pursue it.

Freire states that students caught by their own subjectivity can break through personal walls and move to a collective social perspective through investigating generative themes. Such themes must be selected carefully so that they encourage students to write for a broader, more public audience and empower them to use writing to change their lives. Freire advises teachers searching for themes to involve themselves intimately in their students' culture and minutely observe all the facets of their daily lives, recording "the way people talk, their style of life, their behavior at church and work" (Freire, 1970, p. 103). Analyzing these observations with a team of other educators, the teacher will discern meaningful generative themes.

A stranger, unaccompanied by a "literacy team," I can't follow Freire's advice, and in my ignorance I turn to my students for help. We discuss generative themes, and they each select three issues from their daily lives that they would like to talk, read, and write about for the semester. When they bring in their suggestions, I list them on the board. We debate them briefly and they vote, picking marriage for their generative theme. This theme affects their lives economically, socially, and emotionally. Ninety percent of these women have been raised by two parents in traditional Bahamian homes. Seventy-five percent are now mothers. Two-thirds of these mothers are single parents totally responsible for their children's physical and emotional well-being.

Having chosen their theme, the women break into groups. They discuss the areas of marriage they want to investigate and construct an outline of subtopics, including *housework, divorce, sexuality*, and *domestic violence*. With these subtopics in hand, I start to hunt for reading materials. I look for articles that bridge the distance between students' lives and society. We'll use these articles as a basis for dialogues about individual problems, common experiences, and the larger social world.

My search of the college library yields nothing on contemporary Bahamian marriage. Writing back to the United States for articles, culling my old *Ms.* magazines, and hounding the local newsstand, I collect a packet that fits our course outline. Initial reading assignments come from popular magazines: an article on wife beating from *New Woman*, one entitled "Why Bad Marriages Endure" from *Ebony*. As students' reading skills and knowledge increase, we will use more advanced texts, such as *Our Bodies Ourselves* by the Boston Women's Health Collective; *Sex Differences in Perspective* by Tavris & Offir, 1977. At the end of the semester, we will read a novel by Kamala Markandaya, *Nectar in a Sieve* (1971), about peasant marriage in India.

For the rest of the semester we spend about one week coinvestigating each subtopic of our marriage theme. I introduce each subject by handing out a related article. To help the women understand new information, I discuss the concepts I think unfamiliar, e.g., the historical concept of "Victorian" as a set of sexual attitudes. After reading and talking about the articles, we develop a thesis statement following the procedure we devised when writing essays on the Bahamas. When discussing articles and writing critiques, students do not follow the traditional liberal arts curricula. Their criticism is not bound by the authors' intent or opinion, nor do they consider all articles equally valid. Rather, they judge the reading by whether or not it connects with their personal perspectives and tells them about marriage as a socioeconomic institution. They find much of value in *Our Bodies Ourselves* (1976). They dismiss poet Judith Viorst as a spoiled middle-class housewife.

During our investigation students pass through three distinct phases as they hone their abilities to examine, critique, and write about marriage. They elaborate their own experience more skillfully, and they perceive stronger links between their own lives and the larger social context. They reach outside their own experience to seek new sources of knowledge. Finally, they become critically conscious of the way society affects their lives, and they begin to use writing as a means of intervening in their own social environment.

In the early weeks many women have trouble discerning the connections between their personal life and their social context. They analyze problems using concrete knowledge drawn from experience.

They argue by anecdote. To encourage them to broaden their outlook, I ask for a definition of marriage as a social institution. In response, they describe what marriage should be ("communication," "love," "fidelity), or they recite personal experiences ("men can come and go as they please, women cannot"; "men are violent"). Posing questions targeting a social definition of marriage, I elicit broader, abstract responses: "legal procedure," "age requirements," "union between man and women," "religious sanctioning of sex." Looking over this list, they ask me to throw out their earlier, more personal definitions.

Next, they construct lists of the positive and negative aspects of marriage as a social institution. These lists display a mixture of personal experiences, idealistic yearnings, and social traits.

Positive	*Negative*
Safe from rape and break-ins	Sex against our will
Not coming home to an empty house	Security sours relationships
	Loss of freedom
Community approval of the relationship	

Comparing these lists, the women start to talk about the social aspects of marriage. They conclude that the major benefit of marriage is security and social approval; its major shortcoming, a loss of freedom. Even after our extended dialogue, in their essays on "The Worst or Best Things about Marriage," women either write empty generalizations or briefly recount their own experience.

The Worst Thing About Marriage
By Rosetta Finlay

The worst thing about marriage is security. Whenever a couple is married they tend to become too sure of themselves. One would say, "All is well." I already have whom I want so I don't have to say I love you anymore: I don't have to show that I care as much. We don't have sex as often and you can go out with the boys while I go out with the girls.

This is where one would find time to go out of the home and look for the missing links in his marriage. That's when all the problem arises as soon as this happens, there's no end to problems.

The Best Thing About Marriage
By Eurena Clayton

I enjoyed being with my husband when we were dating and the things we did together drew us closer. After we got married my husband's business prevents us from doing as many things as we used to do together. Usually when we have a spare chance we take off on trips which we simply enjoy together. The feeling of not having to bother with the every day responsibilities is a great burden lifted for that period. We find ourselves taking in the movies, theatre, tennis, golfing or simply sightseeing.

There are special occasions such as anniversary or birthday which are always remembered. Sometimes for no reason you receive a beautiful gift which is always appreciated and thoughtful.

In order to achieve one's goal in life it is safe to pool both resources.

I suggest revisions for these essays, reproduce them, and pass them out. Students critique each other's papers, and each woman rewrites her piece. This time a number of students expand their essays through elaboration. However, at this stage no one goes beyond her own experience without writing platitudes, and few maintain a consistent focus throughout the entire paper. The woman writing this third draft has expanded and improved her mechanics and drawn clearer contrasts in her conclusion. She still reverts to an unrelated generality.

Draft III
By Rosetta Finlay

The worst thing about marriage is emotional security. When a couple is married, they tend to become too sure of themselves. One will say, "All is well I already have whom I want so I don't have to look nice anymore: I don't have to say I love you anymore: I don't have to show that I care as much: we don't have sex as often and you can go out with the boys while I go out with the girls."

Marriage shouldn't be taken so much for granted there's always improvement needed in every marriage. Marriage is like a job, e.g.—one has a job; everything is routine; you have a steady salary; steady hours nine o'clock in the morning to five o'clock in the evening; go to work every day and perform the duties your job position requires.

Marriage is very similar, e.g.—one has a steady companion: cook every day; keep the house and laundry clean; have babies and bring them up. Apart from doing the house chores there's the chauffeuse part to be done and the office work.

I personally think that there is a lot more to be done if you want to have a successful marriage. Therefore if more interest is taken in these areas, marriage would be much better than what it is today.

In the sessions that follow, students evidence similar problems with the reading assignment. The article is about battered wives. Although they can read the words, the women have difficulty distinguishing major ideas from details. Where in writing they recounted personal experiences, now in reading they focus on anecdotes. They underline when, where, or how hard Frank hit Marlene, as opposed to the main concept this example illustrates.

To sharpen the contrast between a main idea and an illustration, I ask them to list causes of domestic violence on the board. Then we start to talk about the difference between causes and anecdotes. It takes students several sessions to learn to select main points correctly on their own. During these sessions they also begin to gain a better grasp of the connections between their own lives and the forces of society.

I am reminded as I consider my students that teaching and learning are part of a single process. To present something in class is not to teach it. Learning happens when students make cognitive transformations, expanding and reorganizing the knowledge in their cerebral filing systems. Only then can they assimilate and act upon ideas.

By the end of Phase One, the women have made several such transformations. They have an idea of their individual differences and a sense of the common ground they share. Although they still rely on personal experience as a source of knowledge, they are beginning to recognize how the outside society affects their lives. This awareness has improved their writing. They use more detail. They separate ideas and events into paragraphs. They sustain a third-person perspective with greater skill. They clarify generations with examples.

A "Typical" Bahamian Marriage
By Rosetta Finlay

"For richer, for poorer, for better, for worse, in sickness and in health, until death do us part." God has commanded his children to join in the holy matrimony and obey these rules. Unfortunately, the majority of the Bahamian marriages tend to focus more on the negative, than the positive aspects of marriage. A Typical Bahamian Marriage will begin with both, the male and female being in love with each other, so much in love that the husband will help with the house chores, such as washing the dishes, doing the laundry, taking out the garbage and making breakfast. It will even get to the point where the husband will stay up at night with their first child. Every Sunday the family will go to church and have dinner together. Later in the evening the husband and wife will go to the movies or a special function.

Weekdays, both the husband and wife will go out to work, usually they both work. After work the wife rushes home to prepare the dinner. The bills are paid by both the husband and wife's salary put together and if possible, a little is saved. For some period of time, the wife will satisfy her husband's need such as, sharing sex, understanding and the house chores. Then all of a sudden, for an unknown reason the husband changes.

He will start staying out X amount of hours and stop putting his share of monies towards bills. Comes home and take out his frustration on his wife and children by snapping at children and beating his wife. He does not even want to spend any time at home to help with the house chores or baby sit. He only comes home to change, if he is questioned about money it will end in a fight. Then he will leave home for another day or two.

The wife, is now in a situation where she does not have enough money to pay the bills and support the children, no husband to lean on and protect the family. She does not have any where to go, because he keeps telling her that she cannot go with out him. Getting a divorce in the Bahamas is completely out of the question. So she will have to, "grin and bear it" until death.

By midsemester most women have entered Phase Two. We pause to take stock of our work. Looking back over their gains, women are sparked with pride. They begin seizing more control in class and start to generate their own theories on the writing mechanics. One night we tackle the problem of pronoun agreement. While aware they often switch back and forth in writing from *they* to *you*, *she/he*, and *I*, students have little success self-editing for pronouns because we don't know the cause of this problem. Then one woman comments she has no trouble writing general points in the third person. However, she says when she illustrates these points or gives advice, she starts mentally addressing a particular person and slips into a second-person referent. Examining several essays, classmates confirm her observation; as a result, they begin to catch and correct these errors.

Women also start to discover punctuation rules. Although I have not stressed punctuation as such, they observe patterns in the reading, and they hypothesize the rules themselves. While working on the use of logical connectors like *however* and *similarly*, a student asks if the first sentence always ends in a semicolon followed by the connector, a comma, and another sentence. After consulting with each other and essays, other students incorporate this rule in their writing.

During this phase students also break away from their total dependence on personal experience. They become more confident about gaining knowledge from class dialogues and reading. One night we debate whether or not women "ask for" rape. Remembering how reading about wife beating changed our stereotypes, one student asks for additional materials on rape. Others second her request. Spurred on by their own curiosity, they assail excerpts from Susan Brownmiller's *Against Our Will* and discuss how her theories and statistics destroy or reinforce their personal myths and beliefs.

Encouraged by their confidence and advancing skills, I begin to introduce the idea of rhetorical forms: cause and effect, definition, comparison and contrast. Rather than concentrating on these forms explicitly, we employ them as a means of pondering, exploring, and writing about various facets of marriage. When looking at the social forces that perpetuate wife beating, we cover cause and effect. To illustrate the relationships between wife beating and rape, we use comparison and contrast. The outline students construct for this topic clarifies the social similarities and differences between these two forms of violence.

Comparison and Contrast on Rape and Wife Beating

Comparison
   brutality to women
   —by men
   —at night
   —police take male side
   —society reluctant to believe women
   —female shame

Contrast
   —husbands vs. stranger
   —predictability
   —sentence more severe for rape
   —provocation

In their essays comparing and contrasting rape and wife beating, the women bring together cognitive skills and social realizations. They now write from a unified perspective with more coherence, fewer sentence fragments, and more complex sentence structure. They combine information gained from discussions and reading with their personal knowledge to create a solid argument by crisp, focused examples.

Comparison and Contrast of Rape and Wife Beating
By Rosetta Finlay

In 1973 over half a million rapes were estimated by F.B.I. along with 14,000 wife abuse complaints in New York alone reached the family courts during a comparable period that same year.

Rape and wife beating are common crimes done by men in our society.

Unfortunately, the women of our society have to turn to the law who are men for help. Very seldom a female will win a rape case to get protection from the law on a wife abuse complaint. Calling the police will not help, not when they ask you questions like, "Are there any witnesses to this assault?" "Look lady he pays the bills, doesn't he?" Only to conclude with "What he does in his house is his business," and "Why don't you two kiss and make up?" They really don't act any different when called upon a rape assault not when they say things like, "Well things certainly seem to be in order here now." "What was the problem?" "What were you wearing, were your pants tight?" On the other hand the female in wife abuse must think about her dependency upon her husband, when she thinks about taking her complaint to family court, e.g.:—who will pay the bills? In most cases the female doesn't work and what will she do without him, where will she turn after not working for years? This is where the female is trapped and cannot win.

Despite the trapping situation the women of our society have decided to fight against that to bring more rights and evidence for the female, for instance Judge Oneglia who as a lawyer specializes in marital problems, recommends that the female should get out of the house, go to a friend or neighbor, and cause as much disturbance as possible. The more witnesses the better. As in a rape case the victim must produce pictures or evidence of (bruises or semen) to corroborate the rape victim's testimony, another prohibits the introduction in court of evidence concerning a rape victim's previous sexual conduct.

The women in society have formed groups and organizations to fight and protect themselves from wife abuse and rape, for instance they have decided to get together with other women in their neighborhood or apartment building and establish a whistle signal. In cases where the female lives alone she should list only her first initial in the telephone directory and also keep all outside doors and windows dead bolt locked mostly used in a rape case. In a wife abuse case the women of our society have recommended to call a special meeting to discuss the problem inviting representatives from the police, clergy and social service agencies to participate. Hopefully, this would contribute to cut down on rape and wife abuse.

In Phase Three, students begin to use writing as a means of intervening in their own social environment. A few weeks before the end of the semester, the women decide to share the knowledge they have gained about marriage with the world outside the classroom by publishing an open "Letter to Bahamian Men" in the island newspapers. Writing this manifesto takes four weeks. In addition to class time, we meet together on Sundays and put in hours of extra work. We start by writing individual letters. We discuss these letters in class, then outline a collective letter.

    A. Introduction
       1. Role of women in Bahamian society
       2. Oppression of women in marriage
    B. Women victims of men's inconsiderate actions
    C. Men's financial neglect of the family
    D. Men's lack of help at home
    E. Men's lack of responsibility for their children
    F. Men's failure to satisfy women sexually
    G. Conclusion: recommendations for Bahamian men

After considering the concerns each woman mentioned in her first letter, I assigned each one a particular topic to develop. I organize the topics into a text, leaving gaps where I think there is a need for further work. From this point on my role is limited to copying, cutting, and pasting. Equipped with her own copy, each woman begins to edit her epistle. They go line by line, spending over an hour on each page. Students all semester defend their contributions vehemently. They argue over punctuation, style, and semantics. They debate whether to separate the list of men's inconsiderate actions with colons, semicolons, or full stops. One woman thinks a reference to *gambling* is too colloquial. Another questions the use of *spend* vs. *squander*.

They consider their audience's viewpoint, calculating the effect of their words. They discuss whether to blame the issue of sweethearts on the men or the sweethearts themselves. One student observes that since the letter confronts the wrongs men perpetuate on women, it would be a tactical error to criticize other women. They finally compromise by using the term *extra-marital affairs*. Wanting to state their case clearly yet not run the risk of censorship, they rewrite the paragraph on sex several times. The final letter appears in both Nassau daily papers.

Bahamian Women Deserve a Change

Dear Bahamian Men:
    The social, spiritual and economic growth of Bahamian society, depends on men as well as women. For a very long time there has been a downward trend in male support of their wives and

children. In the typical Bahamian marriage both the male and the female begin by thinking that they are in love, so much in love that the husband will help with the household chores. The husband will even stay up all night with their first child. Every Sunday the family will go to church and have dinner together. Later in the evening the husband and wife might go to a movie or a special function. Week days both the husband and wife will go to work. After work the wife rushes home to prepare dinner. The bills are paid by putting together both the husband and wife's salaries and if possible, a little is saved. For some time all will go very well in the home. Then all of a sudden, for some unknown reason, the husband begins to change.

We are a group of women who have all been victims of men's inconsiderate actions. We would like to focus on the punishment, deprivation, discourtesy, mental anguish and death of the soul for which Bahamian men are responsible: Punishment because some women are beaten by their husbands: Deprivation because husbands give wives less and less to survive on each month: Discourtesy because extra-marital affairs disturb the home. Mental anguish is humiliation of the mind, for whose mind can be at ease in such a situation! Death of the soul deteriorates the whole body, for women are made to feel they serve no purpose.

These problems arise when the men begin to neglect their homes. The main problems between men and women in the Bahamas are: child raising, housekeeping, finances, and sex. Men are the root of most of these problems.

In most cases the male salary is more than the females. Despite this fact, the majority of Bahamian men neglect the financial upkeep of their families in some way or the other. Because of this, the greater part of the financial burden which includes savings, school fees, groceries, utilities, and even mortgages have been left to women. The male finds other things to do with his salary. Some men wait for the women to remind them about their bills. Others expect the women to pay all the bills. How can the female be expected to do all of this with a salary that is less than the males?

For centuries women have been solely responsible for housework. So men still think that a woman's place is in the home. Men expect women to work all day, come home and cook, wash dishes, clean house, wash clothes, prepare dinner and get the children ready for bed while they sit around and watch. It used to be that women did not work and were solely dependent on their husbands for support. Since women are now working and helping their husbands with most of the financial upkeep, there is no reason why the men can't be a part when it comes to housework. It is both the male's and the female's place to share the responsibilities of the home.

It takes two to produce a child and so it should be two to see to the upbringing of the child. Fathers do not spend sufficient time in the home. The most important stages in a child's life, the most cherished and once in a life moments are when the child says his first word, makes his first step, and claps his hands for the first time. Fathers being around the home when moments like the above mentioned take place are important in children's lives. Here in the Bahamas fathers have failed to be real fathers, and children have been left totally dependent on their mothers. Having children and not supporting them is not a good way to prove one's manhood. A child should have both parents' care and attention. But before men see that their children are well taken care of they prefer to spend money on their own pleasure. Why be responsible for another life coming into the world if men don't care if the children are properly fed, have proper clothing to wear, and get a proper education?

Men tend not to realize the necessity in satisfying their partners when making love. Unfortunately, they are mainly concerned with the fulfillment of their desires. They come home at the most tiresome hours of the night, hop in bed and expect us to respond without any love or affection. Most Bahamian men don't take the time to caress women's bodies before having sex. Therefore, the instant they get into bed—if they're in the mood—women are expected to perform. However, when women are in the mood, they don't respond. This leaves women dissatisfied and angry.

Our recommendations to Bahamian men in relation to the above are as follows:

a) That men join in family worship at least twice a month.
b) That men stop putting most of the financial burden on women. 75% of the household responsibilities should be handled by men.
c) That men at least buy their children's groceries, pay school fees and buy clothes.
d) That men take their children out for recreation at least once a week.
e) That men do an equal share of the housework.
f) That men do not allow extra-marital affairs to damage or destroy their marriages.
g) That men make more effort to sexually satisfy their wives. Talk about the things that please them. Caress their women

until they're ready for sex. Try not to climax until the women are ready.

Men, there is definitely room for improvement in love, affection and communication. Try it.

Sincerely,
English 016-06

Comparing this "Open Letter to Bahamian Men" with women's earlier essays on "Rape and Battered Wives," "The Worst Things in a Marriage," and life in the Bahamas demonstrates how, through the investigation of a generative theme, students can advance their reading and writing skills, recognize links between their own lives and the larger society, and develop ways of using their newfound writing skills to intervene in their own environment.

At the end of the semester all these women passed the College-administered English exam. Most received "B" grades on the essay component. Further, they decided to continue meeting throughout the next spring in order to read about women in other countries, broaden their understandings, and write a resource book for Bahamian women.

The success of this pedagogical experiment demonstrates that advanced literacy teachers can modify Freire's pedagogy to fit the needs of their students and the demands of the college. Through this approach, students will achieve literacy in the truest, most profound sense. They will understand "their reality in such a way that they increase their power to transform it" (de Oliveira & de Oliveira, 1976).

Notes

1. The curriculum described in this article was developed by Nan Elsasser, Kyle Fiore, Patricia Irvine, and Larry Smith.
2. See especially Lev Vygotsky (1962). We would like to thank Vera John-Steiner for sharing with us her knowledge of and commitment to the theories of Vygotsky.

References

Boston Women's Health Collective. (1976). *Our bodies ourselves* (2nd ed.). New York: Simon and Schuster.
Freire, P. (1970). *Pedagogy of the oppressed.* New York: Seabury.
Freire, P. (1978). *Pedagogy in process.* New York: Seabury.
Tavris, C., & Offir, C. (1977). *The longest war: Sex differences in perspective.* New York: Harcourt Brace Jovanovich.
Markandaya, K. (1971). *Nectar in a sieve.* New York: New American Library.
de Oliveira, D., & de Oliveira, R. (1976). *Guinea-Bissau: Reinventing education.* Geneva: Institute of Cultural Action.
Vygotsky, L. (1962). *Thought and language* (E. Haufmann & G. Vaker, Trans.). Cambridge, MA: MIT Press.

6.

Monday Morning Fever: Critical Literacy and the Generative Theme of "Work"

IRA SHOR

From coast to coast, Monday morning fever grips the start of each school week. The old forms of discipline collapse under the weight of new alienation. Teachers and students face each other as confused combatants. What can be done? Where do we begin when the clocks sound for Monday's early class?

Ironically, we have no choice but to begin from the best possible place—where we are. Education for critical thought begins with the concrete situation of each class. It can work only by being grounded in the limits and possibilities of each course, each academic department, each school, and each locale. New theory and new practice will both emerge from sharing reflections on teaching experiments, in an educational project which is definable only as people act and reflect on it in-process.

Because Freire is a rich resource of pedagogical frameworks, it can be helpful to look concretely at the teaching practice of his literacy teams.[1] Prior to scheduling classes, Freirean educators study the life and language of their prospective students. These sociological inquiries permit them to discover a small number of key words from daily life—called "generative words"—that will be used for both problematizing experience and for literacy teaching. The generative words, like "brick," "rice," "slum" or "wealth," suggest social themes around which consciousness can be raised. They are also selected for their trisyllabic structure (tijolo, ti-jo-lo, "brick" in Portuguese), so that each word can be broken up into phonetic pieces and then recombined to make new words. Each generative word is "codified," that is, presented in a visual form, prior to being written out. Visual codification in the form of a slide permits a class dialogue to begin around the thematic content of the word, without preliteracy interfering with the learners' ability to reflect critically. Following a discussion of the cultural situation suggested by the picture, the word itself is presented in written form. In this way, literacy flows from social critique, through images, conversation and writing rooted in the concrete lives of the students.

Before any codification or generative word is introduced, the Freirean teams train themselves in the technique of dialogue, in addition to their study of local conditions. Further, the pictures and words through which writing and reading will be taught are not offered in the first class sessions. The initial meetings are wholly devoted to a group of pictures concerning the distinction between nature and culture. The intent is to raise consciousness about the human power to make culture, as demonstrated in the everyday lives of those people in class. Critical consciousness begins with an encounter between students and their human capacity to transform the world. This dialogue on humans as hunters, farmers, builders, tool-makers, etc., proceeds through a series of ten pictures, the last of which represents the literacy class itself, as the latest act of the students in transforming themselves and their reality, through the activity of learning to read and write. Such an exploration begins the reperception of self and society, in an empowering format. The discovery of self as a culture-maker and of culture as the making of human activity propels the class forward into sessions devoted to literacy. Freirean teams found that using the dialogic method, they need only seventeen generative words and some thirty hours of classes, to provoke basic literacy. The first trisyllabic generative words progressively give way to more complicated ones, in sound and structure, as the students gain facility with the written code of their speech.

This pedagogical style, emerging for preliterate peasants in the Third World, has lessons for educators who work in the metropoles of the West, teaching for an urbanized, post-literate, and industrial constituency. Domination by mass culture, in an advanced society like the United States, has left the population either marginally literate or uncritically literate, and politically undeveloped. The questions of dialogic pedagogy, cultural democracy, critical awareness and structural perception are urgently relevant in this technically advanced culture. The specifics of this pedagogy cannot be mechanically lifted from Brazil or Guinea-Bissau to North America, but need to be evolved right here.

Problematizing Daily Life: Literacy and the Theme of Work

Work! You can't live with it and you can't live without it. My students have a hard time finding jobs, and a hard time keeping the bad jobs they find. They resent their low wages and menial tasks, but how can you live without an income? So, they fade into and out of a wide variety of jobs below their capabilities, as clerks, helpers, "gofers," messengers, typists, loaders, burger pushers, cashiers, pump-jockeys and salespersons. Their experience of work is not happy, but work itself can be a dynamic theme for class study.

In a number of classes, I experimented with the theme of work as the subject matter for language teaching. The project related to a variety of operational goals: self- and peer education, collective work styles, the turn to daily life for material, and the emergence of students as subjects of a structured learning exercise. By examining work as a means to develop literacy and consciousness, I wanted to do more than merge popular experience with awareness. As a literacy project, the study of work was built on the language skills students brought to class. The resources I drew upon were not only experiential. Work autobiography served as the program content of the study, while the students' existing speaking, listening, reading and writing capacities were the linguistic base for deepening literacy.

The approach that emerged was textured, integral and successively more demanding. It combined the activities of composing, editing, verbalizing, conceptualizing and reading. From the verbal and biographical backgrounds of the students, we moved eventually to considerations of work-oriented changes in society as a whole. In the end, I understood this methodology as an alternative to the "back-to-basics" phenomenon, which exalts the value of traditional study in grammar. The liberatory approach—experiential, sequential and integral—does not impose grammar on culture, but rather shapes literacy from resources in student reality.

Preparing for the Study: Easing Alienation, Exercising Resources

It's a tricky business to organize an untraditional class in a traditional school. Freire and his associates took more time to prepare for the start of their class sessions, by studying the student population. The classes they offered to preliterate peasants were carried out in a noninstitutional setting. Once inside a school, many alienating factors come into play, distancing the students from the act of learning. To ease this situation of student hostility on the first day, I say my name and the title of the course, and little else. Instead of delivering a lecture on the course material, I ask each student to come to the board, write his or her name, and spend a few minutes telling all of us who they are, why they are in the class, what jobs they have now or have had, where they live, etc. This introductory sign-in withers my presence while magnifying the voice of the students. They do far more talking than me, from the beginning. In addition, as they introduce themselves to each other, they begin making bonds—some live in the same neighborhood, or are enrolled in the same programs, or have worked in the same places, or need rides to school, or announce their need for a job, which someone else may help out with. I introduce myself last and talk to the kinds of material the students have raised in their own self-presentations. On occasion, I've asked the class to write for me the kind of opening speech they *expect* me to deliver or that they would *like* me to deliver. We read these short compositions aloud, and compare people's expectations from the course.

I do share with the class the style of pedagogy I will offer and explain my commitment to it. One of the first exercises I ask people to do helps concretize the self-educative, nonpunitive approach to literacy: free writing.[2] This technique has become more familiar as a nontraditional writing exercise. The goal is to develop composing skills, by having students write for a timed period, without stopping to correct. This spontaneous writing is an athletic exercise to develop compositional fluidity. In daily life, there are few occasions to write. Depressant English classes have convinced many students that they can't write, read, speak or think correctly. The simple act of composing nonstop is a way to reverse the retarding effects of prior experience. As an impromptu exercise, the free writing is not read, corrected or graded, by the teacher. The nonpunitive milieu surrounding it permits students to exercise their human talent to compose, without feeling threatened by authority. Week by week, the amount of writing students complete in the timed period invariably increases. Their growing facility with words is ego-restorative. It is validating to notice your increasing command of a language activity.

With the sign-ins and free-writing setting a nonauthoritarian tone to the sessions, and with the student voices and composing skills being the predominant action so far, a base has been established for introducing more demanding literacy exercises.

Biography and Prewriting: Resources in Memory

Most students possess more language skills than they will display in school. The turn towards student reality and student voices can release their hidden talents. Autobiography, memory and the power to make mental images are concrete, initial resources for deepening literacy. Two provocative themes on which students write willingly are "the worst teacher I ever had" and "the most dangerous moment in my life." I ask students to write a good sized paragraph on each of these subjects.

For this phase of the writing, I present a "prewriting" method, a tool students can use to help them generate well-written material. Prewriting involves organizing the material prior to putting it into paragraph and theme form. A simple means for this includes three steps: think—itemize—write. First, close your eyes and get a good mental picture of what you're going to write about. Then, begin listing all the things you're seeing. Last, from your written list, write your composition, checking back later to see that you've put into your sentences all the items you listed from your thoughts.

Prewriting offers students a way to systematize their thoughts for writing. The successive activities of mental imaging, itemizing, and then composing, generate written matter in sequentially more demanding phases. The simplest level of making mental pictures moves on to harder levels of transferring images into words and phrases listed on a page. Then, those pieces need to be transformed into coherent sentences and paragraphs. This method makes students aware of resources they already possess. Their visual imaginations can serve as propellants into more difficult acts of composing. The sequential approach avoids the confrontation with the blank page, in front of which students can sit in paralyzed anguish, until they just decide to write chaotically off the top of their heads. Between paralysis and disorder lies the student's own power to systematize what he or she knows. Prewriting helps begin this, while the themes of "worst teacher" and "dangerous moment" offer students appealing topics from their own lives. They have been waiting for a chance to share public blasts at their teachers, and are curious to hear each others' perils.

There is another fundamental means to use student language resources as a support for the best writing students can do. This second method can be called the "dictation sequence." The key feature here is connecting spoken language to written language. Dictation involves not only mental imagery, but also speaking, listening and composing, in a phased technique. The dictation sequence begins by asking students to break into groups of two. One member of the team will be dictating his or her verbal thoughts on the theme for composition, while the second member of the unit will record, on paper, verbatim, what the person speaks. Then, the two change places, the recorder becoming the speaker and the speaker becoming the composer. The students are asked to gain a sharp mental picture of the things they want to speak before they begin talking to their partners, and each recorder is urged to ask the other to speak as slowly as necessary to get every word down. This is a style of writing that encourages peer relations. The students have to cooperate to get the work done;

the teacher does not monitor them. They need to listen carefully to each other, something they are conditioned against through the teacher-centered schooling in their pasts. The same progressive difficulty of the prewriting method is also present in this dictation mode. From simple mental imaging we progress to speaking out loud what we see in our minds to recording on paper the words we hear spoken. In their native idiom, students have strong speaking skills, so it is a great resource to have composition evolve from their verbal talent. Further, it is important to make clear that the written language of our culture is nothing more than encoded speech. Students should make a connection between their speaking language and the act of writing language on paper. That literate activity is now dissociated from them, because they have been required in authoritarian classrooms to encode a language which they do not speak—Standard English. By transcribing the language of a peer, they validate their own native speech, which once it is put on paper with respectful care, turns out to be a far richer resource than they had imagined.

The prewriting and dictation methods are writing techniques that develop self-confidence and awareness. They are also literacy modes that students can "take away" with them from class. They can use these simple exercises on their own, without need of teachers or grammar books. The more they practice it, the better they become, without teacher supervision. Even the style of it in class, as an activity, where you are thrown onto your own memory, images, or ability to listen to a peer, encourages the withering away of the teacher and the subjective emergence of the students. Neither a teacher nor a textbook are the centers of this self- and peer education. These modes naturally support the workshop format for class discussion, in which people write and then read their own work for each other as an audience of peers. This serves to decentralize the responsibility for reaction, criticism, discipline, and correctness from the teacher to the peer group.

These simple exercises in literacy, here developed around the specific experiential themes of bad teachers and dangerous moments, have led to a good deal of discussion in class. The writings on teachers have been especially fertile for deeper scrutiny. It helps for students to get their antischool feelings out in the open, instead of only acting them out in alienated behavior. An open confrontation with teacher-repulsion in students is a way to work through an interference to critical thought. The students have taken the opportunity to pour out a litany of oppressive memories, vis-à-vis their schooling. It has been a relief for me as the teacher and for them as students to be in a school space where this reality need not be hidden. From the sharing of experiences and impressions, we have occasionally moved on to a conceptual exercise based in the same thematic material. I asked several classes to write a short piece which draws on all we've heard so far, and answers the general question: What is a bad teacher? This involves the simple philosophical operation of abstracting a general case from specific details; it's a foundation for structural perception, and a logical base for categorical understanding. The model of the bad teacher that they develop serves me as a caution in designing my demeanor. During this exercise, I act as recorder, standing at the board, listing the qualities that they abstract from their experiences as the paradigm for bad teacher: too much or too little discipline, doesn't allow students to ask questions, doesn't answer questions, talks so fast people can't follow, talks so slow people fall asleep, gives too much homework, always yelling at students, makes fun of students. At this point, some classes have gone on to practice "negation," that is, designing the opposite of the bad teacher, to arrive at a model of a good teacher. Other classes have returned to their personal histories to record the best teachers they have had, and then develop the general category from experience. In either case, they gain a more conceptual command of a rather ordinary feature of their lives. Still, they do not think in a transcendent fashion, even as they practice critical scrutiny; they do not yet articulate the model good teacher as one who practices liberatory values. This kind of thinking is far down the road. With some critical analysis underway through writing and dialogue on experience, the time has been ripe for introducing a second problem-theme, "work," and another self-educating technique, "voicing."

"Once I Built a Railroad": The Self-Correcting Voice

The class writings so far have unearthed and systemized rather interesting material. In preparing autobiographical compositions, the students have not only exercised literacy and conceptual skills, but they have also been working together, and have begun a study process that is validating their lives. Their personal experiences are acknowledged as things worthy of serious attention in class. This is a beginning in restoring self-esteem after the years of depressant schooling they have had. Our next step in this project was my request that students write a composition answering this question: What is the worst job you ever had? For those few who had not yet been employed, I asked for an account of what they considered the worst job around, one they would hate to wind up doing.

I asked that people use the three-step, think-itemize-write prewriting method I had introduced earlier. When their brief chronicles are ready, I take the opportunity to discuss an exercise in self-correction that we employ for the balance of the sessions: voicing. Voicing

MONDAY MORNING FEVER 111

is a self-editing tool that calls on students to use the natural grammar in their speaking voices. The method is simple: after composing, you read out loud what you've written. The grammar in your speech will automatically correct errors made by your writing hand. All you have to do is carefully listen to your own voice as you read, wherever you stumble or hesitate, your strong speaking skills are being interfered with by your less-developed writing skills. This developmental distinction between speech and encoding offers students a self-educating method that uses one of their strengths to remediate one of their weaknesses, without the learning activity passing through a teacher or grammar book. This is possible, epistemologically, because speaking is mastered earlier in life and through a different means than the mastery of reading and writing. The ability to speak a language is a skill normally and automatically acquired as long as a child hears language in the early years of its life. As an older and more exercised language facility, speaking is deeply rooted in children before they begin the formal study of reading and writing in school. In addition, there is a political interference complicating the transition from speaking a language to encoding and decoding it on paper. The child who naturally learns to speak through her or his family environment is taught to read by an institution of the state or church, in a regimented setting, and in a form of language that is dissonant to the conversational rigor of everyday life. These alienating factors widen the gap between the formal study of language and the informal learning of speech. The result is a dissociation of students from their own speech, as a rich communicative resource and as a self-educative tool vis-à-vis strengthening their powers of composition. The practice of self-editing through voicing helps correct this problem.

My students do not know that they already have grammar in their voices. Good grammar has become mystified as something only English teachers and textbooks have. Students feel condemned merely by opening their mouths. It is ego-restoring to value something as crucial as your own speech.

Vocalized self-correction is a simple way to begin literacy study from student resources. It is a form of self-study on several levels: you use it to study your own experience while studying your own speech and writing. Such textured language activity integrates skills development with consciousness-raising. One problem in this method is that student speech has been limited in its styles, dialects and lexicons by mass culture. It is not their autonomous creation, but is rather a socially conditioned product. Still, their speech, as well as their reading and writing, is more developed than they show in traditional school settings. Speaking is also an athletic skill they take for granted. To focus conscious attention on their mastery of talking, I have asked them to analyze speech into components. Speaking involves drawing on images and vocabulary in the mind, moves to the taking in of air and the modulated release of a stream of air through nasal, mouth and throat cavities, across a supple and mobile tongue, to moving lips, which together are expertly trained to form the sounds desired. This sequential action includes knowledge of cadence and rhythm, which is the grammatical way the voice achieves emphasis, phrasing of words and punctuation. By systematically recognizing the virtuosity of their speech, students continue a literacy-provoking self-study. The knowledge gained in this way is empowering. They contain within themselves the resources to gain the literacy that has eluded them.

With an understanding of their own mastery of speech, it becomes easier for students to accept how their voices can be a self-help device. The legitimation of voicing is achieved by the practice of it, rather than through the teacher's delivery of a lecture. One problem that the teacher can point out is that the rigorous voice will *insist* on reading correctly. As students search for their own errors, their demanding tongues will so swiftly read the correct thing that the eye will not be allowed to see the actual errors on the page. The speaking voice is a stronger language instrument than the reading eye, so for voicing to become the best help it can be, the eye has to be strengthened.

At first, students will not even know that they are automatically correcting errors as they speak. While voicing our writings aloud in class, in chorus, each person attending to her or his own words, the individual will unknowlingly speak correctly what has been written incorrectly. To remedy this, we do voicing in pairs. One student reads her or his composition out loud while the other follows silently along, reading with the eyes. Whenever the speaker passes over something that the reader notices, the silent partner points it out to the other. Eventually, as this exercise is practiced, each person's eyes become more alert to the instant corrections of the voice, so that paired voicing is less necessary. Through this kind of language class, students pay more attention to their own writings and to each other's writings than ever before. It's unfamiliar for them to be looking so closely together at what each of them has done. Usually, only the teacher does that, and shares bad news with you, one by one. Like the dictation sequence, voicing withers the teacher and enhances peer relations. With these basic literacy methods, we can move into a discussion of the subject matters, "work," which unified the class at the level of their common experiences.

The Worst Jobs: Composite Theme Development

After asking people in class to compose a piece on the worst jobs they ever had or on the worst job they can imagine, we devote a number of sessions to prewriting, voicing and self-correcting. With the theme developed through these techniques, I ask two students to volunteer to read their compositions to the rest of us. As they read, the saga of bad work experiences stirs a lot of interest. Students spontaneously dialogue on jobs they have held in common. Just about everyone has something to offer to the conversation. To gain a deeper scrutiny of the theme, I ask the class to write two lists. What did the two worst jobs we just heard have in common, and what was different about them? We hear the two reports again before doing this simple structural exercise. At the board, I serve as recorder, making two lists, one titled "in common" and the other "not in common." As a basic conceptual habit of mind, the task of abstracting features of an experience around an organizing principle initiates the class into critical reflection on an ordinary subject. No one in class has trouble distinguishing some similarities from some differences. As each student reads her or his lists, I compile a composite of the responses at the board, as a public record of our deliberation so far.

The two lists need examination. Are they valid? Are there any items in the lists that contradict other items? Any claims made to add or remove an item has to appeal back to the original reports read to us. We sometimes ask the two student volunteers to read their work again, so that we can decide the validity of the lists. The principles underlying the lists are what provoke the development of critical thinking. I ask for careful attention to the items. If one of the personal stories of worst jobs referred to routine kitchen work for low pay in a burger house while a second related digging ditches in summer for minimum wages, then the experiential material allows us to draw general conclusions around salary and the kind of work, but has not offered us enough information to contrast work hours and routineness or interaction with co-workers on the job. If we find details missing that we must know, we are able to ask one of the volunteers to give us more reportage. Critical education in this mode has its sources of data close at hand. An exercise like this one helps clarify what it means to make a reasoned judgment on a body of material. We structure a mass of details into categories of meaning. The mind practices reperceiving reality into meaningful shapes.

Most of my students have never looked this closely at their jobs, their writings, each other, or the teacher. The careful attention to detail is what their English teachers have lectured to them under the rubrics of "paragraph development" and "theme organization."

Studied as a rhetorical lesson instead of as a lesson in critically reperceiving reality, "paragraph development" has of course not developed
inside my students. By preparing composite lists, we construct a systematic breakdown of a discrete corner of life. By asking the original
volunteers for further details, we gain a wealth of information that
leads into a still more advanced phase of conceptual analysis: structural decomposition of "work." I ask the following question after we
have continued unearthing more and more information: What are all
the aspects of a job? This takes us again to the activity of abstracting
a general case from specific examples. The class writes new lists of the
components of "work": wages, hours, benefits, location, duration of
employment, boss, co-workers, kind of work, special training, etc. The
higher level of abstraction sets a model for a structural analysis of any
subject.

Conceptual Composition: Going Deeper and Deeper

With this much practice in developing an idea, we have sometimes
gone on to write more precise analyses of the two job reports, and
sometimes, for a little refreshing change, we have had two new volunteers read their accounts to us, and then have compared their reports.
These early exercises in critical scrutiny begin to produce more thorough writing on the topic, but the development towards conceptual
habits of mind requires more exercise. To go on with our problem
theme and literacy work, I next ask four students to read their worst-
job reports, and call upon the rest of us to attempt a more conceptual
composition: What do the worst jobs have in common as Worst Jobs?
This task involves abstracting a category of knowledge. Students write
on the whole dimension of marginal labor, not on any one or two bad
jobs. This phase of the inquiry has often given me the feel of takeoff,
as I stand at the board, listening to each student read out her or his
piece on worst jobs. I make a composite list again of the qualities they
identify as characterizing dead-end labor. Their thinking here is the
most thorough so far, as they extract from their reality the general
features of alienated work: low pay, no power to make decisions, little
responsibility, routine and repetitious tasks, no creativity or independence, etc. With a well-developed conceptual model for the worst conditions of work, it's simple enough to practice developing the negation.
The students easily produce a characterization of the best jobs around.
These jobs have high pay, creative work, power and prestige, responsibility, and require special training or education. When I ask them to
list which jobs in society fulfill this model of the best work, they come

up with doctor, lawyer, architect, author, singer, athlete, executive, model, artist and pilot. With this material in such developed form, the next exercise is composing an answer to the following question: What's the difference between the best and worst jobs in society?

Up to this point, we have been gaining conceptual and writing skills through the systematic analysis of work in social life. These exercises offer a clear means to perceive what had previously been for students a rather chaotic rush of impressions. The development of critical scrutiny is valuable, but it can remain a largely empirical skill, that is, it can be an act of static knowledge, a training in describing the shape of something. Empirical observation is an important intellectual skill, but it is a foundation for transcendent thought, not the goal. Students who practice these conceptual exercises have been transforming themselves into people who can observe carefully and who can generalize but they do not yet have a commitment to transform what they have abstracted.

Some progress towards transcendent perception can be gained by diversifying the dualisms set up so far. We have been writing about bad and good teachers, worst and best jobs. I next ask the class to consider that terrain of labor known as "union jobs." A convenient place to begin this is to question the economic benefits offered through unionized employment. The list of material advantages in union jobs sets them up as one distinct notch higher than the world of worst jobs. The students compile a benefits list that includes fixed hourly rates plus periodic increments, sick pay, overtime, paid vacations and pension plans, etc. This systematic analysis of the union job is revelatory to all those who have not yet worked in an organized office, shop or plant. The knowledge of trade unionism is uneven and unclear among students, in a society where only a quarter of all jobs are unionized, and where the commercial media spread negative images of strikes and contract negotiations, announcing how wage settlements only increase the cost of living. The simple economic gains offered by unionizing stand out starkly when compared to the situations of the worst jobs we have analyzed. The moment when another section of social life— like trade unionism—takes systematic shape in the imagination is a pedagogical time rich in possibilities. The largely invisible history of labor struggles can be integrated here rather organically; the landmark dates of great strikes (1877, 1886, 1894, 1912, 1934, 1937, etc.) are of course unknown to almost every student. In addition, some imaginative writing can help clarify what class interests are involved in the flow of history. For example, students can be asked to compose a short speech from the point of view of corporate management and from the perspective of the workers, with each explaining in their own idioms why unions are good or bad. By creating persona speaking for each position, the students can clarify what each has to gain or to lose by the progress or regress of unionization. To expand the interdisciplinary character of this literacy exercise, it would be ideal to ask: Do wage increases really cause inflation? The students have a lively interest in this question, which permits the integration of formal economics into the discussion.

Through a consideration of a third shape of work—union jobs—and through interdisciplinary materials from labor history and economics, some transcendent thinking can be initiated into the critical scrutiny underway now for several weeks in class. Three central questions about labor suggest themselves as the obvious areas for a reconstructive dialogue around work—power, production, and distribution. How is work organized? What does work produce? How are the products and profits of labor distributed? These problems are systemic and grandiose. They need a concrete shape that can be phased into the experiential and conceptual studies underway in the class. One simple means to focus attention on power is to ask: If you show up late for work and make mistakes, can the boss fire you? Of course, everyone says. Fine. If the boss shows up late for work and makes mistakes, can you fire him? Of course not, everyone says. Fine. This trivial fact of life provokes serious attention on an habitual injustice rooted in mass experience. How come people who do the same kind of thing at work do not have to pay the same price? This problematic discussion often leads to a dialogue on hierarchy. I have drawn pyramidal structures at the board and under it have put a variety of titles—hospital, school, bank, etc.—denoting some locations where students have worked. For each workplace pyramid, we have named the levels of bureaucratic power. Needless to say, students have systematically discovered themselves to be at the bottom of whatever pyramid we draw. I locate my own position in the college hierarchy, but the question of the bottom remains far more interesting. The bottom is not homogenous; the work force is stratified in a variety of ways that interfere with its solidarity. What I ask next is: In how many ways is the rank and file at the bottom divided? Besides job titles and salary ranks and length of employment and location of work, etc., we also uncover features of sex, race and age as separating the bottom. Not only do power, pay and privilege decrease as we go down the pyramid, but the number of factors segmenting the work force increase. The shape of this dialogue has varied from class to class, sometimes reaching dead ends and sometimes going deeper. To focus continuing attention on the question of power and work organization, I take the opportunity at this point to introduce reading materials that propose transcendent ideas on labor. I also introduce a literacy technique that develops the students' ability to understand printed matter—prereading.

Work Redesign: Prereading and Rebuilding

By this point, the class dialogue has matured enough to support the introduction of readings coordinated with the problem theme. Because the literate act of decoding a text is as troubling for my students as writing a composition, I cannot hand out printed materials without offering techniques for close comprehension. Skill in reading has to be developed as we deal with serious texts relevant to an experiential theme. While I carefully choose reading matter on work changes in society, I present to the class a systematic sequence that exercises their decoding skill. This sequence can be called "prereading."[3]

The simple first step in prereading is to stimulate interest in the text. The sensuous rush of mass media and rock music has so overstimulated my students that they are dishabituated from the careful examination of a "slow" medium like the printed word. Prereading decelerates perception. Before any of them have to look at words, I mention the general topic covered by the reading selection and ask them to invent hypothetical questions that they think this text will answer. At first, this unfamiliar exercise receives a slow response. Having heard only the general topic of the reading, can you really imagine questions it will answer? I mention the topic again and sometimes offer a sample question. Eventually, someone comes up with one or two questions, then a third, fourth, fifth, and in a surprisingly short time, most of my classes have verbalized fifty to a hundred possible questions related to the general topic of the text, prior to having looked at the material. This type of preparation accomplishes a number of things besides using mental imaging and speaking as vehicles to prepare for reading. The speed of imagination and of speaking act as a deceleration bridge between the rush of mass culture and the deliberateness of close reading. Further, the authority of printed material is demystified. Ordinarily, through the authoritarian demeanor of mass schooling, an aura of expertise surrounds the dull texts handed out to students. In the case of prereading, the students' own thoughts and words on the reading topic are the starting points for the coordinated material. The text will be absorbed into the field of their language rather than they being ruled by it. This reversal is a concrete means to stimulate the students' subjective emergence in the learning process. Needless to say, after inventing dozens of potential questions to be answered by the text, the students become extremely curious to read it and find out how many are actually addressed. This stimulation of curiosity is a developmental test for the process as a whole. If students reject the reading material, then the critical process is not overcoming their alienation. If the prereading method of questioning provokes interest in the material, then the process has begun to restore a neglected intellectualism in the students.

The first technique for prereading—prequestioning—is a method students can take away with them. After generating numerous preparatory questions on the reading material, the class can go right ahead and read the selection, taking note of how many questions are actually answered, or more extensive prereading can be used. An expanded form I experimented with in my classes involves a takeoff on the dictation method of prewriting. Before I hand out the printed matter, and after we have recorded all the preliminary questions we can invent about the topic, I ask students to copy down verbatim a few opening passages I read from the material. I read several paragraphs slowly and the students transcribe by dictation. Then, we voice their writings individually and in pairs, for immediate self-correction. Lastly, I hand out the text and ask students to compare their written versions to the original, noting where their encoding deviates from the print. This extended preparation develops close reading habits using the skills of careful listening and transcribing. Then, the eye is exercised in comparing two encoded forms. This is a rich way to extend the conscious connection between spoken and written language. At this point, I ask students to read the whole piece and write a summary of it. We hear each other's summaries aloud, and use this not only to develop comprehension skills, but as the means to begin a critique of the content of the reading.

In deciding what kinds of materials to introduce, I look for a few things. The selections should be in a reasonably colloquial idiom. If the language is jargonish, technical, abstract or formal, then it will alienate the attention of my students. Richly critical ideas and debate can be started from accessible language, so I scour the mass media, books, etc., for articles on the problem theme of work. I like engagingly written things, but they must also suggest a problem, a critique or an idea of transition, for the class discussion to gain transcendent qualities. The range of material has been reasonably broad:

- About a failing steel plant taken over by the union, which managed to increase production 32 percent, saving the mill from bankruptcy
- About a young auto worker from Detroit, whose chronic absenteeism and alienation perplex both the union and the corporation
- About a college president who spends his sabbaticals doing menial work, discovering there the injustice of hierarchy
- About a college teacher who spent time working in a piston plant and resented the absence of democracy on the job and the way he was laid-off without warning
- About the occupational hazards of job stress and alienation, both contributing to heart disease

- About a ghetto student working his way up from poverty and the worst jobs, living out the American Dream
- About the glamorous and controversial pro basketballer Bill Walton, who mixed politics with his profession
- About job redesign at Saab plants, where the work-team approach has been experimented with as an alternative to assembly line production
- About the IGP insurance company in Washington, which has had worker control for a number of years
- About a Michigan plant that eliminated most middle-level management, allowing the rank and file to organize its own work schedule, distributing supervisory wages to the workers as fringe benefits

Each class does not get to read all the articles. There has never been enough time in the semester for that, and the shape of the class discussion has often made further reading not necessary or organic. The pieces that we do read provoke many questions for debate. We have gone on to do short compositions around such issues as: Can people manage their own work without supervisors? What would a fair policy be for wage levels? What alternative is there to hierarchy? While the study of the problem theme of work has been deepening and diversifying, the compositional skill being exercised has so far remained mostly in the realm of short papers. To develop longer writing, we have gone on to write extended profiles of each other.

Profiling: Mining Personal Experience

Two of the articles we have read are in the form of profiles—the one on the ghetto student rising upward and the one on Bill Walton. The first is written personally as autobiography, while the second is a magazine feature by a professional writer. One way to continue the problem dialogue while extending the awareness beyond the classroom is to ask students to write profiles of two working people, one around the age of twenty-five and the other over fifty. The goal would be for students to interview outside people so that they could compose comparative profiles of two generations of workers. To prepare for this ambitious exercise, the two profiles we read serve as preliminary models; yet, they do not go deep enough into the kinds of issues raised so far. For a more probing inquiry into job history, life style, and attitudes towards work and social life, we prepare our interview questions in advance. I ask each person to write down twenty questions they would want to ask their interviewees. We hear each other's lists out loud, and people are encouraged to borrow questions from the large pool they hear. Developing a model of questions is a starting point that helps develop critical scrutiny. Each student needs to draw upon our learning so far to understand the most important things to ask. The list of questions amounts to an in-process "test" of the course. It is a means to evaluate the amount of critical progress up to this point in the study. The design of questions for interviewing is a jointly conceptual and experiential task that grows naturally out of the material developed so far. Just how much structural perception exists now in each student will be dramatized by the listings. One useful means to advance the outside interviewing can be inside interviewing. Students can practice writing profiles of each other from their extended list of questions, as a pilot exercise prior to their doing it on non-members of the class.

The exercise in writing profiles generates a lot of material that will need to be sorted before a long composition can take shape. This sorting process demands conceptual scrutiny of the information each subject will offer the interviewer. An interesting variation of profiling, which can provoke attention on the categorical organization of an information mass, is to have the whole class interview one student. Each recording student will be hearing the same responses, but they will not produce the same profiles. By comparing the variant compositions, the class can have a useful discussion on the effective organization of the material. What were the best introductions and conclusions offered on this person's experience? Who emphasized which details and why? Who left out which crucial information? Which concrete details justified general interpretations made by the writer?

Overall, this problematic study of "work" offers one means to engage students in an extraordinary reperception of something very ordinary. It not only develops literacy skills and consciousness relevant to the problem theme, but it also validates students psychologically, because the exercise is based in their experience and in their language resources. By being sequential as well as experiential, it is a successively more demanding way to gain critical literacy. By using biography, speech and mental imaging, the class can develop conceptual habits of mind with surprising rapidity. Their mastery of reading and writing, the formal decoding and encoding of spoken language, appears to take longer than the development of structural thinking. Because the functions of reading and writing are harder to command than the verbal exercise of critical analysis, the written products of the class at the end of a single term will represent in most cases less conceptual reflection than the students can actually do. The excess skill in analysis will almost always be demonstrated best in the strongest language skill students possess—their speech. Thus, it is common for our class dialogue to remain more critical than our class compositions through most of the process. Both advance from where we started, but at different speeds. The best test of critical thought remains through dialogue, while the activities of reading and writing noticeably progress month by month. In the end, the work world has achieved an unfamiliar shapely presence in thought and language. Work is not made less alienating, but critical thinking is less remote.

Notes

1. For the most concrete account of Freire's work in the classroom, see Cynthia Brown's monograph *Literacy in 30 Hours: Paulo Freire's Process in Northeast Brazil* following Freire's letter in this book. In Freire's translated work, the most detailed description of his methods can be found in *Education for Critical Consciousness* (New York: Seabury, 1973).
2. For discussion of free writing and other student-centered, nontraditional approaches, see Ken Macrorie's *Uptaught* (New York: Hayden, 1970) and Peter Elbow's *Writing Without Teachers* (New York: Oxford, 1973).
3. I am indebted to Bill Bernhardt of Staten Island College for my introduction to prereading and free writing. His book *Just Writing* (New York: Teachers and Writers, 1977) is a valuable resource. See also Bernhardt and Miller, *Becoming a Writer* (New York: St. Martin's Press, 1986).

7.

More Than the Basics: Teaching Critical Reading in High School

NANCY ZIMMET

At Newton North High School where I taught English and reading, Curriculum Two students are usually from white, working-class families. They live in apartments or two-family homes in a Boston suburb where a few blocks away and up the hill are one-family homes that might be mistaken for luxury hotels. Kids from up the hill, Curriculum One kids, will go to Wellesley, Bowdoin, Penn, maybe Harvard. A few of the Curriculum Two students in my class are thinking of going to such schools as Wentworth Technical Institute, Boston State, or maybe the work-study program at Northeastern. Many are in the technical-vocational program at the high school, planning to become car mechanics, electricians, or carpenters. Curriculum One and honors students predominate in extracurricular activities. Curriculum Two students are not only "Two's" *academically*; they are "Two's" *socially* as well. My students have little faith in their own knowledge, tending to discount the importance of what they have learned from their own experience.

For them, a moment's unstructured time is an irresistible temptation for fooling around, for chatting, for trying to persuade the teacher to dismiss class. There is a lot of movement, a lot of noise until the teacher says, "That's enough. Let's get to work." They quickly obey. The fooling around does not bring them closer together, but rather isolates them from each other. They have difficulty listening to one another; extended conversations are rare. They look to the teacher for the one right answer: "You're the teacher: you should know." It never occurs to them to question the structure of the course or the kind of work assigned. There are periodic outbursts objecting to homework, but no one in class expects the teacher to pay attention. They never discuss their placement in Curriculum Two even though they are concerned about not being in the "higher" Curriculum One. They have not been told why they are Two's, but they have the feeling that Curriculum One would be too hard for them, that they are not smart enough. They don't question; they only wonder.

They fight reading—homework, classwork, tests—at each opportunity. They see it not as a way to take control of their lives, but as a task that someone else should force them to complete. The teacher is "good" if he or she makes them learn, makes them read, makes them do their homework, and then makes them talk about the reading.

Teaching these students to be truly literate, to go beyond the most elementary reading levels and evaluate what they read, to incorporate what they learn in forming new ideas, in other words, to read critically, requires more than assigning mechanical exercises in reading skills. It involves a total change of attitude toward reading. Using the ideas of Paulo Freire (1970, 1973) and Harold Herber (1978), I tried to help bring about that change.

Building self-confidence, I realized, would have to be the first step if my students were eventually to take an active, positive role in school. They would have to realize that their skills and their knowledge of life were important. I hoped that they would come to face honestly the limitations reading difficulties would place on them. Most of all, I hoped that by learning to work with and help each other, they would begin to deal with some of those difficulties.

Because my students' alienation and insecurities about school were at the heart of their learning difficulties, I decided to make schooling itself the object of study, to "problematize," in Freire's words, "the existential situation." We used a variety of activities—games, writing assignments, discussions, interviews. Restless fourteen-year-olds don't want to be stuck at one activity for very long. They especially liked one game designed by Herber. Divided into small groups, they wrote as many words as they could associate with the word EDUCATION. After three minutes, each group read its list to the entire class, other groups adding words to their own lists. Most words related to school, but some that hinted at other ways people become educated sneaked in. A few students mentioned skills their parents and grandparents possessed, skills they had learned outside a formal academic institution. We began to talk about what they thought it meant to be educated and about the knowledge their parents and they themselves already possessed. By expanding the definition of education to encompass more than what they learned in classrooms, students eventually realized they and their families were educated, perhaps differently than students in the honors track, but nevertheless educated.

We began talking about experiences in school. Students wrote and discussed papers about their first day in school, about how they saw themselves, and about how they thought other students and teachers saw them. Using cassette recorders, they talked about what they remembered most clearly about each school year. We interviewed students outside our class. We photographed students throughout the day doing everything from munching carrots in the school cafeteria to plugging away at homework in the library, finally putting together a photographic essay of daily life at the high school.

We found much in common. In spite of the "we are totally unconcerned about school" image my students had cultivated with such care, they realized that they had all looked forward to the beginning of school, that they all were excited about the new classes and eager to learn, eager to do well. But the eagerness left them vulnerable to all sorts of fears—of failure to understand what a teacher was saying, of the inability to do classwork or homework, of getting poor grades, of not being able to make friends at school, of getting physically lost in a gigantic school building, fears that each student felt no one else shared. And at the core of many of their fears were reading problems. As these school problems were discussed, chattering, giggling, jostling students became still, speaking only with much anxiety. Clearly, for any changes in attitude, for any feeling of confidence to develop, reading problems would have to be dealt with.

We began a unit of readings about others' experiences in school, an attempt, as Freire urges, to start objectifying situations in students' lives so they might be discussed. Making every effort to encourage active student participation and sharing, I led them through a series of exercises, each of which I knew they could handle successfully. These exercises were designed to take them through what Herber describes as the three levels of reading: literal, in which students simply determine what information is presented; interpretive, in which they look for relationships between statements and derived meanings; and applied, in which they question an author's premises, judge material in light of their own experience, and formulate new ideas. These exercises asked students to work with such patterns as cause/effect, comparison/contrast, time order, and simple listing in order to make them consciously aware of relationships they had already been using successfully.

Using a short story by Otto Friedrich (1974), I designed a set of exercises to teach the cause/effect pattern while focusing on some of my student's fears. The story itself is very short and posed little reading difficulty. George Grass, who the narrator tells us might now be classified as "a little slow," enters a 1940 Vermont classroom. For his first day in school he's dressed in what his mother "hoped would be the most respectable of outfits. He wore a brown tweed suit with a brown cardigan underneath, neatly buttoned. That day and for the few days following, George does "his best to avoid attention." A week later, the teacher, Mrs. Forbes, handing back history test papers, tells the class that she doesn't understand George's paper: "He seems to have answered every question by writing 'vegetables.' " As students begin to giggle, she reads the questions from the test along with his answer—"vegetables"—for each one. There is great hilarity in the classroom while George sits "helpless with a grin frozen on his pale face." "The History Lesson" is finished and George is finished with school: "George Grass didn't come back to school the next day, or ever again."

We had already talked about taking tests: what kinds of tests they had to take, what they thought of tests as a teaching method, how they felt when they weren't sure of an answer, how they responded when they knew they had written a better answer than a friend. I handed out the story and the first exercise, on Herber's literal level, at the same time.

Exercise

Everyone in the class laughed at George Grass. Decide from the list below which caused the laughter and which were the effects of the laughter. Be prepared to justify your choices in class discussion. You might not use all the sentences.

George tried to avoid attention.
George took a seat in the back row.
George wore a brown tweed suit.
Older and dumber children were expected to keep quiet.
George ate lunch alone.
Mrs. Forbes made a left-handed boy write with his right hand.
Mrs. Forbes made kids feel ashamed if they didn't spell
   correctly.
Mrs. Forbes gave a history test.
Mrs. Forbes said she didn't understand George's answers.
George wrote "vegetables" to answer every question on his
   test.
George sat wide-eyed in his corner.
The narrator realized something awful was happening.
Mrs. Forbes told George he would have to do better next time.
George never came back to school.

Students worked first on their own and then in small groups comparing answers. Only after there had been considerable debate did we reconvene as a class. By that time even the shyest student had had the opportunity to try out his or her answers in a small group. After a number of class sessions working in groups, almost every student felt confident enough to speak to the entire class.

Moving to the interpretive level, I asked students to pick from a list those statements which correctly described the relationships between the students and the teacher in the story.

Exercise

Check the statements you think are true. Write at least one sentence explaining each choice you make. Your reasons must refer to information in the story.

The students helped each other.
The students were afraid of each other.
The students were afraid of the teacher.
The students had to compete with each other for the teacher's approval.
The teacher wanted the students' approval.
The teacher helped the students to learn.
The teacher and the students decided together what was going to happen in the classroom.

After we had agreed on a few statements, we talked about causes of these relationships—"Why didn't students help each other?" for example.

The final exercise, at the applied level, asked students to begin to think critically about concepts suggested by the reading material. It asked them to justify their answers with reference not only to the story but also to their own experiences.

Exercise

Judging from your own experiences as well as the experiences of the students in the story, check statements you think are true. You must justify the statements checked with references to the story as well as with references to your own experiences. Use complete sentences.

Giving tests is a good teaching method.
Tests just make students afraid.
Feeling afraid makes you learn faster.
Feeling hurt makes you learn faster.
Poor students have more to be afraid of in school than do rich students.
Students feel relaxed most of the time in school.
The best atmosphere for a school is a relaxed one.
Students learn best when they compete with each other.
Teachers control what happens in classrooms.

> When most students are doing one thing, it is almost impossible not to go along with the group, even when you know what's happening is wrong.
>
> Most teachers and students are not sensitive to the feelings of others.
>
> Lots of times students don't understand assignments in school.

By the end of the third exercise students were able to talk more easily about their fears about school, mention of which had brought near silence before. We concentrated on those aspects of their lives that they now perceived as preventing them from doing things they really wanted to do or from becoming the kinds of people they knew themselves really to be, thoughtful and capable. They felt afraid of not understanding reading material, of not remembering what they read so that when they had to take a test, like George Grass in "The History Lesson," they became petrified. They had no idea of how to prepare for a test other than to "study." When I asked one boy what that meant, he just shrugged his shoulders. They often felt so afraid in school that there was little chance of concentrating: "You're afraid of flunking and you can't think." They often pretended they didn't care about the assignments or about the difficulties they were having in school. To avoid having to deal with their inability to complete an assignment, they often wouldn't even begin. The cool "I don't care about school" image was complete.

For the most part their attitude toward their predicament was what Freire would call "naive." That is, they thought their situation in school, academically and socially, was established and therefore impossible to change. They would never improve in reading, never take control of their lives at the school.

I tried to pose this as a set of problems. How had they handled the situation before? What alternatives were there? If they didn't understand a given reading passage, what could be done about it? If they thought the readings and the tests themselves were inappropriate, what could they do? If they no longer pretended they didn't care about school, about their courses, about being Two's, what could they do? What kinds of action could they take?

We came up with some answers, but really only a few. At the end of the unit, students were still talking about the questions and the problems that had been raised. We had at least begun to discuss those silent themes—the eagerness to learn, the fears, the isolation, and the real desire they had to deal with their problems. Situations they had viewed as unalterable were now problems that might eventually be overcome.

Students had talked about their families with pride. They realized that they already had important knowledge and skills. They had used their knowledge of life in their work at school. They no longer felt quite so inadequate to the problems there. Their attitude toward reading had changed from thinking of it as just a painful chore to believing they had found a way to learn more about themselves and their lives. New reading skills gave them a certain confidence when they approached a school assignment.

Because they had worked on exercises together and learned to value their own experience, they felt more assured as individuals and as a group. They could go to each other for help; no longer did they rely only on the teacher. We could hold conversations for twenty-five minutes, not just five. Even the shyest student had made a number of acquaintances in class and felt more comfortable participating in discussions. By questioning what was happening to them in school, by questioning themselves and how they had handled problems before, they had all become truly active in the classroom. Now my students would have to bring these new ways of behaving and thinking to their lives outside the classroom.

References

Freire, P. (1970). *Pedagogy of the oppressed.* New York: Seabury.
Freire, P. (1973). *Education for critical consciousness.* New York: Seabury.
Friedrich, O. (1974, January 23). The history lesson. *The New York Times,* p. 37.
Herber, J. (1978). *Teaching reading in the content areas.* Englewood Cliffs, NJ: Prentice-Hall.

8.

English and Creole: The Dialectics of Choice in a College Writing Program

NAN ELSASSER and PATRICIA IRVINE

> Whey me dey stretch out pon me lodgin a could sense
> something in de air. A done whey me an me landlard,
> Pantius, gon got it out tomorrow Satidy shen he come long
> dung yah fu he rent (Fraites, 1983[1]).

This excerpt is from an essay that challenged landlord abuse of poor
tenants, sociolinguistic norms that restrict Creole to oral functions,
and prejudice against the use of nonstandard language in English classes.
The author was a freshman honors English student at the College of the
Virgin Islands. When he learned that he could write forcefully in his
native language, Creole, he and other students in an experimental writing course took the first step in challenging assumptions that had rele-
gated Creole to oral use in limited contexts and had created silence in
English courses.

To date there has been limited interest in developing standardized,
pan-Caribbean Creole literacy (Craig, 1980; R. Joseph, 1984), in part
because it is associated with slavery and colonialism (Alleyne, 1976),
and in part because it is underdeveloped for many functions. That
Creole is not recognized as a language contributes to its low prestige
(Keens-Douglas, 1982). Thus, if Creole literacy is to develop, sociolinguistic norms must be challenged.

Spolsky, Engelbrecht, and Ortiz (1981) propose five factors that
together encourage the use and development of vernacular literacy:
those who introduce it must themselves use it; it must be accepted by
traditionally influential members of the community; it should be used
for existing (native) functions; it must be sustained and supported by
a powerful, locally controlled school system; and it must be a living
language. Their model derives from an extensive study of societies

where people speak clearly distinct languages (for example, Navajo/ English and Guarani/Spanish).

In the Eastern Caribbean, however, the factors that affect the development of Creole literacy are confounded because there are a number of language groups and regional dialects. For example, a speaker of Kittitian Creole would say "i gat wan neks haas self," while the same thought would be expressed as "I iivn gat anʌda haas" by a St. Thomian, and by a Barbadian as "hi gɔt ə neks hɔrs self." In English, the sentence would translate "He even had another horse" (Hancock, 1985).

In the U.S. Virgin Islands alone, six main language groups exist:

- Virgin Islands English Creole (including St. Thomian, St. Johnian, Crucian, and the British Virgin Islands versions);
- Cruzo-Rican Spanish spoken throughout St. Croix (especially in Campo Rico and Machuchal);
- Non-Virgin Islands English Creole (including Kittitian, Nevisian, Antiguan, etc.);
- Virgin Islands French Creole (spoken in St. Thomas, especially in Nordside Village and French Town);
- Non-Virgin Islands French Creole (including Dominican, St. Lucian, and, to a lesser extent, Haitian Creole);
- North American English (including White English and Black English).

In addition, there are small communities of Arabic, Hindi, Portuguese, and Spanish speakers (Cooper, 1985b).

Distinctions among these language groups are blurred by a Creole continuum (basilect to acrolect) (Cooper, 1979). A Kittitian speaking in basilectal Creole would say "mi a wan big uman," which in meso- lectal Creole might be "a iz a big woman".[2] The sentence in English is "I'm a grown woman" (Cooper, 1985a). There also exist competing varieties of English: British, American, and educated West Indian (Allsop, 1978).

Sociolinguistic Norms of the Eastern Caribbean

Creole is a vibrant oral language. Varieties of Creole are spoken by virtually all West Indians in informal contexts and by many rural and working-class West Indians in most contexts. However, it is not spoken in formal or professional contexts in the Eastern Caribbean by elites or traditionally influential members of the community; for them, Creole is a low prestige language. In matched-guise tests[3] administered to local high school students, Creole speakers were consistently rated lower than the same speakers using standard English (L. Joseph, 1984): "When a speaker read a passage in English which began 'I have a patient . . . ,' more respondents thought her a competent, intelligent doctor with much common sense who was definitely going to succeed. When the same speaker said, 'I go' dis patient . . . ,' however, a significant number of respondents felt she was a waitress, vendor, or janitor of average intelligence" (p. 26).

Typical of prevailing attitudes towards Creole and English is the following comment in a Virgin Islands educational journal: "Perceptive teachers are aware that to achieve success most West Indian children must be speakers of two 'languages': That dialect of the playground with its succinctness is suitable for relating stories and telling jokes and Standard English which is the language not only of the school but also of business and government" (Rezende, 1984).

Creole is written for a few indigenous functions such as calypso and reggae lyrics. Also, popular poets (Keens-Douglas, 1979) write in Creole, and a number of plays have been written and performed in Creole. The St. Thomas local newspaper, the *Daily News*, carries a weekly column in St. Thomian Creole of which the following is an example:

"Hey Miah—I hope you takin a good ressup after all dat outgladidniss you wus carryin on wid."

"Meh dere Stella—it look like you never goin change from you ole ways to new ways. Nobody in sayin 'outgladidness' no mo—tis havin a good time, mekin youself merry—doan care wat you tink, wen change come you gat to go along wid it—keep up wid time."

"Well, meh dere chile, wedder you rite or you rong, I ain goin downstrive wid you—I know juss how to tark to who wen I want, good anuff to mek dem understan wat I sayin" (Petersen, 1984).

It is noteworthy that although the column appears on the editorial page and usually addresses a serious issue, it is appreciated more for its humorous, folkloristic value than for its editorial content. In fact, when Petersen recently wrote about a prominent local official who had died, she wrote in standard English, reflecting the attitude that Creole may not be appropriate for serious exposition.

Attitudes toward Creole could change as a result of the growing interest in maintaining and promoting West Indian culture, which for some means writing in Creole. Keens-Douglas, a well-known Trinidadian poet, distinguishes between the West Indian writer and the West Indian who writes, "to me, a West Indian writer is a dialect writer" (1982).

Furthermore, the rise of regional nationalism and the presence of a new class of postindependence elites together provide a political climate conducive to the development of Creole literacy. Already school curricula in the independent nations have been modified to include more West Indian language, literature, and history. In the 1978 edition of the Caribbean Examinations Council syllabus for the secondary education certificate (for use during 1981–1982), West Indian literature is present to a significant extent. In Section A, one novel (of three) and one short story are by West Indian authors. The plays are by Shakespeare and Shaw. In Section B, eight books by West Indian authors appear. There are also two books by African novelists and one by an Afro-American writer. Of six volumes of poetry listed on the syllabus, four are West Indian anthologies. In the basic and general proficiency sections, capitalization follows the conventions of West Indian Standard; for example, "Government" and "Principal" are capitalized. The situations depicted are generally West Indian; for example, a child washing his little brother under a standpipe, a table on West Indian migration to the United Kingdom, and an opportunity to argue against wearing school uniforms.

In 1981 St. Lucia developed and adopted a standard orthography for educational purposes, the benefits of which were summarized in these remarks by Carrington (1981):

> The . . . opportunity for the use of creole by the development of a writing system breaks the barrier that has shut out from information transfer, from "languagehood" and from confidence, large numbers of people over several hundred years in this country; has shut them out from full communications within their society. . . . There is a severe need, a very deep need, for communication tools that allow people to share in the development of their society beyond simply being labourers within the situation directed from places of which they have no comprehension (p. 6).

Sociolinguistic Patterns at the College of the Virgin Islands

In order to determine the language background of students at the College of the Virgin Islands (CVI), we distributed a questionnaire to entering freshmen seventeen to twenty years old. The replies showed that students came from all islands in the Eastern Caribbean. Three-fourths of the students were first-generation Virgin Islanders whose parents had immigrated from other islands; seven-eighths came from Creole-speaking backgrounds, but they did not mention Creole when asked which languages they spoke.

Creole is heard in student conversations in the cafeteria, dorms, and library; it is also used in student-sponsored calypso contests and skits expounding cultural themes. Occasionally, the theater department produces a West Indian play with Creole dialogue. Faculty members, on the other hand, rarely use Creole on campus although they acknowledge speaking it informally off campus. The patterns of language used in CVI speech thus conform to the diglossia found in the rest of the Eastern Caribbean: English, not Creole, is used for educational and professional purposes.

As in the larger society, the use of written Creole at CVI is limited. Although written Creole is a subject of analysis in some linguistics courses, it is not used in papers on academic research or as a language of instruction. Students publish some original Creole poetry in the student newspaper, however:

President Freddie!
Over here awhile!
Wha' yuh tink a dat?
Tink it can pass?
Me no tink so, yuh know:
See how it stain up an' ting?
Check a nex' one:
Yuh fine it better?
It look wors' to me!
It can't even reflec
Yuh ugly face.
Put it on de side
An' lewwe check a nex' one:
Wha' yuh tink?
Is any better?
No way: is same ting!
Pull ten one time—
One mus' good.
Not one good, sah,
No, not one!
Well, lewwe keep lookin':
Nex' one: not good
One more: no way
Nex': no . . .
Bu' Freddie, al' gone, yuh know.
No more lef' to examine—
No more lef' to use!
An' ah hungry, you know!
An' not one piece a clean

Cutlery to use in dis cafeteria!
Yuh tink is bes' ah use
Me durty Rebels fingah?
(Farouk, 1984)

Professors in some literature courses also assign West Indian novels,
short stories, poetry, and plays, parts of which are written in Creole. A
linguistics faculty member and native Virgin Islander recently wrote
and produced a play in Creole, *The Bonfire War*, which commemorated
a slave rebellion (Sprauve, 1984):

A flat clearing in the woods. A group of 12 to 14 slaves, including
women and adolescents, form a circle. One half of them are sitting
or kneeling. In the middle Kenta crouches with a pointer in one
hand and a flambeau in the other.

KENTA: Everybody here?
MA TUBGA: Wey paat klaes dey?
KENTA: He go come. He know all a' dis a'ready. OK! Everybody
hearin'?
CHORUS: Yes, Pa.
MA TUBGA: You! (tugging on boy). You list'nin, baay?
BOY: Yes, Ma.
KENTA: Everybody seein'?
CHORUS: Yes, Pa.
BOY: Ma, tain if "everybody seein' and hearin'" he should say
. . . tis if everybody LOOKIN' and LIST'NIN.
MA TUBGA: Hush yo mouth, chile, wen big people talkin.
KENTA: Yo seein' de fo't here (drawing a structure on the
ground) . . .

It is noteworthy that the word *baay* (boy) above is written in
Creole in the dialogue and in English in the prompt. This illustrates
the diglossic relationship between the two languages that obtains even
in writing: Creole is used to represent oral language, while the narrative is in English.[4] So it is in most West Indian literature, where only
the dialogue is in Creole. The story from which the following is ex-
cerpted is unusual in that the entire narrative is in Creole. It is called
"Roun' de Walls of Jericho" and was written by a linguistics faculty
member (Cooper, 1982) who is a native of St. Kitts and who regularly
writes poetry and short stories in Creole:

Soapie stan' de thinking more dan Plato. Is Buckra what mek life
so hard for one suddn like me. He take all we lan' and now we
gat fo' wuk so hard. Me mother suck salt to sen' me to school,

and if it wasn't for the English language ah woulda move up to fif standard, and get a good job. But me no lucky like Buckra son, John, who head so hard that he can't even catch cold. But he wearing tie and collar, anyhow.

Consequences of Sociolinguistic Norms

The acquiescence of educators to these sociolinguistic norms has profound academic, emotional, and aesthetic consequences. Eighty percent of entering freshmen at CVI fail to meet minimum English proficiency standards and must enroll in noncredit, remedial English courses. Three to five semesters of English instruction later, 60 percent or more fail the English exit test required for graduation.

The negative attitude toward Creole is manifest in the conviction of the students that they speak "broken" English or "slang," a bastard-ized nonlanguage in St. Thomas dubbed "calypso." In the students' own words:

The people of the island speak in broken English and they use slangs that may not be familiar to you. Some of the slangs are very funny.

—Denise Coumarbatch

A person born and raised in the Virgin Islands or any of the Caribbean Islands will find themselves handicapped in English. Our native language is broken English.

—Patricia Leedee

The present diglossia has also resulted in the underdevelopment of informal registers of English. Thus, in this sample telephone conversation between family members presented to students on the Caribbean Secondary Education Certificate Examinations, it would be appropriate to write an informal variety of English. However, it is written instead in formal West Indian or British Standard, making it sound stilted:

I have a few bruises to show but I'm alright. They kept Selma overnight in hospital for observation but they sent her home this morning. She probably must have been more frightened than anything else.

Now, your Aunt Elaine should have met Selma at Kennedy Airport last night and is probably worried sick. You know how Aunt Elaine can get worried. Selma cannot get another flight to the States within a week, so she has had to change her plans (Caribbean Examinations Council, 1979, p. 5).

The rigid domain demarcation between Creole and English and between Caribbean and American cultures in the Virgin Islands produces alienation and silence in writing courses. Furthermore, because of the lack of informal registers of English and the stigma attached to Creole in educational institutions, many students produce writing that is "correct" but distant and flat, as in this example published in a student literary magazine (O'Neal, 1982):

> Shakespeare describes England as "This royal throne of kings, this scepter'd isle" and "This blessed plot, this earth, this realm, this England." On the other hand, a certain West Indian singer describes it as "a bitch" when he sings, "England is a bitch." The last statement is clearly different from those before it. Shakespeare, a loyal Englishman, expresses a positive judgement of the worth of his country. The West Indian singer, who has had bad experiences in England, expresses a negative judgement. From this example, I can see that no two people necessarily hold identical values upon a thing or person. The value that an individual places upon a thing or person sometimes depends upon the way the individual experienced it (p. 23).

Students have internalized the assumption that their "dialect" interferes with their writing. The following excerpts are from a student's essay (Liburd, 1982), which appeared in the College literary magazine:

> Many students, both high school and college, are faced with serious writing problems. Students are becoming more and more frustrated as a result of their inability to present a well-written, coherent piece of work.
>
> There are many factors which account for the problems students face. Firstly, the student's use of dialect has become a very significant part of their writing. Students just do not take time out to write standard English. Even if standard English is used, it is combined with the use of dialect. . . .
>
> Most students do not seem to recognize a significant distinction between present and past tense. This is seen most clearly in the students' use of dialect . . . (p. 40).

It is a mistake, however, to confound the ability to write well with the ability to speak or write in English. One can write English without speaking it; conversely, one can speak it and still remain a poor writer, as in these excerpts from placement exams at the College:

> *Essay Question:* Describe the unusual or impressive aspects of the food served at a special occasion.

A Buffet Party

Someone once said, 'It usually takes someone with skill and talent to prepare food for a buffet party.' 'Their's a sense of pride one gets' said another, when one prepares and cooks that special meal for that special occasion. A buffet party in short, is a party, where all the food and drinks are distributed in buffet style.

Sharon Abba Gumba

Essay Question: Describe an object you would like to own.

A Personal Object

The way clothing came into my life was at the age of seven. Every year my father would go to Puerto Rico and tell me to chose what I wanted. So I would pick the prettiest dresses or blouses that I can find. From the age of seven clothing has become a god to me. But that isn't anymore. Sometimes your most personal object can be the most dangerous object in your life.

Laureen Mason

The resistance to teaching Creole literacy derives from three assumptions: (1) students' limited writing ability is due to linguistic interference; (2) time devoted to writing in Creole detracts from students' ability to learn to write English; and (3) teaching Creole literacy violates prevailing sociolinguistic norms that designate Creole for oral functions. In addition, educators justify its exclusion by the lack of existing Creole literature, dictionaries, and a standardized orthography. But their reluctance to teach Creole literacy in turn precludes the development of a standardized orthography, dictionaries, and literature (Craig, 1980; R. Joseph, 1984).

Experience has shown us that the writing problems of West Indian students are not due to "interference" in the structural linguistic sense of the term, rather, we find their reluctance to write directly attributable to the denigration of their native language and to their conviction that they do not, in fact, possess a true language but speak a bastardized version of English. It is difficult if not impossible to write without a language, and it is emotionally draining to attempt to develop voice and fluency in an educational system that has historically denigrated one's own language.

At the college level, resistance to writing and to learning standard English can be mitigated by actively exploiting the tensions between Creole and English in the following ways: (1) providing a framework to distinguish Creole and English as separate, rule-governed linguistic systems, (2) addressing the power relations inherent in language choice and language attitudes; and (3) integrating the study of Creole, and writing in Creole, with learning academic research and writing skills.

The rest of this essay documents our efforts to integrate the study of Creole and English in a writing program at CVI. We wish to emphasize that our curriculum was not transitional nor was it based on contrastive analysis. We taught remedial and honors English courses in which there was ongoing written and oral expression in, and discussion of, both languages. This experimental program taught us that writing and speaking Creole do not necessarily interfere with learning English. On the contrary, students learned to sort, control, and use both languages. The use of written Creole by these students may be a first step towards expanding its functions.

A College Writing Curriculum

We began the classes with a presentation by a Creole linguist who explained the phonological, semantic, and syntactic systems of both English and Creole. For most if not all students, the study of "grammar" had been limited to English; thus the idea of Creole as rule-governed was a revelation. The impact of the lecture was immediate; as one remedial student wrote, "I learned I had a language." In a thank-you letter to the linguist who lectured, the same young woman who wrote the nonsensical essay on the buffet party cited earlier wrote: "The difference between standard and nonstandard Dialect confused us for years, but now we realize that we are not speaking 'broken English' but Creole."

Students' understanding of written language began to shift when they discovered that Creole was a language; up to that time, they had always attributed their lack of college-level writing skills to their "broken English" and to their negative experiences with writing. In one student's words: "As far as I can remember I've never like to write. The reason is because whenever I sit down to write I have to be going back and forth in a dictionary to make sure that I have the correct spelling"—Henry Todman.

After the lecture and discussions about Creole, however, a student wrote the following:

I grew up in a society where dialect is the dominant form of speech; this I believe is the main reason why I lack college level English skills. . . . In school I was taught standard English, but on the outside, on the playground and at home I use English dialect. Therefore, there is a gap between the English that I am taught at school and the English dialect which I use on the out-

side. However, this has not hampered my mastery in other subjects such as math, physics, chemistry and biology in which I
have excelled at the high school level, but it is that I have not
grasped the grammar and mechanics of the English language to
the degree that it is needed at the college level.

Kenneth Smith

Developing literacy in Creole did not impede progress in English. On
the contrary, wrestling with writing in a nonstandardized language
with no official orthography demystified the purpose of grammatical
conventions and grammar "rules." The immediate reaction of several
remedial students to the unit on Creole linguistics and the language's
systematic linguistic structure was a new but equally simplistic response to their writing problems; students claimed that if only they
could write in their own language, writing would be easy. So they tried.
They began by writing a letter to a Creole author who had visited the
class. It took them almost two hours to compose the following letter
in Antigua dialect because they argued about spelling, word choice,
choice of dialect, and appropriate tone:

Deyeeh Mrs. Petarsin:

Ahwe de studnt an de profesar ah de English Class Oll waar fo
sah tank uy fo de spekin pan Wensday.

Ahwe min lub fo heer yu reed de dilek an tark bout de difference ah how people min lib from lang time from how dem lib
teday.

De whoola class tek in plenty from wa yo sey. Ahwe hope yo
injay heerin ahwe plants pan tanded spekin size up to dilek spekin
in de karibyan.

We de class lub yo kalum an glad fo see who writ tum.

Tank yo fo sharin yo litle submn wit awweya clas, and we realy
realy much oblige.

From this and similar experiences, students learned that rules were
not just arbitrary conventions in an English handbook but tools that
contribute to ease of communication. In another instance, after listening to Creole linguist Vincent Cooper discuss the difficulty he found in
making linguistic and orthographic choices for his short story, "Roun'
de Walls of Jericho," an honors student, Lenore Joseph, wrote: "I
hadn't realized that the writing of dialect could take so much thought.
. . . My respect for the written form has been deepened greatly."
   The scarcity of published Creole grammars and dictionaries
forced students to search for their own written models. One student
modeled his orthography and his characters on Arona Petersen's column
in the St. Thomas *Daily News.* In composing an anecdote, he spent an

hour with a group of Creole speakers discussing stylistic alternatives, such as the choice between "de young people dem" and "dem young people," which he finally used. An honors student also reported on the difficulty of writing in her native language: "I had a very hard time writing this essay. . . . At times I forgot the story line, plot, etc. because of the effort I had to put out to write the dialect." She explained some of the problems she faced and how she resolved them:

> I chose to write in mesolect for I knew it would be easier than basilect. . . . I had to think about each word before I wrote it for the spelling was worrying me. . . . In speech instead of the "th" sound there is in fact a "d" sound. I didn't know if words like "dere" and "there" would make the essay basilect. . . . I therefore took my chances with the "th" sound.
>
> Sharylle Richardson

Exploration of Creole spurred students' interest in language in general, and their vocabulary and writing reflected their excitement. In less than six weeks, freshmen in the remedial course wrote about language with ease and sophistication:

> Dr. Cooper was talking about different dialects and why some dialects are accepted while others are stigmatized.
>
> Barbara Registe

> Dr. Vincent Cooper lectured on dialect. He advises us not to discard Creole because of myths advocating that Creole is not a language. . . . In conclusion, Cooper said the Virgin Islands vernacular, like all other language systems, has (1) a sound system; (2) rule-governed; (3) word formation rules; (4) agreement rules; (5) grammar rules; (6) semantics, and (7) can definitely be written.
>
> Cleve Maloon

> Schools have ignored that writing standard English for the people of the Virgin Islands is difficult. We are brought up in our native language, Creole. . . . Therefore the reasons we need standard English are: We are owned by the United States which emphasizes standard English, and we travel in a world that uses standard English. It is the contemporary international language like Latin was a long time ago. . . . But we need to develop fluency in standard English without ignoring or putting down our own language (Smith & Lauchau, 1983).

The remedial students were especially sensitive to the power relations which determine language choice. In single-paragraph summaries of Dr. Cooper's presentation, several chose to include the political and social dimensions of language use:

> He defined the word "dialect" as a variety of language. He also defined standard language as a dialect with an army and a navy to back it up. He said that politics plays an important role in how people use their dialect. People, he said are the problem, not the language.
>
> Deltha Woods

> "Language is the same but people make the difference," stated Dr. Vincent Cooper. To clarify this statement, it means that people who live in a big country that is prospering economically, and with political backing, feel that they are better than people of a smaller country who is not as fortunate as they are. He also went on to say that if you try to do away with Creole language you will stifle the life force and culture identity of the Caribbean people. In the story, "Roun' de Walls of Jericho" he use what is called Non-standard dialect which goes to show that you can write dialect and it is a language.
>
> Henry Todman

Honors students discussed their own attitudes toward Creole and how these were changing. They then searched for ways to modify the negative feelings that permeated their communities. A seventeen-year-old student from Nevis wrote:

> I have lived in the VI for eight and a half years and yet few people ever here me speak in the dialect, and I can speak it fluently. . . . For a long time I used to put people in categories based on their speech. . . . I no longer picture people based on their language but I feel the urge to mentally correct them. . . . While I love the Creole, . . . there are times when I rather not speak it or have it spoken to me. . . . I feel like such a hypocrite when these times come.
>
> Lenore Joseph

In an effort to investigate the origins of her own attitudes, the same student spent eight weeks conducting matched-guise tests at her high school and writing a paper documenting the disparate responses to Creole and standard speakers (L. Joseph, 1984). In the end she wrote: "I am much more aware of people's attitudes about Creole, and I have come to its defense many times since starting my project. . . . I'm working very hard to wipe out the ten percent of me that is negative toward Creole."

Another honors student prefaced his Creole writing with the following cautionary note: "I do not think one should just jump into this kind of writing. I should conduct a more detailed study into the method of how previous books have been written. I am mainly concerned with the reaction of people to these books and why they were or were not accepted by a wider audience"—Vincent Brown.

This student's comments show his awareness of the complexity of the issue. If Creole literacy is to develop, good intentions will not suffice; an understanding of the forces that support the prevailing sociolinguistic norms is necessary.

Remedial students whose responses on their entrance placement exams were immature and incoherent, as in the excerpts cited earlier, learned to use the academic vocabulary with aplomb and published guest editorials in the local newspaper criticizing the educational system. Honors students published original works in Creole and conducted research on attitudes toward Creole and the use of Creole in literature, and documented sociolinguistic norms governing code-switching (L. Joseph, 1984; R. Joseph, 1984; Richardson, 1984). This activity was not only unusual, it was risky, especially for students who hoped to teach in their home communities. By advocating Creole literacy, they exposed themselves to social and economic ostracism. The following editorial was written six months before the author decided to send it to the *Caribbean Contact*, a regional newspaper, and risk the reprisals that might result from its publication:

> Although Creole is the language of the masses, great emphasis is placed on speaking "proper" English in the British West Indies. From the moment we utter our first words, our parents encourage us to enunciate "properly" and to speak Standard English. Throughout our pre-school and elementary school days, our teachers ensure that when we reach junior high, we have a firm grip on the "Queen's" English.
>
> We have allowed ourselves to be absorbed into a quasi-elite society wherein command of the English language is used to measure our intelligence and our academic achievement. From the pinnacle we peer down at the helpless masses and create a language barrier which allows for minimal inter-group communication. This barrier, once created, enables us to forget our own humble beginnings and pretend that fluency in Standard English places us higher on the social ladder.
>
> For many of us, our Creoles are not languages, merely "bad English." This attitude results from having allowed parents, teachers and peers to correct us when we speak our Creoles and we having, in turn, corrected the younger ones. But, what are we really correcting? Our Creoles are perfect as we speak them and have no need for correction. Regretfully, many of us who struggle

to dissociate ourselves from our Creoles only learn to appreciate
them when we go off to university or simply overseas and become
exposed to great works written in other Creoles or dialects.

To date, little work has been written in our West Indian Creoles;
the onus is on us, university students, to take the initiative—to
acknowledge and publicize the historical value of our native languages. We must also write and publish work in our Creoles and
encourage others to do likewise. This can take the form of poems,
stories or plays and we must use the local newspapers wherever
possible as a medium for developing literacy in Creole.

I am not advocating a total disregard for Standard English; I
am suggesting that we stop ostracizing Creoles and Creole speakers.
Jamaicans have made positive steps toward this end; Jamaican
scholars have compiled a Jamaican dictionary. The Dominicans
and St. Lucians have put together a "Kwayol" dictionary, and
in Dominica national radio translates all English into "Kwayol."
There is also one day set aside each year when national radio
broadcasts exclusively in "Kwayol."

Although we will be confronted with much opposition and
perhaps even mockery, each of us has to start somewhere. The
task was no easier for the Alice Walkers, the Samuel Selvons or
the Chinua Achebes. We must persevere and one day we will receive the respect that writers of Creole deserve.

We are now independent nations and we need to develop our
own literary traditions. Our Creoles must form the basis of these.
As we strive to identify with the rich history of our enslaved fore-
parents, as we endeavor to become more patriotic, let us learn to
cherish everything that belongs to us; this includes our Creoles.
They are works of art created by our ancestors in bondage and,
as such, are precious gifts to be treasured by all of us here in the
English-speaking West Indies (Richardson, 1985).

Both remedial and honors students gained an understanding of
the role of grammatical conventions, standardized spelling, and the
rhetorical possibilities of both languages; both groups applied this
knowledge when they researched an aspect of language as it affected
their lives. In the six-week remedial course, inexperienced students
approached and interviewed professors and other people, designed
questionnaires, conducted surveys, and spent time in the Caribbean
Room of the College library reading literature about Creole. The results of their research were published in letters to the editor (for
example, Coumarbatch, 1983; Smith & Lachau, 1983).

In the honors course the research was more extensive and sophisticated; the results, in some cases, were publishable. In fact, the quality

of the final papers belied the lack of experience in academic research with which these honors students began. At the beginning of the semester, they were unaware of journal indexes and did not know how to use bibliographies or the card catalogue to generate specific information. The students had no idea how to narrow a large question into a manageable research proposal; and when advised to include a detailed research plan in their first drafts, several students wrote journalistic entries stating who they went to talk to, whether the person was there, when and how often they visited the library, and so forth. Nevertheless, although they were only freshmen and had taken neither linguistics nor statistics courses, they plowed through works by sociolinguists Labov and Hymes; designed and administered controlled experiments; and eight weeks later, turned in highly polished, original research.

Challenging Sociolinguistic Norms

The prevailing Creole-English diglossia in the Eastern Caribbean is educationally, emotionally, and economically costly. The exclusion of Creole in language arts, history, and social studies curricula leaves students ignorant about their language and its history and unable to write it. Many students drop out of school or graduate from college semiliterate victims of linguistic shame and confusion. Too often, those who succeed in writing standard English do not actually control it; the code instead controls them. Instead of shaping the code to express their experiences and articulate their dreams and aspirations, they channel their thoughts through the conforming mediocrity of an imported, imposed language.

Although many educators acknowledge the problems inherent in the sociolinguistic status quo, they hesitate to challenge it because of the deep-seated belief that any time devoted to Creole literacy takes away time that could be spent in English instruction, and so interferes with students' understanding of English. However, our experience with freshmen remedial and honors students at CVI does not corroborate this assumption. In fact, confronting and challenging sociolinguistic norms through the study and use of Creole effected a change in stance and attitude toward learning in general and writing in particular. Both remedial and honors students wrote more, and wrote more carefully and convincingly, in the Creole-centered courses than did our students in the English-centered classes.

In the remedial course, which lasted only six weeks, class time was spent listening to Creole linguists, writers, and calypsonians, who discussed language, language attitudes, and language choices. Students worked in groups to investigate high school language arts curricula and to write guest editorials for the local newspaper. They read novels and wrote book reviews. A few attempted to write in Creole. Most reverted to speaking it in the classroom, especially during heated discussions. Yet there was no evidence that students suffered or "lost" time they needed to devote to English. By the beginning of the fall semester, 65 percent of the class had passed the placement test and were enrolled in college English.

The honors course was a two-semester sequence that allowed for more extensive experimentation. After a lecture on Creole linguistics halfway through the first term, students read works by Achebe (1967), Baldwin (1963), Keens-Douglas (1979), Okara (1969), Shange (1977), Selvon (1970), and Walker (1982) and analyzed how each author approached and reconciled the issue of language choice. They read significant passages aloud and critiqued each writer's effort. For example:

> The phrase: the black coat wearing man, is so beautiful that to put it in the syntax of English would be like putting acid on a rose.
> Then there is the Black American dialect of the deep South.
> "He don't say nothing. Eat." Two simple sentences, indeed, but the English language in its standard form couldn't begin to give the abrupt finality that they demonstrate.
>
> Lenore Joseph

By the end of the semester, six students had composed essays in Creole. In addition to completing the required essays, the class wrote and produced a 90-minute Christmas radio show, most of which was in Creole. In order to write the script, the students had to share their work. They began meeting once weekly in the evenings. This practice lasted throughout the second semester, by the end of which the honors students had completed the sociolinguistic research cited earlier.

Students' interest in language and writing did not stop with the final examination. A student in the remedial summer course who had written a controversial editorial went on to become the unofficial scribe of her dormitory. A student who was one of the poorest writers when he started the remedial course began to attend the weekly honors evening seminars where students read their work. He brought in two short articles he planned to submit to *Reader's Digest*; one article was in Creole.

Miss Alma and Miss Stella are sitting on a park bench chatting.

MISS ALMA: "Gal, gess who I see today? Michael Jackson! I thought dat wen a big celebrity like dat sho he face in public he wadda get trampled by dem young people."

MISS STELLA: "Meh dere chile, you sho tain somebody else you
see? It got many people who dus dress up just like Michael
Jackson you know."

MISS ALMA: "No, gal, dat person I saw had look everything like
Michael Jackson. . . . Look! look him dere again!"

MISS STELLA: "Meh chil, dat's me son, John."

Simon Modeste

Another was written in English:

After looking everywhere for a job, I saw an ad for a cleaner in
the window for a restaurant. Worn out, I decided this would be
my last stop. Annoyed that there were three men ahead of me, I
picked up a number from the receptionist and sat down just for
the sake of resting. It did not take long for the line to dwindle
because as fast as someone went in for an interview, he came out.
I could not help wondering why; then my number was called.

As I made my way toward the manager's office, I stumbled
over a partially hidden broom.
Unnerved, I heaved the broom aside and entered.
Receiving no more of the manager's time than the others, I
threw my number in the wastebasket and left.
Outside the manager's office, the smug smile on the puny
receptionist's face brought me to a halt.
"Why are you smiling? I grumbled.
"Let me tell you a secret," she confided, "You got the job.
Why? You picked up the broom."

Simon Modeste

The honors students have scattered. One now writes critical observations of Afro-Americans' linguistic assimilation at Stanford University, several have enrolled in linguistics courses, and one has become
a journalist. Two others work in the CVI Learning Center as writing
tutors. And all of the students who wrote the Creole research papers
continue to revise them—one year later.

The work of these students is a first but critical step in changing
prevailing attitudes towards Creole. An educational program that recognizes Creole as a valid language (not as a bastardized or informal
variety of English) could effect a change in West Indian students' self-
perception, willingness to use both languages, and ability to write. Too
often, however, if Creole is used in schools at all, it is only for humorous purposes. The conclusions students draw from this are clear. After
viewing a student "cultural" presentation, one honors student wrote:
"Our dialect . . . is often used to make a big joke. . . . Are we West
Indians merely laughing-stocks? . . . . Are we merely living up to the
predictions of Bro'nasnsi? (Remember Saturday night?) . . . Is that all

there is to a West Indian man's life? A few laughs, a bottle of gin, and a wife and a baby?"—Lenore Joseph.

Another student discussed the humor that she included in a Creole essay on teenage pregnancy: "Even though my essay ends on a sad note, with the baby dying, I found myself with an uncontrollable desire to include some humor. Dialect does not necessitate entertainment e.g. Go Tell It on the Mountain but for me it does." —Sharylle Richardson.

Students learned that Creole can be used for new as well as traditional functions. They investigated the consequences of current language policy on their self-perceptions and on the perceptions of others. They experienced the profound difficulties of reshaping diglossic language patterns. When students in the remedial class discovered Creole could be used for writing, they learned the utility of standard grammars and orthographies and dictionaries. They also learned that, no matter what the language, writing must still be organized. Finally, they learned about the cumulative effects of linguistic supremacy: Creole has not been used and is thus not developed for many academic functions. If the functions of Creole are to expand, advocates must simultaneously convince the public that Creole is a language, demonstrate that current educational practice is counterproductive, and create the dictionaries, grammars, and expository models on which literacy depends.

Acknowledgments

This essay was written with the support of a Mina Shaughnessy Fellowship, Fund for the Improvement of Post-Secondary Education (Grant G 00820013). We dedicate it to Dr. Vincent Cooper, whose commitment to the use of Creole in the Caribbean inspired both our students and us. We would like to thank all of our students and especially to acknowledge several who generously shared their knowledge, experience, and research with us: Edward James, Sharylle Richardson, Lenore Joseph, Ron Joseph, Patrick Fraites, Alison Hector, Vincent Browne, Cleve Maloon, Kelly Charleswell, Henry Todman, and Ellis Webster. We also thank Dr. Gilbert Sprauve, Dr. Cliff Lashley, Dr. Simon Jones-Hendrickson, and Dr. John Holm for their careful reading and comments on earlier versions of this essay.

Notes

1. All quotations from the works of students at College of the Virgin Islands have been reprinted exactly as they were originally written. No editorial changes have been made. —Ed.
2. *Basilect* refers to the variety of Creole whose surface features least resemble the official metropolitan language; *acrolet* to the variety of Creole whose surface fea-

tures most resemble the official metropolitan language; and *mesolect* to the varieties of Creole which fall between the basilect and the acrolect.
3. Matched-guise testing is a method of evaluating language attitudes by recording
bilinguals in both their languages, mixing the order of speakers, and playing the
tape to subjects who are asked to describe attitudes of each allegedly different
speaker as the tape is played. By using the same set of speakers in Language 1
and Language 2, all differences in attitude may be attributed to the language
itself.
4. *Diglossia* refers to the use of two languages for complementary but not overlapping functions in a given society; see Charles A. Ferguson, "Diglossia," *Word*,
15 (1959), 325–340; and Joshua Fishman, "Bilingualism With and Without
Diglossia: Diglossia With and Without Bilingualism." *Journal of Social Issues, 23*
(1967), 29–38.

References

Achebe, C. (1967). *A man of the people.* New York: Anchor.
Alleyne, M. C. (1976). Dimensions and varieties of West Indian English and the
implications for teaching. In V. R. D'Oyley (Ed.), *TESL talk.* [Special newsletter issue].
Allsop, R. (1978). Washing up our wares: Towards a dictionary of our use of Eng-
lish. In J. Rickford (Ed.), *A festival of Guyanese words.* Georgetown: University of Guyana.
Baldwin, J. (1963). *Go tell it on the mountain.* New York: Dial.
Caribbean Examinations Council. (June 1979). *Secondary education certificate
examination: Paper 2—basic proficiency.* Barbados: Caribbean Examinations
Council.
Caribbean Examinations Council. (June 1981). *English syllabus addendum: Eng-
lish B examination.* Barbados: Caribbean Examinations Council.
Carrington, L. D. (1981). A seminar on orthography for St. Lucian Creole, January
29-31. In *Language and development: The St. Lucian context.* Castries, St.
Lucia: Folk Research Centre and Caribbean Research Centre.
Cooper, V. (1979). *Basilectal Creole, decreolization and autonomous language
change in St. Kitts-Nevis.* Unpublished doctoral dissertation, Princeton
University, Princeton.
Cooper, V. (1982). Roun' de walls of Jericho. *CVI Viewpoint.*
Cooper, V. (1985a). A sociolinguistic profile of the Virgin Islands. In V. Clark,
V. Cooper, & P. Stridiron (Eds.), *Educational issues and concerns in the
United States Virgin Islands.* St. Thomas: Virgin Islands Teacher Corps
Project, College of the Virgin Islands.
Cooper, V. (1985b). Personal communication.
Coumarbatch, D. (16 September 1983). Grammar skills a must at CVI. *Daily
News* [St. Thomas], p. 6.
Craig, D. R. (1977). Creole languages and primary education. In A. Valdeman
(Ed.), *Pidgin and Creole linguistics.* Bloomington: Indiana University Press.
Craig, D. R. (1980). Models for educational policy in Creole-speaking communi-
ties. In A. Valdeman & A. Highfield (Eds.), *Theoretical orientations in Creole
studies.* New York: Academic Press.
Farouk. (November 1984). Me durty Rebels fingah. *CVI Post.*
Fraites, P. (1983). Me and me lanlard. *Out of Thin Air, 2,* 31-32.

Hancock, I. (1985). A preliminary classification of the anglophone Atlantic Creoles. In G. Gilbert (Ed.), *Pidgin and Creole languages: Essays in memory of John E. Reinecke.* Ann Arbor: Karoma.

Joseph, L. (1984). *Attitudes of St. Thomas adolescents towards Creole.* Unpublished manuscript, College of the Virgin Islands.

Joseph, R. (1984). *Pan-Caribbean Creole—A need.* Unpublished manuscript. College of the Virgin Islands.

Keens-Douglas, P. (1979). *Tell me again.* Port of Spain, Trinidad: Keendee Productions.

Keens-Douglas, P. (April 1982). Unpublished interview with N. Elsasser and V. Cooper, St. Thomas, VI.

Lahming, G. (1953). *In the castle of my skin.* New York: McGraw-Hill.

Liburd, A. E. (1982, Spring). Some writing problems of students in the VI. *Passages, 7,* 40.

Okara, G. (1969). *The voice.* New York: Africana Publishing.

O'Neal, A. (1982, Spring). The origin and nature of values. *Passages, 7,* 23.

Petersen, A. (May 5, 1984). Some words gone outa style, but dey meaning is dere. *Daily News* [St. Thomas], p. 7.

Rezende, E. (May 1984). A West Indian dilemma in British schools. *Virgin Islands Education Review.*

Richardson, S. (1984). *A case study of a Kittitian's use of the dialect continuum: How language shifts according to audience, topic and context.* Unpublished manuscript, College of the Virgin Islands.

Richardson, S. (1985). A gift to be treasured. Manuscript submitted for publication.

Selvon, S. (1970). *The plains of Caroni.* London: MacGibbon & Kee.

Shange, N. (1977). *For colored girls who have considered suicide when the rainbow is enuf.* New York: Macmillan.

Smith, K. & Lachau, O. (1983, September 23). Creole is a language. *Daily News* [St. Thomas].

Spolsky, B., Englebrecht, G. & Ortiz, L. (1981). *The sociolinguistics of literacy* (Final report, NIE-G-79-0179). Albuquerque: University of New Mexico.

Sprauve, G. (1984). *The bonfire war.* Unpublished manuscript. St. Thomas, VI.

Valdeman, A., & Highfield, A. (Eds.). (1980). *Theoretical orientations in Creole studies.* New York: Academic Press.

Walker, A. (1982). *The color purple.* New York: Harcourt Brace Jovanovich.

9.

The Hidden Curriculum of Survival ESL

ELSA ROBERTS AUERBACH and DENISE BURGESS

The post-Vietnam-era wave of refugees and immigrants to the United States has triggered increased attention to the teaching of adult ESL students. In response to the pressing needs of these students, a new literature of survival English has begun to proliferate. Reflecting the "communicative" trend in language teaching, these materials focus on language use rather than grammatical form. Their goal is to teach "those skills that provide the students with the practical abilities that enable them to function in the new society" (Vaut, 1982, p. 1). They have gained widespread acceptance based on their practical, reality-based, student-centered orientation.

While the survival approach is widely acclaimed as "state of the art" ESL by practitioners and publishers alike, there has been little critical analysis of its theoretical assumptions and implications. This separation between theory and practice is what Raimes refers to when she says, "All too often scholars look at classroom methodology rather than the underlying intellectual assumptions which generate methods" (1983, p. 538). Moreoever, survival ESL exemplifies the type of curriculum that Raimes (1983) claims must be reevaluated in terms of "communicative" character. She argues that many new materials in fact focus on the forms rather than the content of language interaction, continuing to divorce language from thought, and language teaching from the creation of meaning.

In addition, sociologists of curriculum (e.g., Bourdieu and Passeron, 1977; Apple, 1979; Anyon, 1980; Giroux, 1983a, 1983b) call for a critical analysis of adult education curricula in terms of their socio-political implications. They argue that no curriculum is neutral: Each reflects a particular view of the social order, whether implicitly or explicitly. This "hidden curriculum" generates social meanings, restraints, and cultural values that shape students' roles outside the classroom. The choices that educators make reflect their views of the learning process, the social context for learning, and the students' place in society. These choices have a very real impact on students: Giroux (1983a) argues that the failure to examine assumptions about how particular materials mediate meanings between students, teachers, and society very often leaves little room for students to generate their own meanings and develop critical thinking.

Such calls for reexamination are particularly applicable to the survival literature genre because of its increasing popularity, its place in the communicative teaching trend, and its inherent sociocultural nature. While particular texts cannot be equated with curriculum, they often shape practice and reflect curricular orientation. As such, the examination of text materials is a necessary step toward the analysis of goals and directions for adult ESL curricula. Thus, the purpose of this essay is not to review or rank individual texts in relation to each other, but rather to lay the foundation for debate about the theoretical assumptions and social implications of survival models by looking at a range of currently available text materials (see the Appendix for a list of textbooks discussed).

The Roots of the Survival Trend

Although survival skills have been defined as those necessary for "minimum functioning in the specific community in which the student is settled" (Center for Applied Linguistics, 1983, p. 162), in practice, the term has been widely used to refer to literacy and prevocational and basic skills for students with zero to intermediate language proficiency. The single unifying characteristic of this type of text seems to be that it is situationally oriented around daily living tasks (shopping, banking, housing, health care, and so on). Most authors explicitly reject a grammatical framework and focus not on "what students *know about* the language but what they can *do with* it" (Center for Applied Linguistics, 1983, p. 11). A basic tenet of the survival trend is that language learning for adults should be experience-centered and reality-based. "Adults begin by learning for and from the situations in which they find themselves" (Center for Applied Linguistics, 1983, p. 7). The success of learning depends on the degree to which content is useful to students. Thus, "curricula, teaching methods and techniques, test materials, and assessment instruments have been developed to bring both the students and the classroom closer to the language needs of the real world" (Center for Applied Linguistics, 1983, p. 1).

This concern with reality derives from theoretical developments in both adult education and second language teaching. From adult learning theory comes the view that adults must be treated as people with complex individual histories, responsibilities, needs, and goals (Knowles, 1973). The tasks that an adult learner must perform in everyday life have increasingly become the focus of curriculum development (Grognet & Crandall, 1982, p. 3). The Texas *Adult Performance Level Study* (Northrup, 1977) made the notion of experience-centered learning concrete by identifying 65 competencies "necessary for an adult to perform successfully in today's society" (Center for Applied Linguistics, 1983, p. 9). Out of this study, the competency-based adult education (CBAE) model for adult basic education was developed.

This movement in adult education has occurred more or less simultaneously with the growth of the functional-notional and communicative trends in ESL. The latter can be characterized by concern with real language use, a student-centered classroom, humanistic approaches to instruction, and an orientation to language acquisition rather than language learning (Raimes, 1983, p. 543). Out of the parallel trends in CBAE and ESL has arisen the notion of competency-based ESL (CBE/ESL), which has gained increasing popularity in teaching survival English. CBE/ESL curricula teach to "task-oriented goals written in terms of behavioral objectives that include language behavior" (Center for Applied Linguistics, 1983, p. 9). Often these competencies are defined in terms of those identified by the Texas *Adult Performance Level Study* (e.g., Keltner and Bitterlin, 1981; Keltner, Howard, & Lee, 1981). Language learning is broken down into "manageable and immediately meaningful chunks" (Grognet & Crandall, 1982, p. 3). The goal is demonstrated mastery of the language associated with specific skills; performance indicators are associated with competencies so that students can be pre- and post-tested for mastery.

In view of this explicit concern with real-life tasks and their linguistic demands, survival curricula must be examined in terms of how well they live up to the goals of being *situationally* and *communicatively* realistic. As Taylor (1982) points out, what is labeled "reality" in the language classroom may not in fact be reality. Thus, we must ask to what degree the *content*—the "real world" presented in survival texts—reflects what adult ESL students actually encounter outside the classroom and to what degree language *forms*—the types of language interaction that take place in the classroom—replicate those of the outside world. Furthermore, we must examine how the selection and presentation of reality contribute to shaping social roles for students.

Situational Reality

One of the inherent limitations of presenting situationally realistic content at a low level is the need to maintain structural simplicity. As a result of linguistic constraints, model dialogues in survival texts are often oversimplified to the point of being misleading, as Examples 1 and 2 illustrate:

1. A. How can I get a loan?
   B. Why do you want the money?
   A. To buy a car.
   B. How much money do you need?
   A. $2,000.00
   B. Please fill out this application.
   A. When do I get the money?
   B. In a week.
   (Freeman, 1982, p. 101)

2. A. How much is the house?
   B. It's $460 a month.
   A. How much is the cleaning deposit?
   B. $200.
   A. When can I move in?
   B. Next week.
   (Mosteller & Paul, 1985, p. 188)

A more serious limitation of many texts results from not taking into account the socioeconomic conditions of newcomers' lives. Middle-class values, culture, and financial status are often reflected in lesson content; for example, a dialogue describing a student spending his one day off work playing golf fails to acknowledge that golf is a culture- and class-specific sport (Delta Systems, 1975/1976, pp. 21–23). A passage that argues that the advantages of having a telephone include the fact that it facilitates buying by credit card, ordering meals for delivery, and finding out snow conditions for skiing (Cathcart & Strong, 1983, p. 214) is not likely to be relevant to survival ESL students.

Beyond these rather obvious examples of a reality alien to newcomers, more subtle distortions are pervasive in survival texts, as can be seen from an examination of health, housing, and work units. Typical health units focus on the use of the medical system: describing symptoms; making appointments; understanding simple diagnoses, instructions, and prescriptions.

3. A. Hello, Dr. Green's office.
   B. This is Mary Thompson. I'm calling about my daughter, Sarah. She has a fever and a rash.

A. When can you bring her in?
B. Right away.
A. All right. We'll see you in a few minutes.
(Keltner et al., 1981, p. 55)

4. Eat good food.
Stay in bed.
Sleep a lot.
Don't smoke.
   drink.
   work.
   worry.
   stay up late.
   go to bed late.
(The Experiment in International Living, 1983, p. 52)

Example 3 is misleading for several reasons: A newcomer is more likely to go to a community health clinic or emergency room than to a private physician; it is highly unusual for a doctor to see a patient on a moment's notice; and a phone call of this sort would probably require giving more information about symptoms (onset of fever and rash, and so on).

Economic problems associated with health care are ignored in most texts. For example, in one lesson, a nurse asks a first-time patient if he would like to be billed, and he responds that he thinks insurance will cover the visit (Keltner & Bitterlin, 1981, p. 61). Frequently, new patients are asked to prepay; newcomers are unlikely to have insurance, and if they do, it may not cover routine office visits. The advice in Example 4 may be impossible to carry out for someone who must work to survive. As Wallerstein points out (1983a, p. 40), this kind of lesson neither acknowledges possible problems in following doctor's instructions (because the patient cannot afford leisure time) nor recognizes unhealthy conditions that may be contributing to the illness. Not exploring the economic or social context of health problems may reinforce students' sense of helplessness.

Thus, what is *excluded* from curricula is as important in shaping students' perceptions of reality as what is *included*. Failure to address such factors as crowded clinics, long waits, unhealthy living or working conditions, high costs, and communication problems neither prepares students for what they might encounter nor legitimates these experiences when students encounter them. Instead, it may promote the view that these problems are somehow aberrations or, worse, the result of the students' own inadequacies.

English Spoken Here: Health and Safety (Messec & Kranich, 1982b) is noteworthy for presenting a broader view of health care. It elicits discussion about fears of going to the doctor and problems of long waits, expenses, and treatment (Example 5); compares private and public health facilities; and discusses preventive medicine, home remedies, and stress reduction. The student is presented with options rather than formulaic prescriptions for behavior.

5. Talk to your friends about their doctors. Ask them questions about their doctors:
   1. What do you like about the doctor?
   2. What don't you like about the doctor?
   3. Is the doctor easy to see?
   4. Do you have to wait a long time for him or her?
   5. Does the doctor charge a lot?
   6. How does the doctor treat you?
   (Messec & Kranich, 1982b, p. 65)

Housing units typically include information about looking for an apartment, negotiating rental agreements, communicating with the landlord, and describing repair problems; competencies include reading ads, taking care of sanitation problems, and filling out rental application forms. As is the case with health units, lessons on housing often reflect a middle-class perspective. The gap between this perspective and the actual survival issues faced by newcomers can be seen by comparing Examples 6 and 7 with the excerpt from the *Boston Globe* story (Example 8) about the housing problems of Indochinese refugees in Boston.

6. A. The kitchen has a new sink and stove. . . . The bedroom has a beautiful river view.
   B. Yes, it does. How many closets are there?
   A. Three closets and a linen closet. The bathroom is very modern.
   B. Does it have a shower and a bathtub?
   A. Yes, it does.
   B. I like it. I'll take it.
   (Freeman, 1982, p. 53)

7. You have to be quiet in an apartment. You have to clean it and take care of it. Talk to the landlord if you have problems. . . . If you don't like your apartment, or if it's expensive, you can move. (Walsh, 1984a, p. 53)

8.   "We buy the diapers, the Huggies," Le Suong was saying. "In the cold, they are good to stuff in the cracks by the window."
   "But it's not the cold that is the biggest problem," Nguyen Van Sau said. "It is getting somebody to come when things get

broke, when the ceiling cracks or when people get scared of a
fire like there was at number 4.

"We call, 10, 15 times and nobody comes. All I want is them
to clean and make the rats go so children will not be near them,"
he said.

"I tell them once about a rat and the man, he say to eat it,"
Sing Ha, 9, said. "He laugh and say we eat dogs so we can eat
rats too."
(Barnicle, 1984)

The situation of tenants who are forced either to accept poor
conditions or fight to have them changed is usually not mentioned in
survival texts. While tenants' responsibilities in the areas of sanitation
and upkeep are discussed at length, landlords' obligations are largely
omitted. Where housing problems are discussed, there is seldom follow-
up discussion on how to resolve them. For example, although Messec
& Kranich (1982a) includes dialogues about complaining to an unre-
sponsive landlord, the absence of discussion about alternative courses
of action may reinforce the sense that the goal of the lesson is language practice rather than communication for survival.

Examples 9 and 10 illustrate the kind of lesson material that
could serve as a stimulus for discussion about strategies for addressing
housing problems.

9. A. We've just moved out of our apartment. They won't give us
   our deposit back.
   B. Did you leave it clean?
   A. Yes, we did. It was spotless.
   B. Why don't you see a lawyer?
   A. We don't know one. Lawyers are expensive and we're broke.
   B. Try the legal aid society. Someone there can help you.
   (Keltner et al., 1981, p. 167)

10. When you are having a problem with your apartment, notify the
    landlord as soon as possible. . . . If he doesn't make the necessary
    repairs in a reasonable amount of time, write a letter to him ex-
    plaining the problem again. . . . Keep a record of the dates when
    you spoke to him and keep copies of the letters that you have
    sent. If the landlord still doesn't make the repairs, you can often
    get help from a local government agency.
    (Foley & Pomann, 1982, p. 41)

In each of these cases, the authors leave it up to teachers to structure
discussion that relates lesson content to students' own experience.

Units on work often promote the view that finding a job depends
on how well you fill out applications, dress for interviews, make appoint-

ments, and so on. While these skills may be helpful, they are not sufficient. Weinstein (1984, p. 481) suggests that focusing on paperwork tasks (that in fact are often handled by family members) only adds to "feelings of powerlessness in a bewildering new culture" and gets in the way of developing talents that the newcomers may already have. This mechanical, decontextualized view of job finding is exemplified by Examples 11 and 12.

11. Women wear dresses or skirts and blouses; men wear jackets and ties.
    Listen carefully to the questions and answer questions carefully.
    Ask questions about the job . . .
    Have your résumé with you.
    Be confident.
    (Freeman, 1982, p. 92)

12. Miss Nakamura is looking for a job. In her country she was a waitress. Every day she looked in the newspaper. Last week she went to an employment service and they helped her. They sent her for an interview. First she called the personnel department and made an appointment. She also sent in an application. She looked very nice on the day of the interview. . . . [The interviewer] asked if Miss Nakamura wanted to work full-time or part-time. She said she would like to work full-time. Now she has a job. She makes $3.50 an hour plus tips. . . . She is very happy.
    (Keltner et al., 1981, p. 136)

The suggestions in Example 11 are too vague to be useful; in addition, they are presented as universal guidelines when, in fact, they may be inappropriate for many jobs. The hidden message of passages like Example 12 seems to be that if you, like Miss Nakamura, follow the appropriate steps, you will find a job. Conversely, if you have problems, it may be because you did not communicate properly. This idealized version of job finding contrasts sharply with another, more realistic view from the same text series:

13. A. You look tired. What have you been doing?
    B. I've been looking for a job for 2 weeks now, but I can't find anything.
    A. Did you check the want ads?
    B. Yes, but they all say they need someone with experience.
    A. What about the state employment office? Have you gone there yet?
    B. Yes, I went there and left an application. They told me to come back in a week.
    (Keltner & Bitterlin, 1981, p. 132)

Example 13 is exceptional in its portrayal of the frustrations faced by job seekers. Most texts do not prepare students for long lines, for situations where they are treated less than respectfully, or for rejections. They rarely discuss nonpersonal factors like competition with Americans, economic recessions, and discrimination.

Beyond *describing* an oversimplified reality, texts often *prescribe* particular roles for students. As sociologists of curriculum have pointed out, education is an "important social and political force in the process of class reproduction" (Giroux, 1983a, p. 267). The classroom often serves to "parallel and reproduce the values and norms embodied in the 'accepted' social relationships of the workplace" (Giroux, 1983b, p. 9). In survival materials, this hidden curriculum often takes the form of preparing students for menial positions and teaching them the corresponding language of subservience. *Opening Lines* (The Experiment in International Living, 1983, p. 178) makes explicit what other texts imply by outlining only the lowest-paying jobs as options for refugees (busboy, busgirl, waiter, waitress, cook, maid, janitor, factory worker, dishwasher, and so on).

The humorous dialogue in Example 14 captures the essence of the employment conflict for many newcomers.

14. A. What did you do in Laos?
    B. I taught college for 15 years. I was Deputy Minister of Education for ten years and then . . .
    A. I see. Can you cook Chinese food?
    (The Experiment in International Living, 1983, p. 177)

Rather than being used as the basis for a meaningful discussion of the contradictions facing refugees who were professionals, this dialogue trivializes their dilemma by not encouraging students to explore the problem (or even to discuss options like becoming bilingual paraprofessionals). Instead, teachers are instructed to ask students, "Why do refugees have to start their jobs at the bottom?" (1983, p. 387). The presupposition of the question (that newcomers must start at the bottom) in itself precludes consideration of less than menial jobs. The reason given in answer to the question is that refugees lack language skills, contacts, and credentials. Again the broader social context is ignored. The implication of the answer is that refugees start at the bottom because they are somehow inadequate, rather than that structural demands of the economy (for example, the need for cheap labor, which foreign-born workers have traditionally filled) restrict their options (Auerbach, 1984).

Survival on the job is often equated with being submissive; students are taught the language associated with being on the bottom of the power hierarchy. This can be seen in the often expressed position that prevocational ESL students be taught to *understand* the imperative but not to *produce* it because they must obey orders but not give them. Language functions in most survival texts include asking for approval, clarification, reassurance, permission, and so on, but not praising, criticizing, complaining, refusing, or disagreeing. The Hopewell *Work Series* (Husak, Pahre, & Stewart, 1976), which is promoted by the Center for Applied Linguistics as "matter of fact with a minimum of moralizing" (1983, p. 154), provides students with a list of rules for job success in Examples 15 and 16. Example 17, from Part II of *Basic Adult Survival English* (Walsh, 1984b), illustrates that this kind of prescriptivism is by no means a thing of the past.

15. I should be clean and neat.
    I should be friendly and polite.
    I should help other people.
    I should not complain.
    I should not be silly at work.
    I should not lose my temper at work.
    If my boss tells me I made a mistake, I should not get mad.
    (Husak et al., 1976, p. 2)

16. Sarah was a shampoo girl . . . sometimes her supervisor told her she made a mistake. Sarah did not get mad or yell. She told her supervisor she would try harder to do better work. She worked harder than the other employees. . . . Sarah was a good worker. Why?
    (Husak et al., 1976, pp. 34–35)

17. To be a good worker, you should:
    Go to work on time.
    Don't be absent a lot.
    Work hard. Don't be lazy.
    Be friendly. Get along with everybody.
    Be nice to other workers.
    Say hello to them. Smile at them.
    Be clean and neat.
    If you have a problem, tell your boss.
    If you are a bad worker, the company can fire you.
    Then it might be hard for you to get another job.
    (Walsh, 1984b, p. 66)

In each of these cases, workers are told to be obedient and to do whatever the boss asks; at the same time they are told to get along with co-workers. In reality, these two goals may be contradictory: A worker who naively tries to curry favor, works harder than others, and indiscriminately follows orders may be resented or ostracized by co-workers. There is a delicate balance of power in every American work-place, and the new arrival who enters the work force unaware of these dynamics may encounter problems. Moreover, texts that suggest that workers immediately go to their bosses with problems overlook the possibility that the source of many problems may be the supervisors themselves (some of whom may ask workers to do unsafe work, work outside their job classifications, and so on). While claiming to teach students how to get and keep a job, prevocational units rarely address conflict on the job. They focus on the duties and obligations of workers without mentioning their rights or options.

The power relations of the outside society may also be reproduced in the classroom when the tone of materials is patronizing. Despite the persistent claim that the learner must be treated with respect because "his intellectual capacity is that of an adult" (Freeman, 1982, p. v), students are often portrayed as incompetent and addressed like children. Every chapter of *Opening Lines* includes a "humorous" cartoon depicting student errors, for example, a student trying to mail a letter at the drugstore (The Experiment in International Living, 1983, p. 89). Students are taught to use polite forms, although teachers are not re-quired to do so in addressing students (e.g., The Experiment in Inter-national Living, 1983, p. 19); instructions are given in the imperative; and some authors use the *we* form, commonly used with children.

A more subtle form of disrespect to students is the way that cul-tural information is presented. It is commonly agreed that " an adult education program shouldn't require the adult to integrate with the second culture to acquire the language" (Center for Applied Linguis-tics, 1983, p. 55). The introductions to survival texts often stress the need to accept the students' culture (Delta Systems, 1975/1976). At the same time, the stated goal of most survival texts is to teach Ameri-can cultural norms: "skills which the community requires and the stu-dents lack" (Vaut, 1982, p. 1). Many curriculum writers have difficulty reconciling these goals of accepting the students' own culture and teaching about the new culture. In practice, the norms of American culture are often presented without reference to students' experience or exploration of cultural differences. Readings and cultural notes suggest rules for behavior, and lessons chunk these behaviors into skills that students are taught to perform. In many cases, guidelines are pre-sented as invariable standards. For example, under the subtitle "Orien-tation Notes: Transportation," *Basic Adult Survival English* states that "In America you need a car. Almost everybody has a car. Some families have two or three cars" (Walsh, 1984a, p. 85).

18. Brush your teeth after every meal. If you can't brush, rinse with mouthwash or plain water. If you have food between your teeth,

use a toothpick. Use dental floss every day. . . . You should see your dentist twice a year for a check-up.
(Freeman, 1982, p. 43)

In Example 18, from a text that claims to "treat the adult learner with dignity," the author takes on the role of prescribing personal hygiene (in the imperative), a topic that may be inappropriate for discussion in some cultures. Other texts tell students to tie their garbage in plastic bags, to defrost their refrigerators once a week, to make shopping lists, and to use deodorant and insect spray (Walsh, 1984a).

In addition to presenting cultural information as "standards," many survival texts view cultural adaptation as a one-way process. Texts often violate a basic principle of adult education by concentrating on what students do *not* know rather than using prior knowledge and experience as a bridge for learning. Very few survival texts incorporate cultural comparisons and contributions from students about their own experience in a systematic way. Information about differences in such areas as housing, family structure, and job finding is rarely elicited (presumably because the goal is to teach American ways). This approach contradicts the findings of schema theory research that shows the importance of activating background knowledge for reading comprehension (Carrell and Eisterhold, 1983). Some texts do elicit explicit cultural comparisons. The reading in Example 19 is followed by questions about cultural differences.

19. American customs are different from Laotian customs. There are many things here that I find strange and confusing. In America, men and women often walk hand in hand. Sometimes they even kiss in public! We don't do this in Laos.
   People also dress quite differently here. Very often I see women wearing shorts and sleeveless blouses.
   (Kuntz, 1982, p. 6)

Carver and Fotinos (1977) consistently encourage students to examine cultural differences. For example, even in a simple lesson about vegetable names (1977, p. 21), they ask, "Which of these vegetables grow in your native country?" A reading about American dressing customs is followed by the questions in Example 20.

20. How do people dress in your native country to go to school? To go to church? To go to parties? To go to work? Are people in your native country allowed to wear their hair any length they want to? If not, why not? What do you think about the people's clothing in this picture?
   (Carver & Fotinos, 1977, p. 11)

Texts that exclude cultural comparisons and conflicts from curricula define acculturation as a one-way process rather than as an interactive one. They implicitly promote a view of learning about a new culture as a mechanical process of superimposing one set of norms on another. This view does not allow for meaningful cultural transformation, the creation of culture through a process of critical and selective integration of the old and the new. To the degree that survival texts focus on changing behaviors rather than critically examining cultural differences, they may contribute to what Freire calls adaptation. Freire (1981, p. 4) characterizes the difference between *adaptation* and *integration* as follows:

> Integration results from the capacity to adapt oneself to reality *plus* the critical capacity to make choices and transform that reality. To the extent that men and women lose their ability to make choices and are subjected to the choices of others, to the extent that their decisions are no longer their own because they result from external prescriptions, they are no longer integrated. Rather, they are adapted.

Communicative Reality

Because teaching communication, rather than teaching language per se, is a stated goal of survival curriculum developers (Center for Applied Linguistics, 1983, p. 6), it is particularly important to examine the degree to which these materials are *communicatively* realistic. To what extent is realistic discourse modeled in the texts, and to what extent do materials stimulate authentic communication between students?

Raimes's (1983) criticism—that much of the so-called communicative approach is little more than the traditional, form-centered method in disguise—applies to many survival texts. The organizing principle for some books continues to be structure (e.g., Delta Systems, 1975/1976; Cathcart & Strong, 1983). Using structural criteria in sequencing lessons may result in a lack of semantic cohesion between units; for example, a lesson called "Where did you work in your country?" is followed by "We went to the circus" (Delta Systems, 1975/1976). While both lessons focus on the past-tense structure, the juxtaposition of these two topics seems incongruous. Concern with grammatical control rather than discourse constraints can lead to anomalous dialogues, for example, portraying a newly arrived refugee talking to her children in English. The attempt to teach specific forms often leads to communicatively unrealistic passages such as those in Examples 21 and 22.

21. Are you a man?
    a woman?
    (The Experiment in International Living, 1983, p. 37)

22. Hi, Ben. How are you?
    Fine, thank you.
    What day is it?
    It's Tuesday.
    (Delta Systems, 1975/1976, p. [5]12)

Beyond examining whether the model dialogues mirror reality, we must ask if texts create a setting where authentic communication can take place in the classroom. What are the interactive tasks and demands made on students? In most cases, students are provided with grammatical, functional, or cultural information in the form of model dialogues and a series of follow-up exercises designed to help them "master" or reproduce the information. The text provides both the content and the form of language/behavior to be used. Students contribute neither experiences nor ideas new to the teacher or other students. Display questioning, a technique designed to elicit specific information already known to the teacher (Gaies, 1983, p. 208), is used frequently. For example, almost every chapter of *Everyday English* begins with a variation of "Is this a tomato? No. It's an apple" (Shurer, 1980, [Food] p. 1). Although this type of questioning occurs rarely in natural conversation outside the classroom (Long & Sato, 1983), it appears frequently in survival texts. An information gap usually appears only after a long series of "communicative drills" (Raimes, 1983, p. 544). From a language acquisition point of view, the rehearsal of rituals may be inefficient if, as Warshawsky claims (1978, p. 472), forms are best acquired when they assume a critical role in transmitting information.

The concern with assessability may partially account for this lack of attention to the creation of meaning. With the new emphasis on accountability in education, ESL curriculum developers have focused on behavioral objectives and performance indicators as a way to quantify progress (Tumposky, 1984). Since knowledge of the world and thinking skills do not lend themselves to easy measurement, they are not compatible with the expressed goals of creating a curriculum that is "a performance-based outline of language tasks that leads to demonstrated mastery of the language associated with specific skills" (Grognet & Crandall, 1982, p. 3). As Tumposky warns, this behavioral orientation may well result in teaching that concentrates primarily on "the lower order skills which are easiest to measure" (1984, p. 305). Raimes argues that the concern with quantification contradicts a truly communicative definition of language: "We have divided language into discrete units, we have stressed assembling, not creating" (1983, p. 539). Not until language teaching engages the thought and mind of the learners can it be called communicative.

Problem-Solving Versus Problem-Posing

Survival ESL materials have been created in response to very real and pressing social problems and have attempted to be situationally realistic, to treat adult learners with dignity, and to assist their transition into the new culture. However, as this essay has tried to show, there is a great deal of unevenness among texts and within texts regarding these goals. In many cases, survival texts unwittingly present an idealized view of reality, a patronizing attitude toward students, a one-sided approach toward culture, and a model of language acquisition that is only superficially communicative. While attempting to help newcomers to fit into American society, some texts may have the impact of socializing students into roles of subservience. Why is it that despite well-meaning and commendable intentions, survival texts often fall short of stated goals?

The distinction made by Freire (1981) between *problem-solving* and *problem-posing* offers insight into this question. Freire suggests that very often in situations of profound social change and upheaval, educators see their role as one of *assistencialism*; that is, they believe they must intercede on behalf of their students with educational welfare to help them solve their problems. Curriculum developers thus assess students' needs and prescribe solutions. As Goulet (see Freire, 1981, p. ix) puts it, "An expert takes some distance from reality, analyzes it into component parts, devises means for resolving difficulties in the most efficient way, and then dictates a strategy or policy." The teacher's job is to transmit predetermined knowledge or skills that the students need to meet the demands of society. The teacher is the "provider," and the students are the "clients," or "consumers," of the curriculum. Freire calls this view the banking model of education: The teacher makes deposits that accumulate interest and value (Berthoff, 1984, p. 3). The transfer of wealth/information/knowledge is one-way, from the teacher to the students. Solutions are found *for* the students and imposed *on* them. While claiming to be student-centered, "such an approach in fact places all the responsibility for learning on the teacher" (Tumposky, 1984, p. 306). According to Freire (1981), the greatest danger of this approach is that it reinforces the silence and passivity of powerless people, rather than creating conditions that allow them to identify and think critically about problems.

In survival materials, problem-solving often takes the form of chunking reality into competencies corresponding to specific skills judged necessary for successful functioning in American society. The complex reality of the newcomers' world is presented in simplified, reduced form, with almost recipe-like instructions for what to say and how to act. Where problematic aspects of reality are introduced, they are sometimes treated as sources of humor, language practice, or supplemental activities. Only rarely are students asked to develop their own strategies for addressing problems, as in Examples 23 and 24.

23. Who would you call? Where would you go?
   1. If I wanted to find out about care for my children, I would

   _____.
   2. If I wanted to learn a trade or get a job, _____.
   3. If I wanted to locate the nearest playground for my children,

   _____.

   (Keltner & Bitterlin, 1981, p. 185)

24. What would you do in the situations below:
   Your new washable shirt shrinks the first time you wash it.
   The milk you just bought at the store is sour.
   (Carver & Fotinos, 1977, p. 36)

However, even in these selections, the problems are quite straightforward, and there seem to be expected correct answers. For more complex problems, like job-finding difficulties or landlord problems, students are often presented with solutions (like job retraining or legal remedies), rather than encouraged to discuss a range of options and devise strategies together.

By contrast, a problem-posing view of education sees the identification and analysis of problematic aspects of reality as central to the curriculum. The teacher's role is not to transmit knowledge, but to engage students in their own education by inviting them to enter into the process of thinking critically about their reality. The purpose of the endeavor is not to find solutions for students but to involve them in searching for and creating their own alternatives. "Instead of education as extension—a reaching out to students with valuable ideas we want to share—there must be a dialogue" (Berthoff, 1984, p. 3).

The only currently available book that defines problem posing as the starting point for adult ESL curricula is Wallerstein's (1983a). This book, intended as a teacher resource rather than a student text, adapts Freire's outlook to survival issues in the United States. It is based on the premise that education should start with problematic issues in people's lives and, through dialogue, encourage students not only to develop a critical view of their reality but to act on it to improve their lives. Each of the sample lessons codifies in picture or dialogue form an affectively loaded theme which reflects a contradiction in students' lives. The teacher's role is to facilitate the dialogue between students with a series of inductive questions aimed at eliciting students' ideas, assisting them in making generalizations, relating the theme to their own lives, and helping them to take action to effect change where applicable. Unlike many other survival materials, the vocabulary, grammar, and function exercises are subordinated to the process of exchanging and creating meaning. What is remarkable is that even at beginning levels of language learning, Wallerstein (1983b) has found that a problem-posing environment can be created through the use of simple codes, small-group work, the physical acting out of dialogues, and support from bilingual participants.

Conclusion

There is little doubt that newcomers need to know the language associated with finding jobs, housing, health care, and so on. Refugees and immigrants are immersed in a process of profound transformation, and they need the tools to be able to confront changes. The question is not *whether* they should be taught the language of survival, but *how* and *to what ends.* The problem-posing view of education challenges the notion that survival skills should be taught as a body of knowledge (linguistic and cultural) to be transmitted from teachers to students. It suggests that the language of housing and jobs, for example, be taught as a function of the single most important skill needed for survival: the ability to think critically. As London (Collins, 1983, p. 181) has said, "Increasingly a premium must be placed not so much on what to think, but on how to think critically. Preparation for living in a rapidly changing world requires that people learn how to learn."

The transition from a problem-solving orientation to a new, more empowering mode must start with teachers' examining materials already in use and asking simple questions about how reality is portrayed, to what degree student contributions are encouraged, what kinds of social roles are implicit, and how much opportunity for creative and critical thinking is allowed. Only by asking these questions and making explicit the values inherent in the materials we use can we begin to move toward a new mode of curriculum. As Giroux (1983b, p. 11) puts it,

> To acknowledge that the choices we make concerning all facets of curriculum and pedagogy are value laden is to liberate ourselves from imposing our own values on others. To admit as much

means that we can begin with the notion that reality should never be taken as a given, but, instead has to be questioned and analyzed. In other words, knowledge has to be made problematic and has to be situated in classroom social relationships that allow for debate and communication.

By problematizing our knowledge about teaching, we do exactly what is proposed here for students; our own critical self-examination becomes a model of the process we are inviting our students to engage in.

Acknowledgments

The authors would like to thank Ann Berthoff, Neal Bruss, and Donaldo Macedo for insightful comments on earlier versions of this essay. We are particularly grateful to Vivian Zamel and Stephen Gaies for their many valuable suggestions regarding both the substance and style of the essay.

References

Anyon, J. (1980). Social class and the hidden curriculum of work. *Journal of Education, 162*(1), 67–92.
Apple, M. (1979). *Ideology of curriculum.* London: Routlege and Kegan Paul.
Auerbach, E. R. (1984). *Shopfloor ESL: The language of self-defense.* Paper presented at the 18th Annual TESOL Convention, Houston, March 1984.
Barnicle, M. (1984, December 10). Their home in America. *Boston Globe,* p. 25.
Berthoff, A. E. (1984). Reading the world . . . reading the word: Paulo Freire's pedagogy of knowing. *Scholarship in teaching.* Boston: University of Massachusetts.
Bourdieu, P., & Passerson, J.-C. (1977). *Reproduction in education, society, and culture.* Beverly Hills, CA: Sage.
Carrell, P. L., & Eisterhold, J. C. (1983). Schema theory and ESL reading pedagogy. *TESOL Quarterly, 17*(4), 553–573.
Center for Applied Linguistics. (1983). *From the classroom to the workplace: Teaching ESL to adults.* Washington, DC: Author.
Collins, M. (1983). A critical analysis of competency-based systems in adult education. *The Adult Education Quarterly, 33*(3), 174–183.
Freire, P. (1981). Education as the practice of freedom. In *Education for critical consciousness,* Paulo Freire, 1–61. New York: Continuum.
Gaies, S. J. (1983). The investigation of language classroom processes. *TESOL Quarterly, 17*(2), 205–217.
Giroux, H. A. (1983a). Theories of reproduction and resistance in the new sociology of education: A critical analysis. *Harvard Educational Review, 53* (3), 257–293.
Giroux, H. A. (1983b). *Toward a sociology of curriculum.* Manuscript.
Grognet, A. G., & Crandall, J. (1982). Competency-based curricula in adult ESL. *ERIC/CLL News Bulletin, 6*(1), 3–4.
Knowles, M. (1973). *The adult learner: A neglected species.* Houston: Gulf.

Long, M. H., & Sata, C. J. (1983). Classroom foreigner talk discourse: Forms and functions of teachers' questions. In *Classroom oriented research in second language acquisition*, H. W. Seliger & M. H. Long (Eds.), 268–284. Rowley, MA: Newbury House.
Northrup, N. (1977). *The adult performance level study*. Austin: The University of Texas.
Raimes, A. (1983). Tradition and revolution in ESL teaching. *TESOL Quarterly*, 17(4), 535–552.
Taylor, B. P. (1982). In search of real reality. *TESOL Quarterly*, 16(1), 29–42.
Tumposky, N. R. (1984). Behavioral objectives, the cult of efficiency, and foreign language learning: Are they compatible? *TESOL Quarterly*, 18(2), 295–310.
Vaut, E. S. (1982). ESL/coping skills for adult learners. *Language in Education: Theory and Practice, 46*. Washington, DC: Center for Applied Linguistics.
Wallerstein, N. (1983a). *Language and culture in conflict: Problem-posing in the ESL classroom*. Reading, MA: Addison-Wesley.
Wallerstein, N. (1983b). Problem-posing can help students learn: From refugee camps to resettlement country classrooms. *TESOL Newsletter, 17*(5), 28–30.
Warshawsky, D. R. (1978). The acquisition of four English morphemes by Spanish-speaking children. Abstract in *Second language acquisition: A book of readings*, E. Hatch (Ed.), 472. Rowley, MA: Newbury House.
Weinstein, G. (1984). Literacy and second language acquisition: Issues and perspectives. *TESOL Quarterly*, 18(3), 471–484.

Appendix: Currently Available Textbooks Discussed

Carver, T. K., & Fotinos, S. D. (1977). *A conversation book: English in everyday life, Book Two*. Englewood Cliffs, NJ: Prentice-Hall.
Cathcart, R., & Strong, M. (1983). *Beyond the classroom*. Rowley, MA: Newbury House.
Delta Systems. (1975/1976). *English as a second language: A new approach for the twenty-first century*. Arlington Heights, IL: Author.
The Experiment in International Living. (1983). *Opening lines: A competency-based curriculum in English as a second language: A teacher's handbook*. Brattleboro, VT: Author.
Foley, B., & Pomann, H. (1982). *Lifelines: Coping skills in English*. New York: Regents.
Freeman, D. B. (1982). *Speaking of survival*. New York: Oxford University Press.
Husak, G., Pahre, P., & Stewart, J. (1976). *The work series: How I should act at work*. Sewickley, PA: Hopewell.
Keltner, A., & Bitterlin, G. (1981). *English for adult competency, Book II*. Englewood Cliffs, NJ: Prentice-Hall.
Keltner, A., Howard, L., & Lee, F. (1981). *English for adult competency, Book I*. Englewood Cliffs, NJ: Prentice-Hall.
Kuntz, L. (1982). *The new arrival: ESL stories for ESL students, Book Two*. Haywood, CA: Alemany.
Messec, J. L., & Kranich, R. E. (1982a). *English spoken here: Consumer information*. New York: Cambridge.
Messec, J. L., & Kranich, R. E. (1982b). *English spoken here: Health and safety*. New York: Cambridge.

Mosteller, L. & Paul, B. (1985). *Survival English: English through conversations.* Englewood Cliffs, NJ: Prentice-Hall.
Shurer, L. (Ed). (1980). *Everyday English, student book I.* Haywood, CA: Alemany.
Walsh, R. E. (1984a). *Basic adult survival English with orientation to American life, Part I.* Englewood Cliffs, NJ: Prentice-Hall.
Walsh, R. E. (1984b). *Basic adult survival English with orientation to American life, Part II.* Englewood Cliffs, NJ: Prentice-Hall.

10.

Feminist Values: Guidelines for Teaching Methodology in Women's Studies

NANCY SCHNIEDEWIND

There is substantial creative discussion on academic content in Women's Studies, but much less attention is given to how we teach. Florence Howe (1977) notes that she observed surprisingly few innovative teaching methods in her visits to Women's Studies Programs. Students, I believe, learn as much from the process of a course, its hidden curriculum, as from the explicit content. Therefore, the more classroom interaction reflects feminist principles, the greater the congruence between process and content, and the more consistent and powerful students' learning can be.

At least some agreement exists as to appropriate content. Women's Studies courses analyze: (1) the portrayal of women in traditional disciplines; (2) the ways in which women are oppressed and alternatives for their liberation; and (3) how the personal oppression of women is tied to the political, economic, and social structure of society. Additionally, we hope students will gain the knowledge and skills to better control their lives. Finally, we encourage women to push themselves toward academic and personal excellence.

In this essay I examine those educational *processes* that reflect certain feminist principles, as I see them. I define five process goals that have implications for teaching methodology, and give examples of how I use such methods in a number of my Women's Studies classes at the State University of New York College at New Paltz.

The emphasis on democratic classroom processes implicit in feminist pedagogy is similar to other egalitarian forms of education that have been proposed historically by theorists and practitioners. However, egalitarian educational methods have been, and can be, used to teach content that is antidemocratic. Jonathan Kozol (1972) articulates such a critique of the subject matter and values of the mainstream free-school movement of the late 1960s and early 1970s. Feminist pedagogy demands the integration of egalitarian content and process.

Development of an Atmosphere of Mutual Respect, Trust, and Community in the Classroom

When women[1] have opportunities to come to know each other as people, speak honestly, take risks, and support each other in the classroom, feminist values of community, communication, equality, and mutual nurturance are reinforced. While the subject matter in Women's Studies itself is often conducive to such community-building, particular teaching methodologies expedite the process.

At the beginning of a course, I use interpersonal activities so students become acquainted quickly. For example, I ask students to "pair up with a person you don't know and talk to her about a woman who has been a role model to you. Discuss the qualities you respect about this woman. What attributes of hers do you see in yourself? Which would you like to develop?" Through this process students not only share perceptions of women role models but also gain personal insights about themselves and their partner.

To encourage honesty, I teach a simple interpersonal communication skill that is a vehicle for feedback throughout the course. "I-messages" offer women a means for giving positive or constructively critical feedback to each other in a supportive way (Gordon, 1974). The format for an "I-message" is: "When you—(behavior), I feel—(feeling), because—(consequence)." For example, "Sue when you dominate the class discussion, I feel annoyed, because I'm interested in hearing the thoughts of everyone here." This enables a person to tell another how a particular behavior makes her feel without generalizing about her. It doesn't demand, but gives the receiver the choice to change her behavior. "I-messages" are easy to learn, can be shared among peers and between students and instructors, and are effective in producing an honest classroom atmosphere.

Democratic processes among students are important for community and mutual respect. (I will discuss such democracy between students and teachers in the next section.) The more aware each woman is of her use or abuse of time, attention, and power within the class, the more potentially democratic the group process. A useful way to make students conscious of one aspect of group dynamics is to brainstorm a list of function roles people play in groups—organizer, devil's advocate, includer, clarifier, withdrawer—and ask them to decide which they typically play. Explain that a group is most effective when its members take on the function role that is needed at the time. Give students a task to try such rotating leadership. Since people become leaders by taking on a needed role, this theory of groups democratizes typically hierarchical views of leadership. It also gives women an opportunity to try unfamiliar roles in a supportive setting. Student alertness to the group dynamics during the course stimulates democratic participation.

During some semesters I'd teach process skills at the beginning of the course, but failed to help students continually focus on them as we moved along. I have since learned that the little time it takes to raise and have students respond to questions like: "To what extent did leadership rotate today?" or "Does anyone want to give an 'I-message' before we leave?" is well worth it in furthering democratic processes.

Finally, festive procedures are community builders. Refreshments during breaks of long classes, a potluck dinner on occasion, and the integration of poetry and songs into the course, all catalyze energy and build solidarity.

Shared Leadership

Feminist values argue for replacing hierarchical authority with participatory decision-making. This does not imply structurelessness, but structure that is democratic. In the classroom it is possible for a teacher to share leadership with both students and other instructors.

Initially, I take primary responsibility for structuring my courses. Once they are underway, I involve students in the following way. At the outset, students divide into small groups and list on a sheet of newsprint what they want from the course and what they don't want. I do this as well. We post them around the room, read each other's and discuss them together as a group. I often list expectations that are both academic and personal; I want and encourage cooperative projects and papers; I want everyone to come to class having done all the reading; I want us all to take responsibility for both our learning and that of others. I *don't* want to start or end late; I *don't* want gossip (people talking about each other behind their backs rather than to their faces). Students' expectations often include those that are content-oriented, as well as general ones: I want to work; I want to learn ways of dealing with racism and sexism in the classroom; I don't want assignments that are busy-work; I want what I learn to have meaning for me in my life.

When any expectation is unacceptable to me, I suggest that students insisting on these withdraw from the course. Examples of expectations that I have found unacceptable have been: (1) not wanting to participate in small groups; (2) doing an independent paper instead of attending class; (3) not writing any papers. I may modify some of my own expectations to meet students' needs. For example, I've included a journal in some course expectations and students convinced me that they had an overdose of journals in Women's Studies. I understood that and deleted it. We discuss with gusto the ingredients of a challenging class. We set some clear, mutually agreed-upon expectations.

During the semester I periodically ask students for information about how the course is going. While this can be done orally, I prefer students to write anonymously. Typical questions include: "(1) What is helping your learning in this course; what is hindering it? (2) To improve this course, I should _____, the instructor should _____." Representative responses might be: "What is helping my learning is the variety of activities, the energetic pace of the course, and the stimulating subject matter; what is hindering my learning is too much reading, the domination of the discussion by the same people. To improve the course I should spend more time on the reading, be more assertive in class. The instructor should allow more time for small group work, invite other guest speakers." Then I ask a few questions about specific problem areas I've noted. For example, "One thing the group/I could do to encourage participation in discussion from everyone is _____." Examples might be to talk less, to ask other people for their opinion, speak out more, or tell Joan how her critical manner inhibits me from speaking. I read, tally, and make notes of these responses and report them back to the class the next session. In discussing them we work through the problem areas, and both students and I may make needed changes. The written feedback takes only ten minutes and the subsequent discussion somewhat longer. I have found this time to be well spent in my effort to share decision-making.

While I share leadership with students in these and other ways, I don't have a totally egalitarian classroom. I do take more leadership and have more power than any of the students. I have found, though, that students need an arena in which to learn to take responsibility for themselves and the group. For many this is a new experience. I no longer expect that they automatically come to class with those experiences and skills. Upper division Women's Studies students come more ready for reciprocity and in those courses the degree of my influence is less.

Instructors, too, can share leadership. For example, three faculty members team teach our introductory, interdisciplinary course, "Women's Image" (Schniedewind, 1978). While certainly more time-consuming than teaching alone, the benefits of each other's ideas and support buoy up the quality of the instruction. We can: (1) stimulate each other's thinking; (2) exchange perspectives from our various

disciplines; (3) pool knowledge to develop readings; (4) share problems
and possible solutions regarding our discussion groups; (5) continually
critique the course; (6) have an automatic time for contact each week—
something much valued in the world of hectic schedules. Further, lectures are given by numerous women from the college and local community. These include various women addressing the issues mentioned:
an attorney—women and the law; a psychologist—Freud and his critics;
a social worker at Planned Parenthood—women's health issues; coordinator of the local pro-choice group—the politics of abortion; local
women's studio collective member—women in the arts; and director
of a battered women's law project—creating changes for women.
"Women's Image" thus becomes a community endeavor with a wide
variety of women sharing its leadership.

Cooperative Structure

A classroom based on cooperative norms is desirable from both
a feminist and educational point of view. Ample research in education
and social psychology points to the increased cognitive and affective
learning gains of students in cooperatively structured classrooms (Johnson & Johnson, 1975).

Cooperative goal-structuring is one method that facilitates inter-
dependence. An activity has a cooperative goal structure when an individual can complete it successfully if, and only if, all others with whom
she is linked do likewise. In other words, the group sinks or swims
together. For example, when students have done assigned reading,
they form small groups. (I talk with any student who has neglected
her reading and provide her a separate task.) Each group is given a different question that compels them to integrate the material in a creative way. For example, after reading initial chapters from Gordon's
America's Working Women and Lerner's *Black Women in White
America*, students divide into groups and I give each group one of the
following questions to answer: (1) Compare Gordon/Lerner's view of
history, and the way of telling about it, with what you learned in high
school. (2) Compare the value and nature of women's work in the revolutionary period and today—What accounts for the difference? (3)
Imagine yourselves "factory girls" in Lowell, Massachusetts, in the
1830s, writing a letter to a friend, describing your life—What would
you say? (4) What were the key similarities and differences between
the life of working women, black and white, before the Civil War? In
discussing the questions, members must see that each person in their
group is prepared to respond. They are allowed about twenty minutes.

When students return to the large group, I ask any member to present her group's response and the group is assessed accordingly. I usually use a checkmark, checkmark-plus, or checkmark-minus, but grading a group would certainly be possible. In this way each member feels a responsibility to do the reading, critically analyze it with others, and share responsibility for her peers' learning as well.

The major problem I've had in using this method is reinforcing the expectation that it is necessary to do all the reading before coming to class—something that many students are not accustomed to. Once we use this process it becomes clear to students that they must read beforehand. However, initially in one class, a group of seven or eight students couldn't participate. They didn't receive credit for that day's activity and I gave them an alternative activity. Nevertheless, the visibility of that number of nonparticipants dampens the morale of the group. This is usually only an initial problem because the norm to read before class becomes established quickly. In classes where I use this strategy I do so at least biweekly.

Other methods foster collaboration. Breaking the class into small discussion groups is one common approach. Assigning cooperative, rather than individual, term projects is another. For example, in my interdisciplinary course, "Women and Work," students contracting for an A (see below) must develop an action project collaboratively. The projects themselves are comprehensive, results of the efforts of several people. Last semester one group researched, wrote, and distributed to women in the community a handbook about the legal rights of women workers in New York State.

Personal and academic support groups are another vehicle to co-operation. "Education of the Self for Women" is a course that enables a student to: (1) define, analyze, and attempt to change dysfunctional patterns of personal behavior; and (2) define and analyze those social forces that contribute to the development and maintenance of those patterns. In that course, students join a support group of three at midterm. For a portion of each subsequent class, they meet to analyze and attempt to change dysfunctional patterns of their behavior. While such groups are more natural for courses with explicit personal content, they are also applicable elsewhere. For example, at the beginning of any course, I might ask women to choose two goals for personal development that they want to address during the semester. "I want to speak up in discussion," "I want to stop procrastinating and complete my work on time," or "I want assertively to give feedback to my peers and the instructor," are typical. In support groups of three, students discuss their goals, and contract to help each other meet them. I insure brief periods for support group meetings two or three times during the semester and a longer session at the end. While drawing little time away from the major focus of a course, support groups integrate a cooperative structure for personal development.

In most college settings, the grading system reinforces competitive norms. Sometimes, however, a pass/fail option is available for entire courses. I use this alternative in "Education of Self for Women," since it is presumptuous of me to grade the growth of another's self-knowledge. Despite my fears to the contrary in a grade-conscious era, students commend the pass/fail system. I promise at the outset of the course a letter of recommendation for anyone needing evaluative information not reflected in a pass grade.

When letter grades are necessary or preferred, a contract grading system takes most competition out of the evaluation process. In this system I describe in the syllabus what requirements are necessary to receive an A, B, or C. Each student decides the grade she wants to earn and does the appropriate work. I set criteria for the quality as well as the type of work expected. While criteria vary with each course, important general ones for me are that work done: (1) be thorough; (2) reflect an understanding of the appropriate content; (3) be well-written—well-organized, spelled and punctuated correctly, argued logically; (4) show a critical analysis; (5) relate, where relevant, to the student's experience. While I have set the criteria in the past, another alternative would be to develop standards with students at the outset of the course. Students appreciate such explicit expectations, and with the competitiveness eliminated, meet and sometimes surpass the academic performance typical of classes graded in a traditional manner.

One mistake I made when initiating a contract grading system was to set the due date for too many assignments toward the end of the semester. If work did not meet the stated criteria, I was hesitant to return it to be redone since it was the end of the semester. I have since learned that in order to make contract grading effective, various assignments must be spaced periodically throughout the whole semester so students have ample time to improve the quality of inadequate work.

Integration of Cognitive and Affective Learning

Feminism values both intellectual and emotional capabilities. Feminists struggle to change the overly rational premises of male-dominated social relations and institutions and to incorporate priorities appreciative of human needs and feelings. Similarly, we wish to strengthen women's intellectual abilities, so long suppressed by those same sexist norms and institutions. Our teaching can synthesize both vital areas of human learning, the cognitive and affective. Since most academic women are adept at teaching cognitive material, I suggest here ways to incorporate affective learning into the curriculum.

One common device is the journal. In "Women's Image" we require each student to keep a journal in which she analyzes the reading and lectures and then relates the material to her personal experiences. Reading and commenting on journals requires time and sensitivity from the instructor. But the value to students is significant.

Experimental activities—structured participatory experiences to draw out feelings—also enables students to relate personally with course issues. Simulation games are a familiar example. In most disciplines even more simple experiences can be incorporated. In "Issues of Racism and Sexism in Learning Environments," for example, students participate in a common planned activity after reading material on institutional racism and sexism. Here they experience being on the "ins" and "outs" of a power group. I explain that we will do an exercise in which a volunteer, on the outside of a circle, tries to break in. A person volunteers, all others hold hands to form a close circle, and the outsider tries a variety of strategies before she gets in or gives up. I process the activity by asking how people felt during the activity and how they compare their experience to the dynamics of racism and sexism in society. We explore alternatives that both those in the power circle and the outside had but didn't think of or decide to use. We particularly focus on the choices white people and men have but don't act on because an "authority" sets the norms of "the game." In discussing this activity some students discover that they were thinking of challenging the norms, but didn't speak out. I ask people to consider in what ways their personal behavior in the exercise reflects their behavior in real life. Some students who were in the circle mention their willingness to conform to group norms, their lack of familiarity with thinking creatively of all alternatives in a situation, and their fear of taking risks. Such an experimental activity elicits powerful personal and social learning.

Affective learning can be integrated into a cognitively structured course through questions asked about material that require students to make personal connections. For example, after reading *Daughter of the Earth* by Agnes Smedley, two of the many questions I might ask are "What are the key contradictions that Marie struggles with as a woman? How do you relate to and deal with these dilemmas in your own life? Dilemmas students point to include: (1) the tension between family responsibility and ties and the need to escape their limits; (2) a woman's difficult search for a life that includes both independence and loving relationships; (3) the sometimes conflicting priorities between personal needs and the need to be involved in meaningful social change. The poignancy and power of themes in the novel relate to students' experience and significant insights can emerge from a discussion of such a processing question.

Finally, to include literature, poetry, and songs into courses in any discipline infuses material with feelings unevoked by much analytical writing. For example, among the short stories used in various sections of "Women and Work" are: "Louisa," Mary Wilkes Freeman; "I Was Marching," Meridel LeSueur; "I Stand Here Ironing," Tillie Olsen; "In Search of Our Mothers' Gardens," Alice Walker. A significant part of the last class of that course is spent singing some of the fine songs—many of them union songs—about the struggles of working women. I provide words, background music on records, and enthusiasm to urge on the timid. The camaraderie inspired by song is a new and rewarding experience for many of our "modern" students.

Action

As long as we live in a sexist society, feminism inevitably implies taking action to transform institutions and values. Perhaps the greatest threat to feminism in the university is the ease with which we can allow the curriculum to reflect thought without action.

Incorporating field-based action into my courses has been a difficult goal. Action projects are demanded for an A contract in "Women and Work" and required of all in "Issues of Racism and Sexism in Learning Environments." In the latter course, students design, develop, and implement an antiracist and antisexist curriculum project, or inservice program, for classroom or school. They have written and used creative and provocative curricula, games, and children's books (Schniedewind, 1977).

I have also offered "Fieldwork in Women's Studies." Here students intern in an existing feminist project such as the Battered Women's Law Project, Mid-Hudson Pro-Choice Action Coalition, the Women's Crisis Center, or develop a program themselves. A biweekly seminar, incorporated into the course, focuses on strategies for social change, providing space for integrating theory and practice. They read sections of *Feminist Frameworks* by Jaggar and Struhl, discuss various approaches to change, and analyze the projects they work in from these perspectives. These discussions encourage them to look beneath daily workings of a program for its underlying, and often unstated, values and goals.

Conclusion

Feminism is taught through process as well as through formal content. To reflect feminist values in teaching is to teach progressively, democratically, and with feeling. Such teaching rejects what Paulo Freire (1971) calls the banking system that assumes that one person with greater power and wisdom has the knowledge to dispense to others. Feminist education implies that we enter into a dialogue with our students, meeting them as human beings, and learning with them in community.

Initially, such teaching is not easy because as products of traditional education, we must relearn. While ideally a course could reflect all five process goals discussed above, in practice this is difficult. What I have found important is to express openly to students the relationship between the process of the class and the feminist principles I espouse. Such discussion not only demystifies some of the processes, but motivates students to analyze critically social relations outside of the classroom for their hidden underlying sexist values.

Notes

1. Since the majority of students in Women's Studies courses are female, I use the feminine terminology.

References

Freire, P. (1971). *Pedagogy of the oppressed.* New York: Continuum.
Gordon, T. (1974). *Teacher effectiveness training.* New York: Peter Wyden.
Howe, F. (1977). *Seven years later: Women's Studies in 1976.* Washington, DC: National Advisory Committee on Women's Educational Programs.
Johnson, D., & Johnson R. (1975). *Learning together and alone: Cooperation, competition and individualization.* Englewood Cliffs, NJ: Prentice-Hall.
Kozol, J. (1972). *Free schools.* New York: Bantam.
Schniedewind, N. (1977). *Confronting racism and sexism: A practical handbook for educators.* New Paltz, NY: Commonground.
Schniedewind, N. (1978, Winter). Women's image: An interdisciplinary introductory course. *Women's Studies Newsletter.*

11.

Critical Mathematics Education: An Application of Paulo Freire's Epistemology

MARILYN FRANKENSTEIN

Knowledge of basic mathematics and statistics is an important part of gaining real popular, democratic control over the economic, political, and social structures of our society. Liberatory social change requires an understanding of the technical knowledge that is too often used to obscure economic and social realities. When we develop specific strategies for an emancipatory education, it is vital that we include such mathematical literacy. Statistics is usually abandoned to "experts" because it is thought too difficult for most people to understand. Since this knowledge is also considered value-free, it is rarely questioned. In attempting to create an approach to mathematics education that can lead both to greater control over knowledge and to critical consciousness, it is important to have an adequate pedagogical theory that can guide and illuminate specific classroom practices. I want to argue that Paulo Freire's "pedagogy of the oppressed" can provide the theoretical foundation for that practice.

Freire's educational theory is complex. In this essay, I will focus on the problems he poses that are particularly pressing for teachers in schools in the United States. For this reason, I will not treat his theory on why revolutionary party leaders must also be educators, or his assumptions (historically grounded in the reality of the various Third World countries in which he has practiced) that these leaders would come from the bourgeoisie, "committing suicide as a class in order to rise again as revolutionary workers" (Freire, 1978, p. 16). Instead, I want to investigate his epistemology, his theory about the relationship between education and social change, and his methodology for developing critical consciousness. Because of Freire's argument that critical education involves problem posing in which all involved are challenged to reconsider and recreate their prior knowledge, this presentation should be seen as an exploration intended to help extend our thinking, not as "Freire's definitive formulas-for-liberation." A discussion of my own experience teaching urban working-class adults[1] basic mathematics and statistics for the social sciences demonstrates ways in which Freire's theory can illuminate specific problems and solutions in critical teaching, and ways in which mathematics education can contribute to liberatory social change.

The Problems Freire Poses to Teachers in the United States

What Is Knowledge?

Freire's epistemology is in direct opposition to the positivist paradigm currently dominant in educational theory. Positivists view knowledge as neutral, value-free, and objective, existing totally outside of human consciousness. Further, knowledge is completely separate from how people use it. Learning is the discovery of these static facts and their subsequent description and classification (Bredo & Feinberg, 1982). Giroux's (1981) critique of positivism in education theory focuses attention on what is omitted from that paradigm.

> Questions concerning the social construction of knowledge and the constitutive interests behind the selection, organization, and evaluation of "brute facts" are buried under the assumption that knowledge is objective and value free. Information or "data" taken from the subjective world of intuition, insight, philosophy and nonscientific theoretical frameworks is not acknowledged as being relevant. Values, then, appear as the nemeses of "facts," and are viewed at best, as interesting, and at worst, as irrational and subjective emotional responses (pp. 43–44).

Paulo Freire insists that knowledge is not static; that there is no dichotomy between objectivity and subjectivity, or between reflection and action; and that knowledge is not neutral.

For Freire, knowledge is continually created and re-created as people reflect and act on the world. Knowledge, therefore, is not fixed permanently in the abstract properties of objects, but is a process where gaining existing knowledge and producing new knowledge are "two moments in the same cycle" (Freire, 1982). In addition, knowledge requires subjects; objects to be known are necessary, but they are not sufficient.

> Knowledge . . . necessitates the curious presence of subjects confronted with the world. It requires their transforming action on

> reality. It demands a constant searching. . . . In the learning proc-
> ess the only person who really *learns* is s/he who . . . re-invents
> that learning (Freire, 1973, p. 101).

Knowledge does not exist apart from human consciousness; it is produced by us collectively searching and trying to make sense of our
world.[2]

So, for Freire, the world is "giving" rather than "given" (Collins,
1977, p. 82), and subjectivity and objectivity are not separate ways of
knowing.

> To deny the importance of subjectivity in the process of trans-
> forming the world and history is . . . to admit the impossible:
> a world without people. . . . On the other hand, the denial of
> objectivity in analysis or action . . . postulates people without a
> world . . . (and) denies action itself by denying objective reality[3]
> (Freire, 1970a, pp. 35–36).

Because of the unity between subjectivity and objectivity, people
cannot *completely* know particular aspects of the world—no knowledge is "finished." As humans change, so does the knowledge they
produce. But, through constant searching and dialogue, we can continually refine our understanding in the sense that we can act more
effectively.

This action and the reflection upon it that leads to new action
are not separate moments of knowing. Reflection that is not ultimately
accompanied by action to transform the world is meaningless, alienating rhetoric.[4] Action that is not critically analyzed cannot sustain progressive change. Without reflection, people cannot learn from each
other's successes and mistakes; particular activities need to be evaluated in relationship to larger collective goals. Only through praxis—
reflection and action dialectically interacting to re-create reality—can
people become subjects in control of organizing their society. Moreover, this praxis is not neutral. Knowledge does not exist apart from
how and why it is used, in whose interest. Even, for example, in the
supposedly neutral technical knowledge of how to cultivate potatoes,
Freire asserts that

> there is something which goes beyond the agricultural aspects
> of cultivating potatoes. . . . We have not only . . . the methods
> of planting, but also the question which has to do with the role
> of those who plant potatoes in the process of producing, for
> what we plant potatoes, in favor of whom. And something more.
> It is very important for the peasants . . . to think about the very
> process of work—what does working mean? (Brown, 1978, p. 63)

CRITICAL MATHEMATICS EDUCATION   183

For Freire, the purpose of knowledge is for people to humanize themselves by overcoming dehumanization through the resolution of the fundamental contradiction of our epoch: that between domination and liberation.

An additional concept that illuminates Freire's epistemology, by helping unpack the objective and subjective forces that shape knowledge and the reflective and active moments in knowing, is the "dialectic." Giroux (1981) defines this concept as

> a critical mode of reasoning and behavior . . . [that] functions so as to help people analyze the world in which they live, to become aware of the constraints that prevent them from changing that world, and, finally, to help them collectively struggle to transform that world (pp. 114, 116).

The central categories of Giroux's formulation of the dialectic—totality, mediation, appropriation, and transcendence—detail the various dimensions of a Freirean critical knowledge of reality. Totality involves understanding any fact or situation in its historical, socioeconomic, political, and cultural context. So as we come to know a particular aspect of the world, we must be concerned with its causal relationships, with its connections to other phenomena, with who benefits from its continuance, and with how it relates to our humanization or dehumanization. As we explore these questions, the answers we formulate are mediated by the institutional structures of society, by our individual and class histories, by our depth psychology, by our current relationships, and by the specific details of the concrete moment in which we are involved. The category of mediation challenges the "taken-for-granted" by helping us unravel the layers of objective and subjective forces through which we make meaning. The category of appropriation focuses our attention on human agency—on how people's actions both continue and challenge the relations of domination that mark our society. Therefore, critical knowledge involves uncovering the limits and the possibilities of our actions for transforming the world. Finally, transcendence unites commitment with theory, insisting that we refuse to accept domination as a "fact" of existence and that we use our knowledge of the world to reconstruct society so that it is "free of alienating and oppressive social institutions and life forms" (Giroux, 1981, p. 122). Thus, the dialectic as a mode of analysis not only clarifies the critical nature of knowledge, but also points to the connection between critical knowledge and emancipatory social change.

184 FREIRE FOR THE CLASSROOM

Education and Liberatory Social Change

Although Freire insists that "There is no such thing as absolute ignorance or absolute wisdom" (1973, p. 43), he also maintains that in an oppressive society people's knowledge is at different levels. People with the most dominated, "semiintransitive" consciousness have a fragmented, localized awareness of their situation and are unable to think dialectically about it. Therefore, they view their condition as caused by their own failure and/or by "God." People living in more open societies naturally develop "naive transitive" consciousness where they begin to see causes in a broader context, but are still convinced that "causality is a static, established fact" (Freire, 1973, p. 44) and, therefore, not susceptible to change through their actions.

One of the major obstacles that the "pedagogy of the oppressed" must overcome is the participation of the oppressed in their own domination. Freire explores the structural, emotional, and cognitive factors behind this "culture of silence." In Brazil, the people had internalized their lack of participatory democratic experience under Portuguese imperialism. This emotional identification was strengthened by the myths the oppressors created that the status quo represented the only possible situation because the oppressed were completely ignorant and powerless, while the rulers were omniscient and omnipotent. In such situations, the oppressed tend to fatalistically adjust to their condition. Since the relationships they have experienced and internalized involve the oppressor-oppressed division, their visions for a better life were very individualistic and focused on joining the oppressors rather than eliminating them.

However, as Freire insists, "the concept of semi-intransitivity does not signify the closure of people within themselves, crushed by an all-powerful time and space. Whatever their state, people are open beings" (1973, p. 17). One very important aspect of this hope for Freire is people's *conscientizacao*—their development of critical consciousness—which he maintains can only emerge through dialogical, problem-posing education. Since action cannot be dichotomized from reflection, and critical education develops critical knowledge, Freire views education as vital in helping people to become subjects involved in liberatory social change.[4]

An analysis of how education in the United States can lead to people's *conscientizacao* involves a focus on overcoming what Freire has called "massified," as opposed to semi-intransitive, consciousness. People with massified consciousness understand that humans change and control the world. But they believe that each individual acts from rational free choice rather than from a complex interplay of choice and manipulation. Freire (1970b) begins an analysis of how the massified consciousness typical of advanced technological societies becomes the major factor in people's participation in their own domination:

> The rationality basic to science and technology disappears under the extraordinary effects of technology itself, and its place is taken by myth-making irrationalism. . . . People begin thinking and acting according to the prescriptions they receive daily from the communications media rather than in response to their dialectical relationships with the world. In mass societies, where everything is prefabricated and behavior is almost automatized, people are lost because they don't have to "risk themselves." . . . Technology . . . becomes . . . a species of new divinity to which (people) create a cult of worship (pp. 49–50).

Both the (apparent) complexities of technology and the (superficially) wonderful concrete changes it has made in daily life, from washing machines to word processors, convince people that control over our high-tech society must be left to "experts." Critical education in the United States, therefore, must counter this belief by showing people that they can understand how technology works, and in whose interest. Also, critical education must challenge and expose the contradictions in this society's definition of "progress" and "the good life."

The meaning of "massification" in highly industrialized societies is illuminated by the concepts of ideology and hegemony. These concepts can sharpen the analysis of how a massified consciousness is developed and perpetuated and point to ways in which education could help break it down. Kellner (1978), drawing on the work of Karl Korsch and Antonio Gramsci, develops a theory of ideology-as-hegemony and of "ideological regions," which demonstrates how ideology contains "anti-capitalist and oppositional moments—contradictions that produce space for ideological struggle and social change" (p. 59). For Kellner, ideological knowledge, in contrast to critical thought,

> tends to suppress reflection, and resists changing its core ideas in the light of recalcitrant experience. . . . Nonideological thought and discourse exercises consistent and systematic reflection and critique on its methods, presuppositions, doctrines, and goals. It continually tests its ideas in practice, remaining open to experience, flexible, and capable of critique, self-critique, and revision (p. 54).

The ideas and images about "the way the world is" that constitute an ideology become hegemonic when they serve to preserve the status quo, presenting it as "natural, good, and just" (p. 50). Hegemonic ideologies, however, are not simply *imposed* by the ruling classes and believed by the "duped" masses—these ideologies are *constructed* through negotiation so as to incorporate people's ideas in such a way that they are not dangerous to the ruling classes. This process leaves hegemonic ideology with contradictions and open to challenge.

In order to focus on these contradictions and challenges, Kellner refines his theory to detail various "ideological regions"—economic, political, social, cultural—"which reproduce in thought the practices, institutions, and relations in each realm of existence so as to legitimate it and achieve hegemony" (p. 58). Tensions among ideologies in different realms (e.g., the hedonistic consumer ethic vs. monogamy and the family), contradictions between hegemonic ideology—these all help to the ideological notion of equality vs. institutional racism), the fact that there is no *one* unifying hegemonic ideology—these all help to create an opening for education to develop critical theory that can in turn foster liberatory social change.

Content and Methods for Education for Critical Consciousness

In developing a critical pedagogy, we must consider both content and methods. Emancipatory content presented in a nonliberatory way reduces critical insights to empty words that cannot challenge students' taken-for-granted reality and cannot inspire commitment to radical change. Humanistic methods without critical content can make students "feel good," but cannot help them become subjects capable of using critical knowledge to transform their world.

Freire is adamant that the content of an education for critical consciousness must be developed by searching with the students for the ideas and experiences which give meaning to their lives (1970a, p. 118). These "generative themes" should be organized and "re-presented" dialectically so that the links between them, their relationship to the totality of ideas, hopes, values, and challenges of the epoch, their historical context, their relationship to the community, and their raison d'etre, are all clarified. Only as people come to know these themes critically, as they realize how these themes support or contradict the dominant ideologies, do they see that "dehumanization, although a concrete historical fact, is *not* a given destiny but the result of an unjust order" (Freire, 1970a, p. 28). And only then are they motivated to intervene to transform that order.

Literacy becomes an important part of a liberatory curriculum because reading enables people to gain distance from the concrete immediacies of their everyday lives in order to understand more clearly how their lives are shaped by and in turn can shape the world (Freire, 1983, p. 11). Further the study of language is vital because

> the object of the investigation [of generative themes] is not peo-
> ple (as if they were anatomical fragments), but rather the thought-
> language with which people refer to reality, the levels at which
> they perceive that reality, and their view of the world, in which
> their generative themes are found (Freire, 1970a, p. 86).

Apple's (1979) analysis of "labeling" points to the value, in this context, of studying the language used to discuss the condition of the
oppressed. He argues that the labels used in educational settings work
against the development of critical consciousness by mystifying the
situations and relations that they describe, so that causality and complexity are hidden. Labels tend to focus blame on the "victims" and
encourage solutions directed solely at them, while simultaneously
directing attention away from the broader social, economic, and cultural factors that created the conditions being labeled.

Since dominant language can disrupt people's ability to know
reality critically, and illiteracy can prevent them from objectifying
the world in order to gain a nonfragmented, sociohistorical understanding of it, some fundamental themes may not emerge from the
people. Freire sees no problem with teachers suggesting additional
themes, since the dialogical nature of critical education must respect
teachers' as well as students' ideas. The central theme that Freire and
his team added in their work was "the anthropological concept of
culture":

> the distinction between the world of nature and the world of
> culture; . . . culture as the addition made by people to a world
> they did not make; culture as the result of people's labor, of
> their efforts to create and re-create; . . . the democratization of
> culture; the learning of reading and writing as a key to the world
> of written communication. In short, the role of people as Sub-
> jects in the world and with the world (Freire, 1973, p. 46).

With this understanding, people realized they already engaged in many
actions that transformed nature into culture, and, "by understanding
what culture is, [they] go on to understand what history is. If we can
change nature which we did not make, then why can't we change the
institutions which we did make?" (Freire, 1982).

A central theme which Apple (1979) suggests for inclusion in the
curriculum in the United States is "the nature of conflict." He theo-
rizes that a significant block to transforming massified consciousness
into critical consciousness is the ideology that in our pluralistic society
the interests of all groups (e.g., business, labor, unemployed) are the
same, and that policy and institutions are formed by consensus.

A basic assumption seems to be that conflict among groups of
people is *inherently* and fundamentally bad and we should strive
to eliminate it *within* the established framework of institutions,
rather than seeing conflict and contradiction as the basic "driving
forces" in society (p. 87).

Apple goes on to argue that by studying the positive aspects of conflict,
such as its role in promoting creative change and in bringing attention
to injustice, students will develop the critical insight that society is
not static.

Whatever themes emerge as the content of a liberatory curriculum,
Freire's theory insists we pay equal attention to the methods by which
people and teachers co-investigate these ideas. Although his methodology was developed for peasants in various Third World countries, his
focus on problem-posing in contrast to problem-solving—together with
his commitment to dialogical rather than "banking" education—is also
important for teachers in the United States.[5]

When Freire's teams discussed the generative themes with the
people, they posed as problems what they had learned from their investigation. These problems did not have the clear-cut answers typical
of textbook exercises, but were intended to challenge students and
teachers to respond through dialogue and collective action. Traditional
problem-solving curricula isolate and simplify particular aspects of reality in order to give students practice in certain techniques. Freirean
problem-posing is intended to reveal the interconnections and complexities of real-life situations where "often, problems are not solved,
only a better understanding of their nature may be possible" (Connolly, 1981, p. 73).

In addition, Freirean problem-posing is intended to involve the
students in dialogue and coinvestigation with the teachers. Freire insists that people cannot learn through "banking"—expert teachers de-
positing knowledge in the presumably blank minds of their students,
who memorize the required rules in order to get future dividends. He
stresses that this dialogue does not involve teachers' pretending ignorance. Since no one is omniscient and people each have different experiences related to the themes under investigation, teachers and students
can truly learn from each other. Especially since the "Literacy Crisis"
is being replaced in the mass media by the "Critical Thinking Crisis"
in American education (Daniels, 1983, p. 5), we need to stress Freire's
point that, "Our task is not to teach students to think—they can already think; but, to exchange our ways of thinking with each other
and look together for better ways of approaching the decodification
of an object" (1982). However, Freire is equally insistent that his concept of dialogical education does not mean teachers are merely "passive, accidental presences" (1982). They listen to students to discover

themes that teachers then organize and present as problems challenging students' previous perceptions. Teachers also suggest themes they judge as important. Teachers can be strong influences without being "superiors" who totally control the learning environment.

> The opposite of manipulation is not an illusory neutrality, neither is it an illusory spontaneity. The opposite of being directive is not being non-directive—that is likewise an illusion. The opposite both of manipulation and spontaneity is critical and democratic participation by the learners in the act of knowing, of which they are the subjects (Freire, 1981, p. 28).

The aspects of Freire's theory that I have discussed above speak to teachers searching for ways to unite their classroom practice with struggles for social change. In order to develop a "pedagogy of the oppressed," Freire contends that we need to explore the nonpositivist nature of the knowledge we are teaching, and the ways in which producing such knowledge deepens commitment and involves action to transform the world. The next section of this essay relates my experiences using Freire's theory to teach mathematics. The specific details are presented to provide a case study of how Freire's theory can inform critical teaching. They also support the belief that critical knowledge of statistics is vital to transforming our massified technological society.

Freire's Theory for Mathematics Teachers

All people reflect on their practice to some degree; mental and manual labor can never be completely divided. Even mathematics teachers who have never heard of Polya (1957, 1981) or Freire will think about problems such as how to explain the "sampling distribution of the mean" so that students do not confuse it with a distribution of scores within one sample. However, studying theory deepens the nature of these reflections; in particular, I believe that a theoretical framework changes the depth and types of questions one considers when thinking about one's practice. Freire's theory compels mathematics teachers to probe the nonpositivist meaning of mathematical knowledge, the importance of quantitative reasoning in the development of critical consciousness, the ways that math anxiety helps sustain hegemonic ideologies, and the connections between our specific curriculum and the development of critical consciousness. In addition, his theory can strengthen our energy in the struggle for humanization by focusing our attention on the interrelationships between our concrete daily teaching practice and the broader ideological and structural context.

Freire's Epistemology and the Meaning of
Basic Mathematics and Statistics Knowledge[6]

The mass media, most academic social scientists, and "common
sense" assume that mathematical knowledge consists of neutral facts
discovered, not created, by people through their interactions with the
world. Cynics claim statistics are all self-serving lies. A Freirean analysis, different from both of these approaches, directs our reflections
to the relationship between subjectivity and objectivity in producing
mathematical knowledge.

A course such as "Statistics for the Social Sciences" affords
many opportunities for examining how subjective choice is involved
in describing and collecting data, and in making inferences about the
world. For example, Max (1981) and Greenwood (1981) show how
the government makes military spending appear smaller by including
funds held "in trust," such as Social Security, in the portion of the
federal budget going for social services; and by counting war-related
expenditures, such as the production of new nuclear warheads, the
space program, and veteran's programs, as part of various nonmilitary
categories like the Department of Energy budget (the warheads!) and
Direct Benefit Payments (veterans' income). The government calcu-
lates that 25 percent of the budget goes for "National Defense"; Max's
and Greenwood's calculations give a figure of 57 percent of the budget
going to pay for "Past, Present and Future Wars." Atkins and Jarrett
(1979) show how significance tests, one of the most commonly used
techniques in inferential statistics, can be used to "provide *definite* and
apparently objective decisions, in a basically *superficial* way" (p. 103).
One reason this occurs is because a "favorable" numerical result in a
significance test gives no assurance that the measurements used in the
study are *meaningful*. In 1925, for example, Karl Pearson, an important figure in the development of modern statistical theory, found
"statistically significant" differences in Jewish children's physical characteristics and intelligence—leading him to conclude they should not
be allowed to immigrate into Great Britain (pp. 101–102). But, what
substantive significance does this have when these characteristics are
so clearly environmental? Also, the nature of probability *requires* statistical inference to be uncertain—a research hypothesis tested "significant at the 0.05 level" gives the impression of certainty, whereas it
means there is a 5 percent chance that the hypothesis is false. Events
with low probabilities sometimes do occur: significance tests only
allow researchers to be reasonably (say, 95 percent) certain that the
event described by their hypothesis is *not due to chance*. Moreover,
the tests cannot determine which of many possible theories explains
the event. For example, R. A. Fischer, author of a widely used modern
statistics text, uses results from a chi-square test, showing a statistically

significant greater frequency of criminality among monozygotic than among dizygotic twins of criminals, to conclude that this happens because of genetic factors. He ignores any other possible explanation, such as people's treatment and expectations of identical versus similar-looking twins (Schwartz, 1977, p. 28).

Freire's concept of critical knowledge further directs us to explore not merely how statistics are nonneutral, but why, and in whose interest. It is certainly not accidental that official statistics are much more useful to conservatives than to radicals. Nor is it accidental that, in spite of the technical weaknesses of significance tests, many standard social science computer packages lack convenient procedures for estimation, an alternative to significance tests that can be evaluated by statistical and *other* criteria and can facilitate comparison among investigations.

On the other hand, the thousands of government workers and university social scientists who produce this statistical knowledge are not *forced* to use methods whose outcome will uniformly support the ruling classes. An examination of the history of statistics can help explain how statistical knowledge "naturally" arises from the conditions of our society in such a way that its production is controlled by the ruling classes. Shaw and Miles (1979) trace its development to the expansion of commerce and the changing needs of the state. In 16th-century London, the crowded conditions of towns, which arose from the growth of markets, created the climate for widespread epidemics that led to the first collecting of mortality statistics. As these statistics were refined, they became more useful to the ruling classes. For example, William and Mary's government paid for loans to conduct the war against France with life annuities whose value was calculated using statistics on life expectancies of people in various age groups. In the 19th century, the rise of industrial capitalism led to the state's assuming a large role in providing conditions under which private industry could thrive, including the expansion and centralization of statistical knowledge. One consequence of this was that in 1832, the Statistical Department of the Board of Trade was charged with gathering and organizing material concerning British "wealth, commerce and industry."

Giroux's (1981) category of mediation extends this historical analysis by calling our attention to the combination of structural and individual factors that inform the production of this knowledge. One factor involves organizational "efficiency," which results in certain statistics being produced as by-products of administrative systems existing mainly for other purposes. For example, in England, unemployment statistics are based on records kept by employment exchanges, so the workers who fail to register are omitted from the official reports (Hyman and Price, 1979). Another factor involves pressures on social scientists from journals that only accept articles that report statistically significant results, and from universities that grant tenure only to widely published professors. This "naturally" results in an underreporting of results that are *not* statistically significant. Thus, one researcher by *chance* may produce and publish a statistically significant finding, while many others researching the same problem find no statistical significance, but since their work is not published, no conflicts among results can be detected (Atkins and Jarret, 1979). Next, Giroux's category of appropriation focuses attention on how, in spite of many factors resulting in what he calls a "selective affinity" for people to produce statistical knowledge to support the interests of the ruling classes, people can still learn from statistics. This is possible because statistical knowledge can be analyzed critically by examining its underlying interests and methods of collection, description, and inference, and by considering historical, philosophical, and other theoretical insights along with statistical knowledge. Finally, Giroux's category of transcendence insists that we not only criticize existing statistics, but that we also explore what new knowledge might be produced consistent with humanization. Along this line, Griffiths, Irvine, and Miles (1979) suggest that new statistical techniques can be developed. For instance, interactive surveys could, instead of treating the respondents as isolated, passive objects, make them participants in analyzing how they can use the information gathered to improve their lives. Further, Shaw and Miles (1979) hypothesize that in a liberatory society

> we would replace accountancy in terms of money and profit by accountancy in terms of social needs. We would replace the definition of social goals by those at the tops of the bureaucratic pyramids, by democratic self-control over all collective activities. We would then require new ways of measuring our needs and goals, which expressed their great variety rather than reduced them to money values or standards imposed from above (p. 36).

Mathematics Education and Liberatory Social Change

Applying Freire's theory to mathematics education directs our attention to how most current uses of mathematics support hegemonic ideologies, how mathematics education also reinforces hegemonic ideologies, and how critical mathematics education can develop critical understanding and lead to critical action.

A significant factor in the acceptance of this society's hegemonic ideologies is that people do not probe the mathematical mystifications that in advanced industrial society function as vital supports of these ideologies. A mathematically illiterate populace can be convinced, for example, that social welfare programs are responsible for their declining standard of living, because they will not research the numbers to uncover that "welfare" to the rich dwarfs any meager subsidies given to the poor. For example, in 1975 the maximum payment to an Aid for Dependent Children family of four was $5,000 and the average tax loophole for each of the richest 160,000 taxpayers was $45,000 (Babson & Brigham, 1978, p. 37). Also in 1980, $510 million of our tax money paid for new airports so that private pilots would not land their planes at large commercial airports (Judis & Moberg, 1981, p. 22). Further, people's misconception that statistical knowledge is objective and value-free closes off challenges to such data. As Marcuse (1964) argues,

> In this society, the rational rather than the irrational becomes
> the most effective mystification. . . . For example, the scientific
> approach to the vexing problem of mutual annihilation—the
> mathematics and calculations of kill and over-kill, the measure-
> ment of spreading or not-quite-so-spreading fallout . . .—is mysti-
> fying to the extent to which it promotes (and even demands)
> behavior which accepts the insanity. It thus counteracts a truly
> rational behavior—namely, the refusal to go along, and the effort
> to do away with the conditions which produce the insanity
> (pp. 189–190).

Traditional mathematics education supports the hegemonic ideologies of society, especially what Giroux calls "structured silences." Even trivial math applications like totaling grocery bills carry the ideological message that paying for food is natural and that society can only be organized in such a way that people buy food from grocery stores. Also it is rare that students are asked to evaluate their own understanding of math. My students are convinced that they are cheating if they check their own work using an answer key or with other people, and they have no experience analyzing which specific topics are giving them difficulty. In the past, when they could not do an assignment, they just expressed general confusion and gave control of their learning to the teacher to "diagnose" what they needed to review. This reinforces the hegemonic ideology of "expertise"—that some people have (i.e., own) a great deal of knowledge that can only be obtained from them and that they will impart *only if* you "follow the rules."

One of the obstacles that critical mathematics education must overcome in the United States is people's math "anxiety." Since, as Freire stresses, people who are not aware of the raison d'etre of their situation fatalistically "accept" their exploitation, teachers and students must consider the causes behind math "anxiety" as part of developing critical mathematics education. The immediate pedagogical causes of the situation—such as meaningless rote drill, taught so that it requires extensive memorization, and unmotivated applications that are unrelated to the math one actually uses in everyday life—create a situation where people "naturally" avoid mathematics (Hilton, 1980). Discussions with students helped me to reconceptualize these pedagogical causes in terms of misconceptions about learning. One misconception concerns the group process in learning. Students often feel they must be able to solve a problem on their own before they can contribute to the group. They do not realize that collectively they can solve problems that individuals working alone could not solve. Another misconception is the idea that a "wrong answer is totally wrong, nothing can be learned from analyzing it" (Frankenstein, 1983).

Understanding the deeper causes of math "anxiety" involves an examination of how the structures and hegemonic ideologies of our society result in different groups being more affected than others by this "anxiety." It also involves recognition that, to some extent, people participate in their own mathematical disempowerment. Considerable research (summarized in Beckwith, 1983) has documented that

> sex differences in mathematical training and attitudes . . . are *not* the result of free and informed choice. . . . They are the result of many subtle (and not so subtle) forces, restrictions, stereotypes, sex roles, parental-teacher-peer group attitudes, and other cultural and psychological constraints (Ernest et al., 1976, p. 611).

Further research needs to be done. In particular we need to investigate how differential treatment based on race and class interacts with mathematics "anxiety" and avoidance. We also need to explore why the research on math anxiety has focused only on the relationship between sex and mathematics learning.

In addition to the effects of sexism, racism, and classism, the hegemonic ideology of "aptitudes"—the belief, in relationship to mathematics, that only some people have a "mathematical mind"—needs to be analyzed. Women's belief that men have more "mathematical aptitude" has been explored. Tobias (1978) discusses research investigating the hidden messages in math textbook content and images; Beckwith (1983) summarizes studies of media influence on children's perceptions of boys' allegedly superior math abilities. However, Apple's (1979) discussion of labeling suggests that more research needs to be done on the contradictory effects of the term "math anxiety." Students are initially relieved that their feelings about mathematics are so common that educators "have a name for them." But in fact this label focuses the problem, and therefore the solutions, on individual failure rather than on the broader societal context that plays such a significant role in producing personal "math anxiety."

Bisseret (1979) demonstrates how language functions ideologically to support the belief that "a difference in essence among human beings ... predetermines the diversity of psychic and mental phenomena" (p. 2). Her analysis illuminates the role that this ideology of aptitudes plays in people's beliefs that the given structure of society is "natural" and "inevitable," and suggests further research to be done in uncovering the complex factors behind the ideology of "a mathematical mind." Bisseret argues that this ideology results in class-specific language; we need to consider how this language encourages dominated groups to believe and act as if they have "nonmathematical minds."

Critical mathematics education can challenge students to question these hegemonic ideologies by using statistics to reveal the contradictions (and lies) underneath the surface of these ideologies by providing learning experiences where students and teachers are "coinvestigators" and where math "anxious" students overcome their fears. Further, critical mathematics education can link this questioning with action, both by illustrating how organized groups of people are using statistics in their struggles for social change and by providing information on such local groups as students may wish to join. Above all, critical mathematics education must take seriously Marcuse's (1964) injunction that

> The trouble is that the statistics, measurements, and field studies of empirical sociology and political science are not rational enough. They become mystifying to the extent to which they are isolated from the truly concrete context which makes the facts and determines their functions. This context is larger and other than that of the plants and shops investigated, of the towns and cities studied, of the areas and groups whose public opinion is polled or whose chance of survival is calculated. . . . This real context which the particular subjects obtain their real significance is definable only within a *theory* of society (p. 190).

Content and Methods in Critical Mathematics Education

In order to apply Freire's theory to critical mathematics education we need to consider what mathematics knowledge is implied by, and would clarify, our students' "generative themes." In most school settings, teachers cannot get to know their students as well as Freire's teams got to know the communities in which they taught. However, teachers can ask students about the issues that concern them at work,

about the nonwork activities that interest them, about topics they
would like to know in more depth, and so forth. These discussions
can indicate the starting point for the curriculum. Then the teacher's
contribution can be to link up the students' issues with an investigation of the related hegemonic ideologies. Any topic can be so connected;
for example, art can lead to an exploration of such areas as the ideology of "high status" knowledge, the ideology of "taste," and the com-
modification of culture.[7]

In addition, most basic math and statistics skills and concepts, as
well as the critical nature of statistical knowledge, can be learned in
the context of working on applications that challenge the contradictions involved in supporting hegemonic ideologies.[8] For example, Max
(1981) and Greenwood's (1981) critiques of the official statistics on
the military portion of the federal budget can be used to learn percents and circle graphs. In addition, students can discuss how they
would decide to present the critiques, and what aspects of this research
and presentation they control. Would they choose to present their
critiques using raw data, percents or graphs? Do they agree with Max
that the space program should be considered part of the cost of "Past,
Present and Future Wars"? Discussing how to present the statistics to
demonstrate that the United States is a welfare state for the rich can
include practice of arithmetical operations; students need to divide in
order to describe the tax loophole data as "each of the richest 160,000
taxpayers got nine times as much money as the maximum AFDC grant
for a family of four." His same data helps students learn about the
meaning of large numbers; they can consider the services that the total
taxes not paid by these rich 160,000 ($7,200,000,000 = $7.2 billion)
could have provided if this money were included in the federal budget.
For a final example, Gray (1983) presents positive uses of statistical
techniques (such as chi-square and regression analysis) in legal cases.
In one situation, such techniques were used to show that in jury selection "a hypothesis of random selection, that is, of no discrimination,
is so improbable as to make it likely that some other process must
have been at work" (p. 72).

Not only can math skills and concepts be learned in the classroom
from applications that challenge the hegemonic ideologies, but interested students can also work with the many groups uniting reflection
about statistics with action for social change. The Coalition for Basic
Human Needs, in Boston, uses statistics (for example, those showing
that actual shelter costs in every major Massachusetts city exceed the
AFDC welfare grant) to fight for decent conditions for (poor) welfare
recipients. The International Association of Machinists had a statistician
prepare a report on "The Impact of Military Spending on the Machinists Union" (Anderson, 1979) that documents that "as the military

budget goes up, and procurement contracts rise, Machinists jobs in military industries steadily decline" (p. 1). Counter-Information Services (CIS), a London-based group of journalists, trade unionists, and statisticians, reconceptualizes information in official corporate reports at the request of workers at the companies involved. CIS issues "Anti-Reports" that present a critical analysis of the company's statistics. CIS's (1978) Anti-Report on Ford, for example, used that company's data to show that Ford had been exaggerating the profitability of its West German operation and understating that of its British plants. Since the United Kingdom workers were more militant in their demands than the German workers, Ford used its doctored statistics to threaten the UK workers with their alleged poor performance. For another example, CIS's (1972) Anti-Report on Rio Tinto Zinc (RTZ) Corporation used RT's data that 42 percent of its profits were made in South Africa, whereas only 7.7 percent of its assets were located there, along with additional information CIS researched, to support its charge that these high profits came directly from the low wages paid to RTZ's black miners.

As these math examples challenge students to reconsider their previously "taken-for-granted" beliefs, they also deepen and increase the range of questions they ask about the world. Once the idea of comparing the results of military vs. civilian spending on jobs is introduced, one can then ask that same question of other government spending. For example, are more jobs created through spending on energy conservation or nuclear power? Further, by learning and recreating a theory of math education and social change with their teachers, students can develop their ability to critique ideology in general.

Freire's methodology shares much in common with humanistic ideas on student-centered teaching but his ideas go beyond those methods in terms of their *intent*. They are not merely the techniques that any teacher who respected his or her students might use. Instead, they are intended to be part of the process of developing new social relations in the struggle for humanization. Freire's methodology directs math teachers' attention to how students with large gaps in their mathematical background can in practice coinvestigate the statistical aspects of their "generative themes." It also directs teachers to consider how students can become independent at decoding the problems coded in the barrage of quantitative data encountered in their lives.

By exploring the statistical aspects of students' themes in such a way that the mathematics involved starts at a very basic level, and by having students pose problems about the data even if they cannot yet solve those problems, teachers and students are *truly* coresearchers. Since math teachers will probably not have previously investigated

Median Income of Black and White Families (1969–1977)

	1969	1972	1974	1975	1976	1977
Black	$5,999	6,864	8,006	8,779	9,242	9,563
White	9,794	11,549	13,408	14,268	15,537	16,740

Source: Census Bureau, Current Population Reports, P-60 Series.

many of the suggested themes, students are likely to ask questions that teachers will have to research together. For example, the median income chart can be used to start a dialogue with students who have previously suggested the theme of racism. Students can initially be asked to describe what the main point of the chart is—an exercise in which they can practice such skills as comparing numbers, subtraction, or finding what percent one number is of another number. As the investigation deepens, students and teachers are equals in problematizing what other statistics would clarify the theme of racism (e.g., comparisons by race of maternal mortality rates; comparisons by race of unemployment statistics; comparisons of latinos with blacks and whites.) The importance of statistics in revealing institutional patterns, in contrast with personal instances of racism, is also brought out by this research. Further depth is added to the investigation by students and teachers jointly finding and considering various social science studies that use more advanced statistical techniques to clarify the theme. Reich (1978), for example, uses correlation coefficients between various statistical measures of racism and white incomes to show that racism results in lower wages for white as well as black workers, and higher profits for the capitalist class. Finally, any thematic investigation must include more than just statistical data. As Reich comments in this case

> the simple economics of racism does not explain why many workers seem to be so vehemently racist, when racism is not in their economic self-interest. In noneconomic ways, racism helps to legitimize inequality, alienation, and powerlessness—legitimization that is necessary for the capitalist system as a whole. . . . Through racism, poor whites come to believe that their poverty is caused by blacks who are willing to take away their jobs, and at lower wages, thus concealing the fact that a substantial amount of income inequality is inevitable in a capitalist society (p. 387).

The above example also illustrates how a dialogical analysis involving the interpretation of statistical data helps students practice the slow, careful thinking necessary to produce any critical knowledge. This practice, combined with opportunities to reflect on the learning process, helps students to become independent learners. Many such opportunities come from involving students in evaluation. For example, as students work on review problems they can answer keys that pose questions about potential errors. Thereby, students are encouraged to pinpoint their own misunderstandings and determine how well they understood each problem. They can be asked to choose between "wrong answer because confused about _____"; "correct answer but unsure of method"; and "understand well enough to teach others." Students can also learn a lot about posing problems by evaluating the clarity, the difficulty, and the interest of other students' and teachers' problems. Finally, having students keep a math journal is another method of having them reflect about their learning process. Journals can be vents for students' feelings about math and can act as a concrete record of progress for students who too often belittle their successes and focus on what they cannot do. The journal helps students realize that they can now accomplish what one month ago they thought was impossible. It helps them clarify which learning techniques worked best and why, and can give them personal feedback from the teachers and/or other students offering encouragement and alternative perspectives. The journal is also another way for students to be involved with the teacher in planning the curriculum, as their comments about their learning and their reactions to the class are considered future lessons. Following is an example from one of my students' journals:

> *Class #6:* I know that I ended my last entry into this journal as saying that "I am ready to tackle the next class," but I wasn't. I was very tired and became bored at the very start of class. I have to learn to control my feelings of being critical of other people problems in Algebra. I found myself thinking of the questions that some of the others asked as being elementary. I just assumed that if I understand, everyone should. Some of the problems I did have a little difficulty doing them, but I did not mention it in class because I felt that I would sound stupid or should I say unable to comprehend what was being said. Finally I began to fight the feelings that I had about other people problems and started being more attentive of what was being asked. I began to understand more and more and at one point, the questions that I wanted to ask were answered so, it wasn't so stupid after all.

My comments in the margin noted that it is hard to be patient with others' problems, but after all, you want others to be patient with your problems. I suggested that it might be more interesting for her if she tried to answer the other students' problems, helping them to see exactly what was confusing to them. I also challenged her use of the label "stupid," and praised her insight into the learning process. I ended by asking if she would read this entry to the entire class as a way of introducing a discussion on what we can learn from collective work. This journal entry taught me about the importance of such discussions in helping everyone understand how much can be learned whenever anyone poses a problem.

Conclusion

The context in which we are working in the United States is quite different from the culture-circle context in and for which Freire developed his theory. In this essay, I have attempted to convince people working in U.S. schools that Freire's theory contains many insights that we can use to inform our practice. Here I want to pose some problems arising from practice in our context that suggest areas of Freire's theory we need to develop further. These include the roles and responsibilities of students, the pressures on teachers, the complexities of moving students from massified to critical consciousness, and the tenuousness of the link between an emerging critical consciousness and radical social change.

Freire focuses on the responsibilities of teachers to challenge students' taken-for-granted beliefs, while simultaneously ensuring that students become their "coinvestigators" in this process. What responsibilities, then, do students have? How do we deal with the daily concrete reality of adult students whose work and family commitments make it difficult for them to do their "homework" or even attend class? How do we work within the enormous tensions created in our society between students' desire for individual "advancement" and our radical vision of collective progress?

Teachers, of course, are also affected by the pressures of daily life and the structures of our workplace. Freedman, Jackson, and Boles (1983) have shown how the conditions that elementary school teachers encounter in their day-to-day school situation—conditions such as the overwhelming emphasis on quantification (both in scoring children and in keeping records), the growing lack of control over curriculum (separating conception from execution), the isolation from their peers, the condescending treatment by administrators, and the massive layoffs of veteran teachers—"naturally" produce the frustration and anger that the mass media labels as "burnout." In what struggles must we engage in order to change these conditions and sustain our energy to teach?

It is often tempting to abandon dialogical education, because of these pressures on students and teachers, because students have internalized misconceptions about learning and about their intellectual abilities from their previous schooling, and because we can get such quick positive feedback and (superficial) positive results by "banking" humanistically. But students' desire for "banking" education in an academic setting does not mean that they are not independent learners in many other situations. Freire discusses how in the transition from semiintransitive consciousness, myths from the former stage remain even as the consciousness becomes more critical and open to new ideas (1970b). In addition to this overlapping of levels of consciousness, my practice calls attention to the nonlinear character of the levels of consciousness, and poses the problem of how to make a bridge from the critical insights my students have in some areas to their developing and overall critical approach to knowledge. My students' journals show how difficult it is for them to maintain a totalizing movement: entries show frequent "ups" and "downs" in self-image, and move between critical insight and myth. It seems clear that if the dialogical classroom experience is isolated and students are treated as objects in most other situations, then only fragments of critical consciousness can develop.

Further, these fragments are often theoretical, unconnected with practice. In both my experience and that of others (Rothenberg, 1983), the critical use of quantitative data can crack open hegemonic ideologies and students do become angry and intellectually committed to social change. But that does not necessarily mean they then join organizations working against oppression. Some even take jobs in business after getting their degree. Critical individual change does occur— when students overcome their math anxiety and learn math, they have a concrete, deep experience that *"things can change."* They also develop the ability to critique and they increase their questioning of the conditions in which they live. It may be that the most critical collective change that a pedagogy of the oppressed can bring about in our circumstances is a subtle shift in climate that will aid in the progress of liberatory social change.

Understanding the limits of our situation can increase our energy to focus on the radical possibilities of education as a force to promote emancipatory change. Using Paulo Freire's ideas as the theoretical foundation for our classroom practice situates that individual practice within the larger ideological and political struggle for humanization. We become more deeply committed as we realize how our actions are connected to this collective struggle. Using the term "militants" for people committed to justice and liberation (1978, p. 73), Freire argues that:

Militancy forces us to be more disciplined and to try harder to understand the reality that we, together with other militants, are trying to transform and re-create. We stand together alert against threats of all kinds (1978, p. 146).

Notes

1. The students at my school are adults who have a clear commitment to work in public or community service. Their average age is 35, about 70 percent are women, and about 30 percent are people of color.
2. Mathews (1981) traces Freire's emphasis on the social nature of thought to Karl Mannheim's philosophy that strictly speaking it is incorrect to say that individuals think; it is more correct to insist that they participate in thinking further than what others have previously thought.
3. One of Freire's first comments at the Boston College course he taught (1982) concerned his debt to the many American women who wrote to him praising *Pedagogy of the Oppressed* but criticizing his sexist language. He has changed his language; I, therefore, change his quotes in this respect.
4. Freire's writings on the details of how critical consciousness leads to radical change (e.g., "This pedagogy makes oppression and its causes objects of engagement in the struggle for their liberation" (1970a, p. 33) leaves him open to Mackie's critique that by ignoring "the political economy of revolution in favor of an emphasis on its cultural dimension . . . (Freire's) talks of revolution tends to become utopian and idealized" (Mackie, 1981, p. 106). However, Freire's comments at his 1982 Boston College course (e.g., "in meetings like this we cannot change the world, but we can discover and we may become committed") convince me that he recognizes the limitations as well as the possibilities of education in bringing about liberatory social change. His writing, possibly, concentrates on the role of human consciousness in changing the world as a counter to overly determined structuralist theories of revolution.
5. For a discussion of the specific conditions in Brazil under which Freire developed his theory and practice, see Barnard (1981). For a detailed presentation of Freire's methodology, see Freire, 1973, pp. 41–84.
6. Although this paper focuses on basic mathematics and statistics, Freire's theory can also illuminate other areas of mathematics knowledge. Some of these connections are suggested by the ideas about the nature of abstract mathematical knowledge in Gordon (1978) and Kline (1980). In his introduction, Kline quotes Herman Weyl, one of the most prominent mathematicians of the 20th century, "Mathematizing may well be a creative activity of man, like language or music, of primary originality, whose historical decisions defy complete objective rationalization" (p. 6).
7. Any topic can be connected to mathematics also; there are always statistics about that topic. In this case, there are even a number of contemporary artists whose work is based on specific mathematical structures (Frankenstein, 1982).
8. For more basic mathematics examples, see my article which focuses on contents and methods (Frankenstein, 1981). For more statistical examples, see Horwitz and Ferleger (1980).

References

Anderson, M. (1979). *The Impact of military spending on the machinists union*, Lansing, MI: Employment Research Associates.

Apple, M. W. (1979). *Ideology and curriculum*. Boston: Routledge & Kegan Paul.

Atkins, L., & Jarrett, D. (1979). The significance of "significance tests." In J. Irvine, I. Miles, & J. Evans (Eds.), *Demystifying social statistics*. London: Pluto.

Babson, S., & Brigham, N. (1978). *What's happening to our jobs?* Somervile, MA: Popular Economics.

Barnard, C. (1981). Imperialism, underdevelopment, and education. In R. Mackie (Ed.), *Literacy and revolution: The pedagogy of Paulo Freire*. New York: Continuum.

Beckwith, J. (1983). Gender and math performance: Does biology have implications for educational policy? *Journal of Education, 165*, 158-174.

Bisseret, N. (1979). *Education, class language, and ideology*. Boston: Routledge & Kegan Paul.

Bredo, E., & Feinberg, W. (Eds.). (1982). *Knowledge and value in social and educational research*. Philadelphia: Temple University Press.

Brown, C. (1978). *Literacy in 30 hours: Paulo Freire's process in Northeast Brazil*. Chicago: Alternative Schools Network.

Collins, D. (1977). *Paulo Freire: His life, works and thought*. New York: Paulist.

Connolly, R. (1981). "Freire, praxis and education." In R. Mackie (Ed.), *Literacy and revolution: The pedagogy of Paulo Freire*. New York: Continuum.

Counter Information Services. (1972). *Rio tinto zinc anti-report*. London: Author.

Counter Information Services. (1978). *Ford anti-report*. London: Author.

Daniels, H. (1983). Notes from the interim: The world since CLAC. *Conference on Language Attitudes and Composition, 8*, 2-7. Elmhurst, IL: Illinois Writing Project.

Ernest, J., et al. (1976). Mathematics and sex. *American Mathematical Monthly, 83*, 595-614.

Frankenstein, M. (1981). A different third R: Radical math. *Radical Teacher*, No. 20, 14-18.

Frankenstein, M. (1982). *Mathematics patterns and concepts that can generate art*. Unpublished manuscript.

Frankenstein, M. (1983). *Overcoming math anxiety by learning about learning*. Unpublished manuscript, University of Massachusetts.

Freedman, S., Jackson, J., & Boles, K. (1983). The other end of the corridor: The effect of teaching on teachers. *Radical Teacher*, No. 23, 2-23.

Freire, P. (1970a). *Pedagogy of the oppressed*. New York: Seabury.

Freire, P. (1970b). *Cultural action for freedom*. Cambridge, MA: Harvard Educational Review Press.

Freire, P. (1973). *Education for critical consciousness*. New York: Seabury.

Freire, P. (1978). *Pedagogy in process*. New York: Seabury.

Freire, P. (1981). The people speak their word: Learning to read and write in Saó Tomé and Principe. *Harvard Educational Review, 51*, 27-30.

Freire, P. (1982, July 5-15). *Education for critical consciousness*. Boston College course notes taken by M. Frankenstein.

Freire, P. (1983). The importance of the act of reading. *Journal of Education, 165*, 5-11.

Giroux, H. (1981). *Ideology, culture and the process of schooling*. Philadelphia: Temple University Press.

Gordon, M. (1978). Conflict and liberation: Personal aspects of the mathematics experience. *Curriculum Inquiry, 8*, 251-271.

Gray, M. W. (1983). Statistics and the law. *Mathematics Magazine, 56*, 67-81.
Greenwood, D. (1981, June 17-30). It's even worse. *In These Times.*
Griffiths, D., Irvine, J., & Miles, I. (1979). Social statistics, towards a radical science. In J. Irvine, I. Miles, & J. Evans (Eds.), *Demystifying social statistics.* London: Pluto.
Hilton, P. (1980). Math anxiety: Some suggested causes and cures. Part I. *Two-Year College Mathematics Journal, 11,* 174-188.
Horwitz, L., & Ferleger, L. (1980). *Statistics for social change.* Boston: Southend.
Hyman, R., & Price, B. (1979). Labour statistics. In J. Irvine, I. Miles, & J. Evans, *Demystifying social statistics.* London: Pluto.
Judis, J., & Moberg, D. (1981, March 4-10). Some other ways to cut the budget. *In These Times.*
Kellner, D. (1978). Ideology, marxism and advanced capitalism. *Socialist Review,* No. 42, 37-65.
Kline, M. (1980). *Mathematics: The loss of certainty.* New York: Oxford University Press.
Mackie, R. (1981). Contributions to the thought of Paulo Freire. In R. Mackie (Ed.), *Literacy and revolution: The pedagogy of Paulo Freire.* New York: Continuum.
Marcuse, H. (1964). *One-dimensional man.* Boston: Beacon.
Matthews, M. (1981). Knowledge, action and power. In R. Mackie (Ed.), *Literacy and revolution: The pedagogy of Paulo Freire.* New York: Continuum.
Max, S., (1981, May 27-June 3). How to make billions for arms look smaller. *In These Times.*
Polya, G. (1957). *How to solve it.* New York: Doubleday.
Polya, G. (1981). *Mathematical discovery: On understanding, learning, and teaching problem solving.* New York: Wiley.
Reich, M. (1978). The economics of racism. In R. C. Edwards, M. Reich, & T. F. Weisskopf (Eds.), *The capitalist system.* Englewood Cliffs, NJ: Prentice-Hall.
Rothenberg, P., et al. (1983). Teaching *"racism and sexism in a changing society":* A report. Unpublished manuscript.
Schwartz, A. J. (1977). The politics of statistics: Heredity and IQ. In Ann Arbor Science for the People, *Biology as a social weapon.* Minneapolis: Burgess.
Shaw, M., & Miles, I. (1979). The social roots of statistical knowledge. In J. Irvine, I. Miles, & J. Evans (Eds.). *Demystifying social statistics.* London: Pluto.
Tobias, S. (1978). *Overcoming math anxiety.* Boston: Houghton Mifflin.

Appendix:

Classroom Examples from a Math Course

First, class discussions that use math to analyze complex, adult issues increase students' intellectual self-image. Touching on a wide variety of topics adds to the students' background knowledge and therefore improves their ability to argue effectively. As students gain confidence in their own intelligence, they become more willing to voice their opinions and challenge what they have been taught.

Second, radical math is an ideal subject for practicing the slow, careful thinking that people need to examine critically the structure of our society. Because a math text must be read slowly, by filling in steps between the lines, students are forced to slow down their intake of information. Because small visual changes in the symbols can totally change the meaning of a mathematical expression, students are forced to slow down their perceptions. Because the political application problems in this course either contain more information than needed, or require finding additional information, students get practice examining and searching for data, rather than immediately spitting out an answer. And because this course asks students to formulate their own math problems, they get practice examining the consequences of many possible situations before determining what questions they can ask and answer.

Third, since the applications come from a wide variety of areas, it is more than likely that students will raise subject matter questions that the teacher cannot answer. This provides students with an important experience: realizing that the teacher is not an "expert" with all the answers. It encourages students to become skilled at searching for information to answer their own questions. Thus, students become what Freire calls "critical co-investigators in dialogue with the teacher" (Freire, 1970b, p. 68).

Finally, radical math challenges the fragmented view of society presented in its traditional curriculum, which breaks knowledge into separate, unrelated issues, to be discussed only by specialists. When math is taught as a necessary part of a careful analysis of the conditions of society, students have a clear example of how knowledge of specific subjects can be integrated to give a critical understanding of the world.

The following sample problems illustrate how to integrate the teaching of basic mathematics with the raising of political consciousness, and how to foster critical thinking by expanding traditional problem-solving techniques to include definition of problems and gathering of required information.

Applications of Operation with Decimals

According to the *Boston Globe* (12/27/80), an unpublished Department of Energy study states that since its beginning nuclear power has benefitted from federal aid in five major areas: $23.6 billion for research and development, $237.4 million to promote foreign reactor sales, $2.5 billion for uranium market promotion, $7.1 billion in fuel enrichment pricing aid, and $6.5 billion for management of wastes, mining spoils cleanup, and unpaid decommissioning costs.

1. Find the total federal subsidy to the nuclear power industry.

(This addition problem requires understanding how decimals are used with the words million and billion. It can also help improve students' intuitions about large numbers. A powerful way of describing the gigantic amount $40 billion is to have the class compute that, spending at the rate of $1,000 per hour, it would take over 100 years to spend just $1 billion! There are many good charts, put out by organizations like SANE [514 C St., Washington, DC 20002], that give specifics on how much in human services our nuclear power and nuclear armament spending costs.)

2. (a) Write a brief statement of your opinion about nuclear power. (b) Work in a group with three or four others who have similar opinions. List the kinds of numerical data that would support your opinion. (c) Find at least one of the facts that you feel would support your opinion and describe how you would find the others.

(The goal of this exercise is to make students aware of how people find and use numbers to support their arguments. For example, this study reported that without these subsidies nuclear power would be twice as costly [4.7¢ per kWh] and unable to compete with oil-fired electricity, currently the most expensive power [3.75¢ per kWh]. A pamphlet, "Nuclear Economics: An Invitation to Ruin," can be obtained from the Clamshell Alliance, 595 Massachusetts Ave., Cambridge, MA 02139.)

Applications of Percent

According to Lucille Sandwith (1980), fifty out of the 32,000 U.S. food manufacturing firms make 75 percent of the net profits. Of these top fifty corporations, thirty-one bought 63 percent of the national media advertising, or roughly $5 billion in 1977. Of the top twenty-five advertisers from all industries, eighteen were food companies.

1. What percent of the U.S. food manufacturing firms makes 75 percent of the net profits?

(This question requires careful reading since the many given percents might be confused with the percent asked for. And its solution serves a purpose: changing 50/32,000 to 0.2 percent highlights the fact that only a tiny percent of the firms make most of the profits. The information in the question can lead to a political discussion of agri-business and corporate monopoly in general, as well as to a math-related discussion of the advertising industry [70 percent of television food advertising, for example, promotes low-nutrient, high-calorie foods, whereas only 0.7 percent promotes fresh fruits and vegetables].)

2. Based on the information given, create and solve a math problem whose solution involves using percents.

(Students will fully understand percents when they understand which percent problems can be created from given information. For example, here students must realize that you cannot find out how much profit the top fifty firms make, but you can find out how much money is spent on national media advertising. Also, it is unclear whether the national media advertising figure refers to the total spent by food manufacturing firms or by all industries. Students must find more information in order to clarify this.)

3. Read the entire article (on reserve at the library). Discuss at least three points in the article that are supported by the use of percents.

(For more facts, contact Lucille Sandwith, Director, Center for Farm and Food Research, Box 88, Falls Village, CT 06031.)

Methods

Because, as Freire says, "a project's methods cannot be dichotomized from its content and objectives, as if methods were neutral and equally appropriate for liberation or domination" (1970a, p. 44), new methods, as well as content, are important in teaching a radical math course.

Traditional teaching methods convince students that they are stupid and inferior because they can't do arithmetic, that they have no knowledge to share with others, and that they are cheating if they do their school work with others. Such methods effectively prepare students to compete for work at boring jobs over which they have no control.

The methods that follow are intended to begin to undo the training students have received from traditional schooling, to give students a positive intellectual self-image, and to encourage them to work together to accomplish the task at hand. The techniques are most effective when the reasons behind them are discussed in class.

Analyzing Error Patterns

All wrong answers (except those guessed wildly from pure anxiety) involve some correct, logical reasoning. For example, there is logical thinking behind these incorrect subtractions:

$$95 \qquad 64 \qquad 82$$
$$-48 \qquad -29 \qquad -36$$
$$\overline{53} \qquad \overline{45} \qquad \overline{54}$$

This person realized that you subtract each place-value column separately and that you must subtract smaller numbers from larger numbers. However, he didn't know how to "borrow," so he guessed by subtracting the only way he could imagine. The class not only analyzes this student's reasoning, but also discusses how to convince him that the method was wrong and how to teach him correct methods. Analyzing error patterns provides nonrote reinforcement of computation skills, and shows students that you respect their intelligence and will not think they are stupid when they make errors. This, in turn, encourages students to respect their own and each other's intelligence.

Keeping a Math Journal

Journals are an effective means of reducing students' math anxiety. They serve as vents for feelings and act as concrete records of progress for students who, too often, belittle their own successes and focus on what they cannot do. The journal helps students realize that they can now accomplish what one month ago they thought was impossible and helps them clarify which learning techniques worked best. Students are expected to write in their journals for five to ten minutes, three to four times a week. Topics vary: how they feel in class, how they attempt to do the homework, how they use math outside school, how they feel about their progress, and so on. I collect the journals frequently and comment on them. My comments offer encouragement, alternative solutions or perspectives, and explanations of how students' remarks on learning math often apply to learning in general. Students' comments on the class are very helpful for my lesson planning. I find time to read and comment on journals when I don't collect homework assignments but instead give students the answers to homework problems and encourage them to work on them in class and evaluate their learning together.

Quizzes

I start most lessons with a review and a one- or two-question quiz. I correct the quiz in class while students solve class-work problems, return the quiz, and review it immediately. The quizzes tell me which topics the students understand and which topics confuse them. They give the students a clear message about what they were expected to learn from the previous lesson. Also, giving students many quizzes and then discussing feelings about taking tests, the fairness of the questions, and techniques for working under pressure gradually diminishes their test anxieties. In addition, when end-term grades are required, an abundance of quiz grades can be helpful to students.

Students Teaching

In order to teach a math problem to someone, you must be able to recognize all the correct methods of solving it as well as the logic behind incorrect methods. At the beginning of the term, I have students explain problems at the board and then, after discussing the difference between explaining and teaching, I gradually train them to teach. As various students practice teaching, they begin to involve many other students and to ask them to justify their answers. I remain quiet; the class checks itself and rarely lets a mistake go by. The students get very involved, arguing constructively and thinking creatively about solutions to the problems. The student teachers effectively involve even the quiet students, who are more willing to participate when it helps a classmate. A feeling of solidarity develops in the class as students, learning from each other, come to respect one another. After many students have had a chance to teach problems at the board, the class attitude begins to reflect their greater understanding of my role as teacher. Students realize how difficult it is to think on one's feet, to write at the board, and to talk to people who aren't paying attention. Having students teach helps break down the authoritarian image of the teacher and simultaneously builds true respect for the hard job good teachers do.

Students Working in Groups

In order for the class to work in groups, certain understandings need to be developed: that people learn at different rates, that they learn by asking questions and analyzing their mistakes, and that every problem can be solved in several correct ways. While the class works in small groups, I circulate among them to facilitate cooperation and to help students who are ahead realize that they can learn by sharing their knowledge.

I suggest a structure for group tasks by writing the task breakdown, with times, on the board, and having the class evaluate how the groups worked after each assignment. The following are sample group tasks:

1. Group evaluation of homework.

(a) Working in groups of three or four, determine which homework problem was easiest (5 min.).

(b) Determine which homework problem was hardest (5 min.).

(Evaluating homework questions is a good lead into having students create their own math problems. Also, this task shows students that because people learn in different ways, they find different problems easy or hard.)

2. Group creation of quizzes:

Working in groups of three or four, create two quiz questions based on the previous lesson (15 min.). I will then choose from your questions to create today's quiz.

(Once students learn to create fair, comprehensive test questions, they will be able to anticipate the test questions teachers will ask and therefore be able to study effectively for tests. Hopefully, the more practice students have in creating questions, the more they will become used to asking questions, in school and in their daily lives.)

References

Freire, P. (1970a). *Cultural action for freedom.* Cambridge, MA: Harvard Educational Review Press.
Freire, P. (1970b). *Pedagogy of the oppressed.* New York: Continuum.
Sandwith, L. (1980, Sept.–Oct.) Eating better for less. *Food Monitor*, pp. 8–12.

12.

Letter to North-American Teachers

PAULO FREIRE (translated by Carman Hunter)

My dear friend Ira Shor asked me to write a brief letter to the North-American teachers to whom this collection of essays is primarily addressed.

I believe I should make a preliminary statement by which I will attempt to be consistent with my own ideas and to introduce a dialogic relation between me and the probable readers of this book. In no way do I want this letter to be an arrogant message from a Brazilian teacher to his North-American colleagues, nor am I making a subtle effort to give prescriptive advice. On the contrary, this letter has only one purpose—that of continuing the dialogue, begun so long ago and constantly being renewed, with countless North-American teachers. I would like to do this by repeating some reflections on the teacher's role that I presented recently in a seminar at UCLA.

One fundamental insight I want to stress now, as I did in the seminar, is that since education is by nature social, historical, and political, there is no way we can talk about some universal, unchanging role for the teacher. This point becomes very clear if we think about what has been expected of teachers in different times and places.

The idea of an identical and neutral role for all teachers could only be accepted by someone who was either naive or very clever. Such a person might affirm the neutrality of education, thinking of school as merely a kind of parenthesis whose essential structure was immune to the influences of social class, of gender, or of race. It is impossible for me to believe that a history teacher who is racist and reactionary will carry out his or her task in the same way as another who is progressive and democratic. It is my basic conviction that a teacher must be fully cognizant of the political nature of his/her practice and assume responsibility for this rather than denying it.

When the teacher is seen as a political person, then the political nature of education requires that the teacher either serve whoever is in power or present options to those in power. The teacher who is critical of the current power in society needs to lessen the distance between the speeches he or she makes to describe political options and what she/he does in the classroom. In other words, to realize alternatives or choices, in the day-to-day classroom, the progressive teacher attempts to build coherence and consistency as a virtue. It is contradictory to proclaim progressive politics and then to practice authoritarianism or opportunism in the classroom. A progressive position requires democratic practice where authority never becomes authoritarianism, and where authority is never so reduced that it disappears in a climate of irresponsibility and license.

There is, however, one dimension of every teacher's role that is independent of political choice, whether progressive or reactionary. This is the act of teaching subject matter or content. It is unthinkable for a teacher to be in charge of a class without providing students with material relevant to the discipline. But if both a progressive and a reactionary are equal in their obligation to teach, if both agree that it is unthinkable to be a teacher without teaching, nevertheless they will differ with regard to their understanding of what teaching really is. They will differ in their practice, in the way they teach. Professional competence, command of a subject or discipline, is never understood by the progressive teacher as something neutral. There is no such thing as a category called "professional competence" all by itself. We must always ask ourselves: In favor of whom and of what do we use our technical competence?

At the risk of repeating myself, let me emphasize that a progressive teacher, in contrast to a reactionary one, is always endeavoring to reveal reality for her/his students, removing whatever keeps them from seeing clearly and critically. Such a teacher would never neglect course content simply to politicize students. From the progressive teacher's point of view, it is not some magic understanding of content by itself that liberates, nor does disregard for subject matter liberate a student, as if political insight could be achieved all by itself. Political clarity is crucial, but it is not enough by itself.

Whether a progressive teacher works in Latin America or in the United States, we cannot neglect the task of helping students become literate, choosing instead to spend most of the teaching time on political analysis. However, it is equally impossible to spend all of the class time on purely technical and linguistic questions, trusting that critical consciousness will follow as a result of being literate. Clearly, those who are illiterate need to learn how to read and write. However, reading and writing words encompasses the reading of the world, that is, the critical understanding of politics in the world, a fact I have noted many times in the past.

As I said above, progressive and reactionary teachers do have one thing in common—the act of teaching some course content. But if they share this obligation to teach, their comprehension of teaching differs, and if they are consistent with their own views, their methods of teaching also differ.

Teaching from a progressive point of view is not simply the transmission of knowledge about an object or about some subject. This kind of transmission is usually a description of a concept or of an object, which is intended to be mechanically memorized by students. Also, from the progressive teacher's perspective, teaching students how to learn can never be reduced to some operation where the goal is merely how to learn. Teaching someone how to learn is only valid in a progressive class when the learners learn how to learn as they learn the inner meaning (the raison d'etre) of an object or subject of study. It is by teaching biology or economics that the teacher teaches students how to learn.

For progressive teachers, pedagogy implies, then, that the learners penetrate or enter into the discourse of the teacher, appropriating for themselves the deepest significance of the subject being taught. The indisputable responsibility of the teacher to teach is thus shared by the learners through their own act of intimately knowing what is taught.

And the progressive teacher only truly teaches to the degree that he or she has also appropriated the content of what is being taught, learning it critically for herself or himself. In this way, the act of teaching is an act of reknowing an already known object. In other words, the teacher reexperiences his or her own capacity to know through the similar capacity to know that exists in the learners. To teach, then, is the form that knowing takes as the teacher searches for the particular way of teaching that will challenge and call forth in students their own act of knowing. Thus, teaching is both creative and critical. It requires inventiveness and curiosity by both teacher and learner in the process.

To teach content in a way that will make subject matter appropriated by students implies the creation and exercise of serious intellectual discipline. Such discipline began forming long before schooling began. To believe that placing students in a learning milieu automatically creates a situation for critical knowing without this kind of discipline is a vain hope. Just as it is impossible to teach someone how to learn without teaching some content, it is also impossible to teach intellectual discipline except through a practice of knowing that enables learners to become active and critical subjects, constantly increasing their critical abilities.

In the formation of this necessary discipline, the progressive teacher cannot identify the act of studying, learning, knowing with entertainment or game-playing that has very relaxed or nonexistent rules. Neither can it be identified with a learning milieu that is boring or unpleasant. The act of studying, learning, knowing is difficult and above all demanding. But, it is necessary for learners to discover and feel the inherent joy that is always ready to take hold of those who give themselves to the process of learning.

The teacher's role in nurturing this discipline and joy is enormous. Authority and competence both play a part. A teacher who does not take pedagogy seriously, who does not study, who teaches badly what she/he does not know well, who does not struggle to obtain the material conditions indispensable to education, that teacher is actively inhibiting the formation of intellectual discipline so essential to students. That teacher is also destroying herself/himself as a teacher.

On the other hand, this intellectual discipline is not the result of something the teacher does *to* the learners. Although the presence, the orientation, the stimulation, the authority, of the teacher are all essential, the discipline has to be built and internalized by the students. Therefore, any teacher who rigidly adheres to the routines set forth in teaching manuals is exercising authority in a way that inhibits the freedom of students, the freedom they need to exercise critical intelligence through which they appropriate the subject matter. Such a teacher is neither free nor able to help students become creative, curious people.

This collection of essays organized by Ira Shor is a testimony to creativity in the classroom. It deserves careful reading and study.

São Paulo
September, 1986

Appendix

Literacy in 30 Hours:
Paulo Freire's Process
in Northeast Brazil

CYNTHIA BROWN

Learning to read is a political act. In a literate society being able to read is a necessary step toward making decisions and sharing power. A nonliterate person may be very powerful within a nonliterate subculture, but within the dominant culture a nonreader is marginal. She/he cannot fill out tests and applications, cannot determine what is in contracts without a trusted adviser who can read, has no access to information controlled by professionals, and often is denied the right to vote. Learning to read gives access to information, protection against fraud, and participation as a citizen.

Learning to read is a step toward political participation. But how people exercise their ability to read reflects in part the political attitudes of their teachers. If nonreaders learn to read by writing and reading their own words and opinions, then they learn that their perceptions of reality are valid to others and can influence even those in authority. If, on the other hand, their teachers require them to learn the words and ideas in a primer that is donated by those in power, then the learners must accept that experience as more valid than their own. They must accept the concepts of social and economic structure transmitted by the teacher—or decide not to learn to read.

By understanding the political dimensions of reading, Paulo Freire developed materials that enabled adults to learn to read in thirty to forty hours. Freire was born and lived until 1964 in Recife, on the northeast coast of Brazil. In 1960, Recife had 80,000 children from seven to fourteen years old who did not attend school. Adult illiteracy was estimated at sixty to seventy percent. Crusades against illiteracy had been waged repeatedly without much effect. But Freire believed that adults could learn to read rapidly if reading were not part of a cultural imposition on them. After all, adults speak an extraordinarily rich and complex language which they could set down graphically if only they were given the tools to do so.

For more than fifteen years Freire had accumulated experience in adult education. In 1959, he received a PhD degree from the University of Recife and stayed at the university as a teacher of philosophy and education. He envisioned the university as a base for the education of all people, not merely for the rich and the educated. While teaching there he coordinated the Adult Education Program of the Popular Culture Movement, which set up circles of culture in slum areas and encouraged popular festivals and performances. In February, 1962, Freire became director of the university's newly established Cultural Extension Service.

The political realities of early 1962 supported Freire's hope that the Cultural Extension Service could be a resource for all the people. In October, 1962, a coalition of the Socialist, Labor, and Communist parties elected the mayor of Recife, Miguel Arraes, to the state governorship. Arraes appointed the founder of the Popular Culture Movement, Germano Coelho, to be state secretary of education. As the Cultural Extension Service developed its literacy program, it received financial assistance from the United States Agency for International Development (USAID)—enough to run a pilot project and to train seventy people in the use of the materials. USAID terminated its assistance in January 1964.

By that time the upper class and the small middle class in Brazil had become frightened by signs of growing political awareness among the masses. On April 1, 1964, the military leaders of Brazil took control of the government at all levels. Freire was under house arrest until June, imprisoned for seventy days, and finally sought refuge in Chile. After a year in Santiago he spent a year in Cambridge, Massachusetts, and in February, 1970, he went to Geneva to work for the World Council of Churches.

In the circles of culture set up by the Popular Culture Movement, Freire and his colleagues arranged discussions of such topics as nationalism, development, illiteracy, democracy. They introduced these topics with pictures or slides, then led a dialogue in which they exchanged points of view with nonliterates. Amazed by the results, Freire became ever more convinced that for adults, learning to read should be a process of analyzing reality, that adults can become critically conscious of their situation, and that when this occurs enormous energy is available for learning to read.

Yet Freire and his teams found many Brazilian nonliterates so submerged in their daily struggles that they had no awareness of whether or how they could change their lives in any way. They resisted being told they had problems. They believed that the conditions of their lives were due to God's will or to fate. In order to change this passive attitude Freire introduced the anthropological concept of culture, that is, the distinction between nature and culture. Freire believed that discussing this distinction would lead nonliterates to the discovery that they are makers of culture as much as literate people are, that aspects of their lives are man-made and therefore subject to change. The distinction between nature and culture included for Freire the difference between men and other animals and the importance of oral and written language in that difference.

Freire asked his friend, the well-known artist Francisco Brennand, to draw a series of pictures that could be used to stimulate discussions about nature and culture, men and animals, and culture in the lives of people. Brennand painted a series of ten pictures. Eight appear below, made from slides in Freire's possession. The originals were taken from him. To complete the series two pictures are included from a later version of the series drawn by Vicente de Abreu and published in Paulo Freire's *Education for Critical Consciousness*.

This sequence of ten pictures is tightly analyzed and structured. The first picture (Fig. 1) is carefully designed to elicit an initial distinction between culture and nature, while succeeding pictures are sequenced to draw out various subtleties of the distinction, namely: the difference between man and other animals being man's culture-making and communicating capacities (Figs. 2–5); nature transformed into culture by man's work (Figs. 3, 6, and 7); communications as culture (Figs. 2 and 8); and patterns of behavior and traditions as culture (Fig. 9). The final picture (Fig. 10) challenges the group to analyze its own behavior—the most distinctive capacity of people.

Figure 1 provides a familiar image from which a nonliterate from northeastern Brazil can use his knowledge to distinguish between nature and culture. The coordinator begins the discussion with the question: "What do you see in the picture?" This naming of the objects is important because people not accustomed to graphic representation may not easily identify what is meant to be shown. Notice that Brennand painted the pictures in one dimension without the conventions used by schooled artists for showing perspective. The coordinator then leads the discussion into the distinction between nature and culture by asking questions like: "Who made the well?" "Why did he do it?" "What materials did he use?" The questions continued: "Who made the tree?" "How is the tree different from the well?" "Who made the pig, the birds, the man?" "Who made the house, the hoe, the book?" Gradually the discussion moves to the conclusion that people use natural materials to change their situation, to create culture. Nonliterates know this distinction, but the discussion gives them the words to name and clarify it. At the conclusion of this discussion participants are already conscious of being cultured.

Figure 1

Figure 2

Figure 3

Figure 4

Figure 5

Figure 6

Figure 7

Figure 8

Figure 9

Figure 10

The second discussion, provoked by Fig. 2, concerns the relationship among people. People can make culture while animals cannot, and people, unlike animals, can communicate extensively with each other, both orally and graphically. Nature mediates the relationships and communications of people. The natural world is real and can be known by investigation and dialogue; human disagreements can be checked against the natural reality. The proper relationship among people is discussed as being that of subjects communicating with each other, not as objects being used by anyone. This communication must take place as dialogue between equals, with the perception of each person having equal validity. If one person assumes a superior position to another, he issues communiques instead of communicating, and the dialogue is broken.

The next three discussions (Figs. 3, 4, and 5) refine the concept of culture and raise the question of how culture is transmitted to younger generations. The group is asked to name what represents culture in Fig. 3. Characteristically, the group mentions the bow and arrow and the feathers. When asked if the feathers do not belong to nature, they answer that feathers belong to nature when on the bird, but people change them into culture by making clothing of them. The Indian teaches his skills to his son by direct experience, without writing, and the group discovers that those unable to read and write belong to a nonliterate culture like that of the Indian, even if they are part of a literate culture such as that shown in Fig. 4. Here the hunter is using a tool so complex in its construction that directions for making it must be recorded, and only those who can read can learn to make it. Moreover, in this culture only those who can read can earn enough money to buy guns, so access to their use is controlled by the literate members of this culture. Participants discuss the technological advance represented by the rifle compared with the bow and arrow, and they analyze this hunter's growing possibilities for transforming the world. This transformation makes sense only to the degree that it liberates and humanizes people. Finally, the group discusses the implication of education for technological development.

Figure 5 reinforces man's culture-making capacity by showing a cat who cannot make tools to extend his hunting capabilities. A nonliterate from Brasilia pointed out: 'Of these three, only two are hunters—the two men. They are hunters because they made culture first and then hunted. The third, the cat, who did not make culture either before or after the hunt, is not a hunter (*cacador*). He is a pursuer (*persequidor*).' The series of the three hunters always provoked many observations by the participants about people and animals, and about such things as instinct, intelligence, liberty, and education.

After this somewhat general discussion of culture referring to other places (countryside) and time (Indian preliterate culture), Fig. 6 ensures that participants in a circle of culture discover themselves as makers of culture. Here they see their brothers from the people making clay pots, and they realize that clay pots are as much culture as the work of a great sculptor. "I make shoes," said one participant, "and now I discover that I have as much value as a professor who makes books."

Figure 7 shows the use to which someone has put a clay pot. Here not only is clay transformed into culture, but flowers, which in the field are part of nature, have been changed into culture by the person who arranged them. "I make culture. I know how to do that," recognized a woman, very moved, in a circle of culture in Recife. A graphic signal is introduced for the first time in this picture. The flowers in the vase are represented by a drawing of them on the clay of the vase. Nature, transformed into culture, has been transformed once again into a written symbol.

Figure 8 is the next step in graphic representation. It shows that words known by and put together by nonliterates can be written down and are as much poetry as poems by educated people. This poem is a popular song, part of an elaborate tradition among nonliterates in northeast Brazil whereby the news is spread from town to town by singers. These singers play guitars and sing in pairs, each challenging the other to invent another verse incorporating the latest news. This picture is highly exciting to nonliterates because it shows them that they can learn to read the words and songs they already know.

Figure 9 shows two cowboys, one from the south of Brazil who is dressed in wool and the other from the northeast who is dressed in leather. This scene is designed to expand the idea of culture by showing that clothes and ways of behaving are also part of culture. The discussion focuses on the clothes of the cowboys. The southern cowboy makes his clothes of wool because sheep are available and wool keeps him warm. The northeastern cowboy uses leather because cows are available and leather is tough enough to protect him against cacti and scrubs. By discussing the cowboys' clothing and why it is different, participants realize that patterns of behaving are created by people in response to necessity. Sometimes this picture leads to a discussion of people's resistance to change—that traditions, such as clothing, develop out of necessity, but the necessity may pass while the tradition stays.

Figure 10 enables the group to develop its critical consciousness—to look at itself and reflect on its own activity. This picture shows a circle of culture functioning; participants can easily identify it as representing themselves. The coordinator introduces the phrase "democrati-

zation of culture" to be discussed in the light of what has been happening in the circle of culture. As one participant concluded: "The
democratization of culture has to do with what we are and with what
we make as people. Not with what they think and want for us." The
function of the circle of culture is examined by everyone– what the
experience has meant, what dialogue is, and what it means to raise
one's consciousness. By the time the group had reached this tenth
picture, participants had regained enormous confidence in themselves,
pride in their culture, and desire to learn to read.

The coordinators conduct the discussion of the ten situations
orally without using any kind of text or written representation. The
fact that participants could not read was not allowed to prevent their
considering highly complex issues. Since they could not read, ideas
were introduced in the graphic representation they could understand–
pictures. Because the participants were given a chance to express their
real knowledge and were not demeaned by their inability to read, they
were able to recover their eagerness for learning to read.

Freire called the process just described *conscientizacao*, usually
translated as "conscientization." For him conscientization is a process
in which people are encouraged to analyze their reality, to become more
aware of the constraints on their lives, and to take action to transform
their situation. For Freire education is either liberating or domesticating, teaching people either to be critical and free of constraints or to
accept things as they are. If literacy is not to be domesticating, Freire
believed, then it must be part of a process of conscientization.[1]

Freire and his colleagues developed the linguistic materials for
their literacy program from two premises: (1) Adults can learn to read
with ease words that are highly familiar and meaningful to them. (2)
It ought to be possible to select a brief list of words that would contain all the phonemes in Portuguese, so that learning this minimal linguistic universe would enable a reader to sound out any other words
or to record any words he knew orally. (This premise appeared possible
because Portuguese is for the most part a phonetic, syllabic language.)

In order to prepare for teaching reading in any specific community, Freire's teams visited the community to investigate its culture.
They explained why they had come and solicited help from volunteers
from the community, whom they called coinvestigators. Together
they examined all the familiar activities of the community, cross-
checking their perceptions and analyzing the significant words used
by the community. From these lists of words they developed a short
list of words chosen by a double criterion: (1) a word's emotional impact and capacity for provoking discussion, and (2) its phonemic value
in presenting all the sounds of Portuguese. Freire and his colleagues
observed, both in Brazil and in Chile, that no more than seventeen

words are necessary for teaching adults to read and write syllabic, phonetic languages such as Portuguese and Spanish. They called these words "generative," in the double sense that the words could generate among nonliterates impassioned discussions of the social and political realities of their lives (in Freire's words, they could engage the learners in "problematizing their existential situations"), and by breaking the seventeen words into syllables and rearranging the syllables nonliterates could generate other words and transcribe their own words.

After choosing sixteen or seventeen generative words, Freire and his colleagues found they must analyze carefully the sequence in which to present the words. Three principles guided their order of presentation. First, the initial word must be trisyllabic, such that each of the three syllables consists of one consonant and one vowel. Second, less common and more difficult phonetic material should appear toward the end of the list. For example, words with "x," "z," "q," and "ao" tend to appear late on the list. Third, words that name concrete and familiar objects should appear early, while words naming more abstract social and political realities should appear later on the list. These principles can be seen in the word lists (Lists 1–4) used by Freire or by teams using his process.

Freire believed the ideas represented by the words must be critically discussed before the words themselves were analyzed as graphic symbols. So his teams prepared a picture to illustrate each word. For example, for the word *tijolo* (brick) a picture of a construction scene was prepared. This picture was shown first without the word *tijolo*. Only after the group had discussed building with bricks, their own houses, housing as a community problem, obstacles to better housing, and whatever other topics were generated, was the second picture introduced showing the construction scene together with the word *tijolo*. In the third picture or slide the word *tijolo* appeared alone. In the same manner pictures were prepared for each of the sixteen words in order to ensure full discussion of the significance of the words before any linguistic or grpahic analysis was made.

On every word list the first word has three syllables. The reason for this is that one of Freire's colleagues discovered that a chart could be made of the syllables of trisyllabic words in a way that helped nonliterates grasp the structure of Portuguese words. For example, after introducing *tijolo* the coordinator broke the word into syllables. After reading aloud the individual syllables with the group, the coordinator presented the first one, "ti," like this "ta te ti to tu." At first the group recognized only "ti," but by reading these five syllables aloud they learned that the "t" sound was constant and they learned the sound of the five vowels. Next, "jo" was introduced in the same manner, "ja je ji jo ju," and was followed by "la le li lo lu." Finally these three presentations were combined in a chart, called the "card of discovery":

ta	te	ti	to	tu
ja	je	ji	jo	ju
la	le	li	lo	lu

List 1

Used in Cajueiro Sêco, a slum in Recife

tijolo	brick
voto	vote
siri	crab
palha	straw
biscate	odd job
cinza	ashes
doença	illness
chafariz	fountain
máquina	machine (sewing)
emprêgo	employment
engenho	sugar mill
manque	swamp
terra	land, soil
enxada	hoe
classe	class

List 2

Used in Tiriri, an agricultural colony in the city of Cabo

tijolo	brick
voto	vote
roçado	manioc field
abacaxi	pineapple
cacimba	well
passa	raisin
feira	market
milho	corn flour
maniva	kind of manioc
planta	plant
lombriga	roundworm
engenho	sugar mill
guia	guide (for a blind person)
barracão	small store rooms near market place
charque	dried meat
cozinha sal	kitchen salt

List 3

Used in Maceio, a city on the sea

tijolo	brick
voto	vote
casamento	wedding
carroça	cart
peixe	fish
jangada	fishing boat
balança	scale for weighing fish
Brasil	Brazil
máquina	machine (sewing)
farinha	flour
coco	coconut
fome	hunger
comida	food
sindicato	union
trabalho	work
limpeza	cleanliness

List 4

Used in the state of Rio, a rural area and satelite of the city of Rio de Janeiro

favela	slum
chuva	rain
arado	plow
terreno	plot of land
comida	food
batuque	popular dance with African rhythms
poço	well
bicicleta	bicycle
trabalho	work
salário	salary
profissão	profession
govêrno	government
manque	swamp
engenho	sugar mill
enrada	hoe
tijolo	brick
riqueza	riches, wealth

After one horizontal reading and one vertical reading, the coordinator asked the group to put together other words by combining the syllables on the chart in different ways. Often the group began to do this with no suggestion. For example, they might recognize *luta* (struggle) or *loja* (store). Other possibilities are: *tatu* (armadillo), *jato* (jet), *lula* (squid), *lote* (lot), *talo* (stalk), *lata* (tin can), and *tule* (tulle). Sometimes they combined syllables in ways that were not actual words, which did not matter so long as they discovered the mechanism of combining syllables. Coordinators were trained to accept any combination of syllables and to let the group discuss which words were actual ones.

In the state of Rio Grande do Norte a group called combinations of syllables that were actual words "thinking words" (*palavras do pensamento*) and others "dead words" (*palavras mortas*). In a circle of culture in Angicos, Rio Grande do Norte, one of the participants went to the blackboard on the fifth night of meetings to write, he said, a "thinking word." Easily he wrote: *o povo vai resouver os poblemas do Brasil votando conciente* ("the people will solve the problems of Brazil by informed voting").[2]

It is important to notice that Freire and his colleagues chose not to use books, or primers, as the format for their program. Instead they used large posters, filmstrips, or slides. They found Polish slide projectors available at about $13 each, and they used the whitewashed stucco walls common to community buildings for screens. They avoided primers on the grounds that they are mechanical and do not lend themselves to much flexibility in discussion. Furthermore, primers discourage people from expressing and writing their own ideas and words. The generation of words, the decision about which formations are actual words, the use of the words, and the messages that the words should convey—all these decisions should be, they believed, jointly undertaken by nonliterate adults and the coordinators of the discussions.

Two colleagues of Freire's in the Popular Culture Movement felt differently about this issue and wrote a *Primer for Adults*. In this primer five words—*povo* (people), *voto* (vote), *vida* (life), *saúde* (health), and *pão* (bread)—are introduced, broken into syllables, and varied in the style used by Freire's teams. The first sentence reads: *O voto é do povo* ("The vote belongs to the people"). The words and messages continue: "People without a house live in shacks." Then the final word "peace" and its messages "The northeast will only have peace when the roots of its ills have been eradicated." "Peace grows out of justice."[3]

This primer is extraordinarily better than the usual ones. Anisio Teixeira, the director of the Brazilian National Institute of Pedagogical Studies, said of it in 1962:

This book effectively teaches reading as if the northeastern non-literate were introducing his own life. The words, the sentences, the phrases are those that would inevitably occur to the nonliterate if he himself were writing his own primer. . . . Learning to read ought to be a simple transposition of one's actual oral language to a written language. This has been realized to an unprecedented extent in the *Primer for Adults*. . . . Those who consider it subversive must consider life and truth subversive and deceit and nonsense orderly.[4]

But the very excellence of this primer reveals the basic difficulties of primers as a format: the phonetic variation becomes tedious and the messages are not the direct opinions of the learners. Because the ideas are those of the teachers, the book is an instrument of propaganda; in supporting what nonliterates may believe, it tells them what they should believe. As long as the message is donated, it domesticates those who accept it to the uncritical acceptance of whatever teachers and writers say should be believed.

Applying Freire's Process

To summarize a bit, the following preparations were made by Freire and his colleagues before convening a meeting of nonliterates to be taught.

1. Acceptance by the political authorities of the necessary conditions was sought. Freire's requirements of mayors and governors were: no partisan interference, technical independence, and acknowledgment that the education provided would cause an internal and external liberation of the people.
2. The life and vocabulary of the community were investigated.
3. The sixteen or so generative words were "codified," that is, a poster, slide, or filmstrip of the local situation described by each of the chosen words was prepared.
4. A card of discovery for the initial word was formulated.
5. A place to meet—a church, school, or whatever community building was available—was arranged.
6. Coordinators, not teachers, for each group were selected and trained. This was a major problem in setting up the program. The technical aspect of the procedure was not difficult to impart, but the creation of a new attitude required a period of supervision to help coordinators avoid the temptation of "antidialogue."
7. A circle of culture, not a school or class, was organized consisting of twenty-five to thirty nonliterates who would be participants, not pupils.

Once the groups convened the procedure went as follows:

1. Meetings were held every weeknight for one hour during six to eight weeks.
2. The first two to eight sessions were devoted to analyzing the ten pictures illustrating the distinction between nature and culture.
3. At the next session the first generative word was introduced, as described above. At the end of this session participants were asked to make up more words from the card of discovery and to bring their lists to the next meeting.
4. At the remaining sessions the other sixteen or so generative words were introduced one at a time. Participants practiced writing and reading aloud, they expressed opinions and wrote them down; they examined newspapers and discussed local issues.

Those who finished the literacy course, perhaps three-quarters of those who began, could read and write simple texts, make something of the local newspapers, and discuss Brazilian problems. On one occasion, a woman in a circle of culture in Rio Grande do Norte read aloud a telegram in a newspaper as an exercise. The telegram discussed the exploitation of salt in Rio Grande do Norte. A visitor to the circle asked the woman, "Lady, do you know what exploitation means?" "Perhaps you, a rich young man, don't know," she replied. "But I, a poor woman, I know what exploitation is."

It was most important to Freire that the discussion of problems did not lead to demagogical solutions. The woman who spoke of exploitation did so not with hatred but with a legitimate determination to overcome conditions that seemed to her and to all the participants highly subversive to the interest of the people.

Another participant in Rio Grande do Norte discussed the fact that he and his comrades knew how to "brand" (*ferrar*) their names. When asked by a guest what it meant to brand their names, he explained: "It means to copy our name, which the landlord writes on a paper, until we get tired, and the landlord keeps saying more! more! until we learn it by heart. Then we have to brand our names—the landlord gets us a voting certificate and sends us to vote for whom he wants." (Brazilian law refuses the vote to nonliterates, but at that time a person could qualify as literate merely by signing his name to an application form.) "But now," he continued, "we are going to unbrand out names, to really learn to write, and then vote for whom we want."

Freire and his colleagues were planning a post-literacy curriculum based on the investigations of Brazilian themes carried out by the circles of culture. They expected that 20,000 literacy circles would have been functioning in Brazil in 1964 if the military coup had not terminated the program.

Notes

1. No verbatim record from Freire's circles is available, but the process of conscientization is clearly illustrated in the account of Stokely Carmichael's speech class, held for field workers of the Student Nonviolent Coordinating Committee in 1965, reprinted in Miriam Wasserman (Ed.), *Demystifying School*, pp. 327-330 (New York: Praeger, 1974).
2. This may be compared with accepted literate Brazilian Portuguese: *O povo vai resolver os problemas do Brasil, votando consciente.* Of the three variations, two are because Portuguese is not perfectly phonetic, i.e., the "l" in *resolver* sounds like "u," and "c" records the "s" sound in *consciente* without requiring the "s." The third variation is a difference in speech; the man from Angicos says *poblemas* rather than *problemas.*
3. This primer was written by Josina Maria Lopes de Godoy and Norma Porto Carreiro Coelho. I was given a copy in 1965 by officials of USAID in Recife. The military confiscated all known copies, but USAID saved one to show how communistic the area had been before the takeover.
4. From an interview with Dr. Teixeira reprinted in the *Revista Brasileira de Estudos Pedagogicas* XXXVIII, 88, October–December, 1962, pp. 158-159.

Selected Bibliography

Adams, F., & Horton, M. (1975). *Unearthing seeds of fire: The idea of Highlander.* Winston-Salem, NC: Blair.

Apple, M. W. (1979). *Ideology and curriculum.* London: Routledge and Kegan Paul.

Apple, M. W. (1982). *Cultural and economic reproduction in education.* London: Routledge and Kegan Paul.

Aronowitz, S., & Giroux, H. (1985). *Education under siege.* South Hadley, MA: Bergin & Garvey.

Ashton-Warner, S. (1979). *Teacher* (First edition, 1963). New York: Bantam.

Auerbach, E., & Wallerstein, N. (1986). *ESL for action: Problem-posing at work.* Reading, MA: Addison-Wesley.

Auerbach, E. R., & Burgess, D. (1985, September). The hidden curriculum of survival ESL. *TESOL Quarterly, 19*(3), pp. 475–495.

Avrich, P. (1980). *The modern school movement: Anarchism and education in the United States.* Princeton: Princeton University Press.

Bastian, A., Fruchter, N., Gittell, M., Greer, C., & Haskins, K. (1985). *Choosing equality: The case for democratic schooling.* New York: New World Foundation.

Berlak, A., & Berlak, H., (1981). *Dilemmas of schooling: Teaching and social change.* New York: Methuen.

Berthoff, A. E. (1981). *The making of meaning.* Upper Montclair, NJ: Boynton/Cook.

Bisseret, N. (1979). *Education, class language and ideology.* Boston: Routledge and Kegan Paul.

Bourdieu, P., & Passeron, J. C. (1977). *Reproduction in education, society and culture.* Beverly Hills, CA: Sage.

Bowles, S., & Gintis, H. (1976). *Schooling in capitalist America.* New York: Basic Books.

Brown, C. (1975). *Literacy in 30 hours: Paulo Freire's process in Northeast Brazil.* Chicago: Alternate Schools Network.

Carnoy, M. (1974). *Education as cultural imperialism.* New York: McKay.

Carnoy, M., & Levin, H. M. (1985). *Schooling and work in the democratic state.* Stanford, CA: Stanford University Press.

Collins, D. (1977). *Paulo Freire: His life, thought and work.* New York: Paulist.

Cuban, L. (1984, Winter). Policy and research dilemmas in the teaching of reasoning: Unplanned designs. *Review of Educational Research, 54*(4), pp. 655–681.

Dewey, J. (1963). *Experience and education* (First edition, 1938). New York: Macmillan.

Dewey, J. (1966). *Democracy and education* (First edition, 1916). New York: Free Press.

Donald, J. (1983, Winter). How illiteracy became a problem and literacy stopped being one. *Journal of Education, 165*(1), pp. 35–52.

Fisher, B. (No date). What is feminist pedagogy? *The Radical Teacher*, No. 18, pp. 20–24.

Freire, P. (1970). *Pedagogy of the oppressed*. New York: Continuum.

Freire, P. (1973). *Education for critical consciousness*. New York: Continuum.

Freire, P. (1978). *Pedagogy-in-process*. New York: Continuum.

Freire, P. (1985). *The politics of education*. South Hadley, MA: Bergin & Garvey.

Giroux, H. (1978). Writing and critical thinking in the social studies. *Curriculum Inquiry, 8*(4), pp. 291–310.

Giroux, H. (1983). *Theory and resistance in education*. South Hadley, MA: Bergin & Garvey.

Goodlad, J. (1983). *A place called school*. New York: McGraw-Hill.

Greene, M. (1978). *Landscapes of learning*. New York: Teachers College.

Gross, R., & Gross, B. (Eds.). (1985). *The great school debate: Which way for American education?* New York: Simon and Schuster.

Heath, S. B. (1983). *Ways with words: Language, life, and work in communities and classrooms*. New York: Cambridge.

Hirshon, S., & Butler, J. (1983). *And also teach them to read: The national literacy crusade of Nicaragua*. Westport, CT: Lawrence Hill and Company.

Hoggart, R. (1957). *The uses of literacy: Aspects of working-class life*. London: Chatto, Windus.

Hunter, C. S. J., & Harman, D. (1979). *Adult illiteracy in America*. New York: McGraw-Hill.

Illich, I. (1972). *Deschooling society*. New York: Harper and Row.

Jencks, C., et al. (1972). *Inequality*. New York: Basic Books.

Katz, M. B. (1971). *Class, bureaucracy and schools: The illusion of educational change in America*. New York: Praeger.

Kohl, H. (1969). *The open classroom*. New York: New York Review of Books.

Kohl, H. (1984). *Basic Skills*. New York: Bantam.

Kozol, J. (1972). *Free schools*. Boston: Houghton Mifflin.

Kozol, J. (1980). *Children of the revolution: A Yankee teacher in Cuban schools*. New York: Delta Press.

Kozol, J. (1985). *Illiterate America*. New York: Doubleday.

Levin, H. M. (1978). Why isn't educational research more useful? *Prospects, 8*(2), pp. 157–166.

Levin, H. M. (1981, February). The identity crisis in educational planning. *Harvard Educational Review, 51*(1), pp. 85–93.

Levin, H. M., & Rumberger, R. W. (1983, February). *The educational implications of high technology* (Project Report 83-A4). Stanford, CA: Stanford University, Institute for Research on Educational Finance and Governance.

Mackie, J. (Ed.). (1981). *Literacy and revolution: The pedagogy of Paulo Freire*. New York: Continuum.

Miller, V. (1985). *Between struggle and hope: The Nicaraguan literacy crusade*. Boulder, CO: Westview.

Ohmann, R. (1976). *English in America*. New York: Oxford University Press.

Ohmann, R. (1981). Where did mass culture come from? The case of magazines. *Berkshire Review, 16*, pp. 85–101.

Ohmann, R. (1985, November). Literacy, technology, and monopoly capital. *College English 47*(7), pp. 675–689.

Ollman, B., & Norton, T. (Eds.). (1977). *Studies in socialist pedagogy.* New York: Monthly Review.

Pincus, F. (1980, August). The false promises of community colleges: Class conflict and vocational education. *Harvard Educational Review, 50,* pp. 332–361.

Pincus, F. (1984, Winter). From equity to excellence: The rebirth of educational conservatism. *Social Policy,* pp. 11–15.

Schniedewind, N. (1987). *Cooperative learning, cooperative lives: A sourcebook of learning activities to promote a peaceful world.* Somerville, MA: Circle Press.

Schniedewind, N., & Davidson, E. (1984). *Open minds to equality.* Englewood Cliffs, NJ: Prentice-Hall.

Schoolboys of Barbiana. (1971). *Letter to a teacher.* New York: Vintage.

Shor, I. (1986). *Culture wars: School and society in the conservative restoration, 1969–1984.* New York: Routledge and Kegan Paul/Methuen.

Shor, I. (1987). *Critical teaching and everyday life* (3rd printing). Chicago: The University of Chicago Press.

Shor, I., & Freire, P. (1987). *A pedagogy for liberation.* South Hadley, MA: Bergin & Garvey.

Spring, J. (1972). *Education and the rise of the corporate state.* Boston: Beacon.

Wallerstein, N. (1984). *Language and culture in conflict: Problem-posing in the ESL classroom.* Reading, MA: Addison-Wesley.

Willis, P. (1981). *Learning to labor: How working class kids get working class jobs.* New York: Columbia University Press.

Vygotsky, L. (1977). *Thought and language* (First edition, 1962). Cambridge, MA: MIT Press.

Wirth, A. (1983). *Productive work—in industry and schools: Becoming persons again.* Lanham, MD: University Press of America.

Notes on Contributors

Elsa Roberts Auerbach is an ESL and bilingual education lecturer at the University of Massachusetts (Boston). She has worked in the electronics and auto industries, where she taught ESL to co-workers from foreign countries. With Nina Wallerstein, Elsa has coauthored *ESL for Action: Problem-Posing at Work* (Reading, MA: Addison-Wesley, 1986).

Cynthia Brown is an associate professor of education at Dominican College in San Rafael, California. Her recent writing includes editing and introducing *Ready from Within: Septima Clark and the Civil Rights Movement* (Navarro, CA: Wild Trees Press, 1986).

Denise Burgess is a bilingual resource teacher in the Pajaro Valley Unified School District in Watsonville, California. She has taught adult and secondary ESL in Northern California and the Boston area since 1980. Currently, she is involved in peer coaching and teacher training in cooperative learning and sheltered English.

Nan Elsasser has practiced and written about liberatory teaching for the past decade. After teaching at the College of the Virgin Islands, she has returned to Albuquerque, where she has set up an educational consulting service with coauthor Patricia Irvine. Nan has also consulted with the Bilingual-Bicultural Program in Bluefields, Nicaragua.

Valerie Faith has taught writing, reading, literature, and speech for over twenty years. Since 1978, she has applied Freire's ideas successfully at a number of U.S. colleges. She has also worked as a business writer for the National Geographic Society and the National Audubon Society. Currently, Valerie teaches freshman composition at George Washington University while writing a book on wheelchairs for the Veterans Administration. She lives in Herndon, Virginia, with her husband and three children.

Linda Finlay is an associate professor of philosophy at Ithaca College, New York. Her interests are education, epistemology, feminism, and peace-making. She writes and speaks about these interests, while living in Ithaca with her husband and two children. Linda is also fond of movies, chocolate, and karate.

Kyle Fiore has practiced liberatory education in a variety of settings in Albuquerque, and has now resettled to the Bay Area of San Francisco.

Marilyn Frankenstein is an editor of *Radical Teacher* magazine. She taught at various public alternative schools, including Park East High School in East Harlem, New York. Currently, she teaches "radical math" at the College of Public and Community Service—University of Massachusetts (Boston).

Patricia Irvine is coauthoring a new book with Nan Elsasser on liberatory writing methods. She taught with Nan at the College of the Virgin Islands, out of which they wrote their essay on Creole. Pat and Nan have started a writing consulting service based in Albuquerque.

Vera John-Steiner is a noted psycholinguist whose work studies the relation between learning, culture, language, and creativity. Her numerous publications include her recent book *Notebooks of the Mind* (Albuquerque, NM: University of New Mexico Press, 1985). She has taught at UCLA, the University of Rochester, and Yeshiva University. She is currently a presidential professor at the University of New Mexico.

Nancy Schniedewind is an associate professor at the State University of New York, New Paltz, where she teaches courses in the Women's Studies Program and in the master's program in Humanistic Education. She has received a Chancellor's Award for Excellence in Teaching. Nancy has coauthored *Open Minds to Equality: Learning Activities to Promote Race, Sex, Class, and Age Equity* (Englewood Cliffs, NJ: Prentice-Hall, 1983). Most recently, she published *Cooperative Learning, Cooperative Lives: A Sourcebook of Learning Activities to Promote a Peaceful World* (Somerville, MA: Circle Press, 1987).

Ira Shor is professor of English at the College of Staten Island. His books include *Critical Teaching and Everyday Life* (Chicago: University of Chicago Press, 3rd printing, 1987), *Culture Wars: School and Society in the Conservative Restoration, 1969–1984* (New York: Routledge and Kegan Paul/Methuen, 1986), and with Paulo Freire, *A Pedagogy for Liberation* (South Hadley, MA: Bergin & Garvey, 1987). He was a Guggenheim Fellow in 1983 and Chancellor's Scholar-in-Residence in 1986 at the City University of New York.

Nina Wallerstein uses her Master's in Public Health to teach occupational and community health education at the University of New Mexico. She has worked in Freirean education since 1973, taught ESL for ten years, and served as consultant and teacher-trainer in problem-posing ESL, literacy, and workplace education in the United States, Canada, a Philippines refugee camp, and Brazil. Her books include *Language and Culture in Conflict: Problem-Posing in the ESL Classroom* (Reading, MA: Addison-Wesley, 1984), and with Elsa Auerbach, *ESL for Action: Problem-Posing at Work* (Reading, MA: Addison-Wesley, 1986). Currently, she is applying Freire's ideas to alcohol abuse and other prevention programs.

Nancy Zimmet is currently on leave from her teaching position at Newton North High School in Massachusetts, where she teaches English and reading. She is now writing a book on foreign adoptions in the United States.